CONVERSATION IN A TRAIN

CONVERSATION
IN A TRAIN
AND OTHER CRITICAL
WRITING

FRANK SARGESON

Selected and edited by
Kevin Cunningham

AUCKLAND UNIVERSITY PRESS
OXFORD UNIVERSITY PRESS

First published 1983
© Christine Cole Catley 1983
Editorial matter © Kevin Cunningham 1983

Published with the assistance of
the New Zealand Literary Fund

Printed in New Zealand
at the University of Auckland Bindery
Typographical design by Neysa Moss
ISBN 0 19 648023 X

ACKNOWLEDGEMENTS

My searching for Frank Sargeson's critical writing began for a bibliography of his non-fiction prose prepared for the requirements of a Diploma of the Library School of the New Zealand National Library in 1977. That bibliography, in shortened form, is printed at the back of this book.

Frank Sargeson gave me generous assistance during and after that work, and in the selection of material for this edition. He answered many questions and gave me much useful advice.

Dennis McEldowney has been a patient and very helpful editor. Robin Dudding read the proofs, compiled the index, and assisted in other ways.

For permission to reprint material I am grateful to Frank Sargeson's literary executor, to the editors of *Islands, Landfall*, the *New Zealand Listener*, and *Parsons Packet*, to Dr Allen Curnow, and to the Alexander Turnbull Library and the Broadcasting Corporation of New Zealand.

None of this work would have been possible without the help of Charlotte Paul.

CONTENTS

INTRODUCTION

I

Frank Sargeson's critical, autobiographical, and occasional writings over forty-five years range very widely, from stray satirical notes to the major imaginative achievement of the three volumes of memoirs. In between is a considerable number of reviews, essays, commentaries, and interviews which tell us much of the remarkable writer he was.

II

I would often feel bitterly my regret that I began writing reviews. I can think of nothing more permanently damaging to a writer who has his own work to do, more likely to efface even a semblance of integrity, than that he should be required to drudge out comments upon books which he would never of his own volition have chosen to read: and all his work worry and doubt will be rooted in the knowledge that no matter how good his intentions, neither he nor anybody can ever be sure about the justice of a pretence to judge contemporary work. (*More than Enough*, p.125.)

Sargeson's critical and occasional writings in journals began in *Tomorrow* in 1935. *Tomorrow* had published Sargeson's first sketches. He soon became a regular contributor to the magazine. 'I wrote for years for *Tomorrow*. I wrote as "A Radical Man About Town"; I wrote all sorts of comments and so on. It was almost like Wordsworth you know, "Bliss was it in that dawn . . . / but to be young was very heaven!" ' (p.183 in this book).

Including his fiction, Sargeson made seventy contributions to the 178 issues of *Tomorrow* between 1935 and 1940, when wartime censorship closed down the radical Christchurch journal. A sense of common enterprise and excitement is obvious in Sargeson's contributions, in his occasional pieces, verse, parodies, and commentary.

He wrote for *Tomorrow* because he wanted to: it did not pay contributors. That distinguishes his work there from his second burst of non-fictional activity between 1948 and 1955 when he published forty reviews and articles, most of them in the *New Zealand Listener*. It is to that period that the quotation above refers. Further, during this period Sargeson did a considerable amount of broadcasting.

In *More than Enough* (pp.124-5) Sargeson describes the circumstances in which he accepted reviewing work for the *Listener* from its editor, Oliver Duff. *More than Enough* also describes the end of his work for the journal, arising out of his dispute with M. H. Holcroft, who succeeded Duff as editor in 1949.

The activity of 1948-55 was from financial need. A scrawled note on the typescript of one of his radio talks reads 'I remember I did these . . . to pay the damn rates'. Sargeson's *Listener* reviews were often merely brief notes on current books. This was never true of his contributions to *Landfall* during this period, where reviews and essays alike reflected Sargeson's genuine interests, and were considered pieces of writing.

After 1955 what little reviewing Sargeson did was in *Landfall* and *Islands*, with a few more imaginative essays such as 'Conversation in a Train' and 'An Imaginary Conversation'. Interviews with Sargeson became more common in the nineteen-seventies, reflecting his considerable status as a fiction writer.

III

There is a great difference between a poet who seeks the particular for the sake of the universal and one who sees the universal in the particular. From the former method comes Allegory where the particular is used only as an example, an instance of the universal; but the latter is the true method of poetry. It expresses a particular without a thought of or a reference to the universal. But whoever has a living grasp of this particular grasps the universal with it, knowing it either not at all, or long afterwards.

Sargeson describes pinning this quotation from Goethe above his writing table in the nineteen-thirties (*More than Enough*, p.93). Quite apart from its obvious interest as a comment on Sargeson's fiction, it furnishes a good example of the consistency of his interests. Among the essays included in this book it is alluded to in a talk of 1948 on Katherine Mansfield (see p.30) and quoted in an interview of 1970 (p.156). Elsewhere it is quoted in a review of a Karel Capek play in 1938, in a review of a book on the theatre in 1957, and in a reply to a questionnaire in 1975 (items 26, 96, and 121 in the bibliography). Particular ideas, names, and interests keep cropping up in Sargeson's critical writings and reviews.

First is Sargeson's interest in 'little Bethel', as he called it, that part of New Zealand's social make-up which he saw as derived from a perversion of the non-conformist Christian spirit. This preoccupation of Sargeson's was explored most fully in his fiction, if in more particular terms. He worried away at the subject in his critical and autobiographical writings over many years, and it was expressed in a variety of contexts: personal, historical, political, and imaginative.

In *Once is Enough* he analysed its manifestations in the personalities of his own parents.

> My father was in fact genuinely religious and moral: he believed in an order that was not of this world: my mother believed only in the worldly order which she considered to be the right and proper one: my father was the pure puritan who believed that all the heavenly absolutes as he conceived them could and should be made to prevail on earth: my mother was the impure puritan to whom the bargain of social convention was entirely satisfactory. My mother was indeed truly representative of the prevailing general sentiment about what life in New Zealand should be—the sentiment which powerfully shapes and dominates New Zealand life to this day (pp.92-93).

Writing in 1950 of D. H. Lawrence, Sargeson identified the puritan's ways of behaviour, which he thought Lawrence shared with New Zealanders, as a neurotic quest for perfection, a distrust of pleasure, and a social unease (see p.47). Sargeson sought to analyse the historical origins of this puritanism. His remarks on a collection of New Zealand short stories (pp.71-77) are an attempt to trace the malady back to its imported English causes.

Puritanism in its political embodiment also concerned him. In his *Landfall* interview of 1970 he worried that 'now you have this drive for the view that every human being has his own dignity and his own rights and that he should share and so on; in extreme form you have the socialist idea that we should all be, economically, anyhow, equal. Now is this too a form of puritanism? I think it probably is' (p.168).

Much of his writing on New Zealand literature is also concerned with the question of puritanism. Dan Davin's *Roads from Home* is praised for its having 'taken the puritan spirit for granted' (p.37-38); Roderick Finlayson's *Tidal Creek* for celebrating the values that puritanism has destroyed (pp.39-41). James Courage's *The Young Have Secrets* is likely to be ill-received by a local readership which has a 'prosaic fact-obsessed New Zealand mind' (p.90).

How then is the imaginative writer to survive in such a society? Sargeson's concern for the survival of the writer is a natural corollary of his pessimism. His own imaginative and financial struggle to survive was recognized very early. In 1953, in 'A Letter to Frank Sargeson', sixteen of his fellow fiction writers, addressing him on his fiftieth birthday, spoke of the example he had provided. 'You have worked with patience and endurance at a task which has never provided as much as a living wage, a task which in our community has provoked suspicion and derision more often than sympathy or understanding. . . . Your dedication is an example and an inspiration.' (*Landfall*, March 1953 (v.7, no.1), p.5.)

Anyone who doubts that tolerance for writers and artists has been lacking at certain times in New Zealand could do no better than browse through the files of the *New Zealand Listener* between 1945 and 1950. At that time any favourable reference to Sargeson's writing, or Colin McCahon's paintings, provoked angry letters. There can be no doubt of the feelings of frustration which writers must have experienced at this time.

Sargeson's own frustrations are most fully recorded in his memoirs, particularly in the second and third volumes, but his reviews and essays consistently express his sympathy for his fellow writers. In 1935, writing of Sherwood Anderson, he spoke of Anderson's relevance to New Zealand writers: Anderson 'has lived his life in an environment similar to our own, raw, aesthetically hostile' (p.16). In 1945, introducing the stories in the anthology *Speaking for Ourselves*, Sargeson praises their authors for having continued to write in a country 'which so far can't exactly be described as over-generous in its encouragement of its own writers'. The writers in the 1953 World's Classics collection were similarly praised for writing in a 'sceptical and indifferent' environment. In 1971 Sargeson understands the neglect of Ronald Hugh Morrieson's novels as 'another comment on the present-day neglect, comparatively speaking, of the writer who endeavours by his craft to extract some sort of meaning from the chaos of popular "documentary" ' (p.189).

The good writer's attempt to cope with a hostile environment was not simply a matter of individual frustration: it was an act of integrity which offered a hope for national redemption. Janet Frame's first book was praised for its vision of New Zealand society and the skill of its writing, but, more than that, 'from now on our literature is the richer . . . Janet Frame becomes one more light to help diminish the vast region of darkness by which we are surrounded' (p.67).

If, in many of his reviews and essays on New Zealand fiction, Sargeson's interest in the way writers cope imaginatively and practically with puritanism was his dominant concern, that is not to say that purely literary appreciation was absent. Sargeson has been constantly attentive to the craft of writing. Technical competence was, if you like, a question of morale. James Courage's *The Fifth Child*, a novel which Sargeson otherwise thought badly flawed, is praised for the accomplishment of its telling. 'There isn't a single hint of the technical ineptitude, the earnest amateurishness, that has disfigured so many of our best "efforts" ' (p.35).

The two concerns, survival and expertise, are perhaps not finally separable. The later writers in the 1953 World's Classics anthology of New Zealand stories were praised for achieving a 'tightening' in technique which is in Sargeson's view closely connected with the writers 'becoming more and more defensively over-conscious of their isolation' (p.76-77).

Many of the reviews and essays reveal that appreciative understanding of craft which a practitioner can bring to a fellow-writer's work. This is especially true of those writers for whom Sargeson feels a special affection, and from whose writing he learned something of his own craft. The loving and perceptive tribute to Sherwood Anderson, for example, in its analysis of Anderson's use of repetition, pace, short sentences, implication and emotion is certainly telling us as much of Sargeson's own writing at that time as it is of Anderson's, and does not suffer by that. The writings on A. P. Gaskell, Rolf Boldrewood, and Henry Lawson (and on Australian literature in general) are likewise informed by a sympathy and enthusiasm which reveal as much of the author as the subject.

What is so valuable in the best of Sargeson's writing about the craft of fiction is its clarity. In 'Conversation in a Train', for example, he speaks of that kind of naturalism which with its 'literal-minded no-nonsense exactness and clarity, will at times prompt us to that intensity of feeling which is always a reliable sign that an important communication has reached us' (p.143).

'I can only make marginal comments in the form that seems to suit me best—that is, by creating fictions', Sargeson has said (p.169). The critical as well as the autobiographical writings act as a small but valuable qualification of that statement.

IV

The present selection gives what is in my view the most enduring of Sargeson's reviews, critical essays, and broadcasts. These pieces are of first interest as an illuminating supplement to Sargeson's central concerns as a writer of fiction, but they are not merely supplementary. At best they offer the lively care which so distinguishes the fiction.

Kevin Cunningham

A NOTE ON THE TEXT

This selection is presented in chronological order. Texts are printed as they were first published, except for items 5, 11, 15, and 18 which have been taken from Sargeson's manuscripts in the Alexander Turnbull Library, Wellington.

Supplied titles have been replaced by simple descriptive titles. Notes on sources have been given after each item.

SHERWOOD ANDERSON

Exporting printed paper from the United States of America must be really Big Business. You can tell from our bookstalls. I wish the big-wigs in this printed paper trade would get on to the idea that a country should export its best products. Then there wouldn't be the glut in cowboy and other untrue romances, the relative scarcity of faithful stories by writers of Sherwood Anderson's quality.

One of the things that Anderson understands is the value of repeti-tion. He never explores the important incidents of a story at one hit. He will say enough to set your imagination working, and have you looking for the page where he will return to the incident and fill in the gaps that he has deliberately left you wondering over. I think he got the idea from some of the story-tellers of the Old Testament.

Anderson also exploits the short, suggestive sentence. What fascinates him about words is their enormous suggestive power, and he uses them to liberate the imagination; certainly not, as some writers do, to restrict and pin it down. The defect of the method is that page by page you get the impression that you are about to receive a new revela-tion of life, a revelation which never quite turns up. You may feel a little disappointed at the end, and conclude that there is a lot to be said for the restrictive qualities of words after all. Some writers demand little more of you than that you should read. But Anderson expects you to be susceptible to suggestion and implication, to eke out his imagination with your own.

Anderson's technical abilities are novel and arresting, but he has made his reputation primarily through his emotional power. His style is one that can be used to great advantage by an emotional writer. There is a parallel in music. Music, more exclusively than literature, is concerned with emotional expression, and there is enormous value in a short, arresting statement that will lend itself to repetition and development. The composer must, of course, be a man capable of experiencing something more than mere shabby emotion. That Anderson is such a man cannot be disputed. His stories are told in the commonplace words and phrases that you find in the Old Testament, but they have nothing of the flatness of life. In life the third dimension often appears to be missing. Anderson makes it his job to put it in.

There is no clever dialogue, there is very little dialogue at all. Anderson's method is the reverse of Ernest Hemingway's. The latter reports his characters' conversation, and from that you have to infer their emotions and everything else it is necessary for you to know. But Anderson makes you understand how his characters feel by placing himself inside their skins. It isn't necessary for you to know much about their conversation. That he appeals by his emotional power is proved by the interest he arouses in different classes of men. Erudite professors who guide the Young towards Literary Appreciation write him grave letters of approval. And the shop assistant who finds that he understands and expresses something of his experience cannot resist the impulse to write and tell him about it.

In late years Anderson has turned newspaper proprietor. His Virginian small-town weekly paper is a potty enough little affair, but it has a vast subscription list now that it is taken by all intending writers in the United States of America. From it Anderson has collected material into a volume entitled Hello Towns! In a sense I think he intends it as a counterblast to the Lewis of Main Street. It is a racy commentary on American small-town life. It is certainly one of the most American books published in English.

It is a pity that Sherwood Anderson's work is not better known in New Zealand. Anderson has lived his life in an environment similar to our own, raw, aesthetically hostile; yet by his courage and his sincerity he has become a first-rate artist. A few of the stories of this ungainly, sympathetic, Middle-Western ex-labourer and ex-businessman are as good as anything you will find in Maupassant, Chekhov, O. Henry, Maugham. But Anderson is more than a short story writer. He is a poet.

It matters little that his poetry does not always shape itself into the more familiar poetical forms. How valuable his journalism is it is difficult to say. It is at any rate like nothing on earth.

Tomorrow, 6 November 1935 (v.2, no.2), pp.14-15.

]2[

MR RHODES' HEROIC NOVELISTS

Concluding his 'Heroes In Fiction' Mr Rhodes makes his point. It was easy enough to guess that it was coming, but hardly in the way that it is put. For Mr Rhodes very nearly says that the true heroes of the novel are certain novelists living today. 'They are not merely observing and writing, they are experiencing and writing.' And it is clear that 'experiencing' means being tied to one or other of the anti-human jobs that mass production involves.

Now leaving aside that last sentence for the moment, I'd say that there are good novels of observation. Babbitt, for instance, is observed, it is written from the outside in, and it is a good novel. And it is so because of Mr Sinclair Lewis' superb capacity for observation. On the other hand you get bad novels of observation, ones like Mr Upton Sinclair's. And the same holds good of novels of experience, novels written from the inside out. You get the good and the bad, it depends on the capacity for experience of the novelist. And I'd go further and say that novels equally good about the same subject matter could be written from both the inside and the outside. They'd be very different in their treatment naturally, but they could both be good in the sense that they'd convince you of the soundness of their re-creation of life.

Mr Rhodes, however, does not admit anything like this. Dickens, for instance, was 'feeling, observing, remembering, not experiencing'. In other words he'd have done better if he'd stuck to his blacking factory. And this is what Mr Rhodes' novelist heroes do today. They work in mines and factories, and after knocking off, unless there's a political meeting on, or political work to do, they sit down and bang away at their typewriters and use up the energy that their fellow-workers let loose in being human in whatever way appeals to them most. They are the workers writing, the people being vocal, and the future of the novel is with them and their company.

Well, it's difficult to argue with anyone as romantic as Mr Rhodes, but I'll try.

The question boils down to this. Can a worker be a writer, and remain essentially a worker? I'd say no, for the reason that the bare fact of a worker's being moved to write marks him out as different from his fellow-workers; or, as Mr Rhodes would put it, as not a true proletarian who can live only by selling his labour in the industrial market; or, if you like, as not the stunted creature mentioned in Mr Rhodes' quotation from Engels. Moreover should he act on that impulse he immediately becomes a different sort of worker. He has, in fact, to learn a new job, that of working in words; a job so difficult, and demanding so much time, so much energy and so many qualities, that out of hundreds of millions of people only a handful are any good at it. It is surely obvious that workers who become writers are gifted individuals who have discovered and developed their gifts. And they make this discovery in an environment where all the chances are against them, a fact which further marks them out as being far from ordinary workers.

Furthermore it is a question whether the discovery of such a gift will turn out to be an advantage. Mr Ramsay MacDonald and Mr J. H. Thomas were workers who discovered their gifts for politics, but it would perhaps have been better for the people of England if they hadn't. And workers who become novelists run the same risks, though as the gift of an unusually thick skin isn't a gift that's of much use to novelists, the risks that they run aren't as a rule so serious. And, apart from deeper sympathies and beliefs, gratitude for a store of incident, vernacular and experience, may alone be sufficient to save them from being demoralized. That being so it is surely a bit too much to expect them to deny themselves certain advantages that the exercise of their talents may bring them, to expect them to limit themselves to the mean world of the spirit that mass production jobs necessarily involve. And in point of fact so-called proletarian novelists refuse to so deny and limit themselves. They sell their stories to *Esquire* and *The Saturday Evening Post*, they make the best bargains they can with their publishers, they sample the life of Greenwich village and Bloomsbury—things unimportant in themselves, but indicating a seeking after the larger world of the spirit. A seeking which should be open to all men, but which in this mechanical age is distorted where it isn't stamped out.

If Mr Rhodes had indicated that he is aware of this large world of the spirit, and the fact that men do seek after it, I wouldn't be arguing with him. He might have said, for instance, that the limitations of Haworth didn't prevent Emily Brontë from finding it and exploring it in a novel of extraordinary genius, and that one of his proletarian novelists might conceivably do the same thing among the tenements and meat works of Chicago. But *Wuthering Heights* is a novel that Mr Rhodes doesn't mention for the very good reason that it does exhibit a vast world of the spirit that cannot be explained, let along explained away, by the use of Marxian principles.

And that is the only point in my argument that I really care about. Like Mr Rhodes I look forward to more and more novels of the type that he describes. Lord knows we need them badly enough, particularly in our own country. But the history of the novel alone will show that there are places in the human spirit where the Marxian word doesn't run.

Tomorrow, 4 August 1937 (v.3, no.20), pp.632-3. This essay is a comment on three articles on 'Heroes in Fiction' by Winston Rhodes, in *Tomorrow*, 9 June, 23 June, and 7 July 1937. Rhodes replied to Sargeson's article in a letter to *Tomorrow* (1 September), which was answered by Sargeson (15 September).

]3[

MR FAIRBURN AND THE MODERN WORLD

In his recent review of Mr Fairburn's poem, *Dominion*, A. C. touched on an important point. He says that Mr Fairburn has produced a 'synthesis'; but he does not enlarge his statement much beyond that. It would, however, appear to have been one of Mr Fairburn's purposes in writing the poem to produce this synthesis (for the purpose of my argument, I would rather call it 'form'); so it may be of some interest to readers if I make some enquiry (slight, I admit) as to whether a valid form has been produced.

This question of form is one which has very much engaged the attention of philosophers, particularly Thomist philosophers; but I don't want to go into all that, mainly for the reason that I know very little about it. I would say, however, that Thomist influence is evident in the poem, as these lines show:

> Our minds are molecules
> awaiting detonation: in that moment
> they shall become the pure act that, being,
> so ends itself.

It is more to my purpose to quote the following passages from Lewis Mumford's *Herman Melville*. Mr Mumford talks about post-

Civil War America being 'characterised by a single figure: the failure to achieve form. . . .' 'the energies of the country went into purely quantitative achievements: their only formal equivalent was money . . .' 'Where there is form and culture, there is true conservation of energy through the arts: where there is only energy without end or form, the mechanism may be speeded up indefinitely without increasing anything except the waste and lost motion.'

That seems to me an extremely important statement.

Now a few years ago, Hart Crane, an American poet, in an extraordinary poem entitled 'The Bridge' (a poem unfortunately very little known or appreciated in New Zealand) set himself the colossal task of imposing this form that was lacking—the task, as it were, that Dante in his day succeeded in. Crane failed in his task but he probably failed because the material offered by the modern world, so unlike Dante's material, made his failure inevitable. And so much the worse, perhaps, for the modern world.

In one of his essays, however, Crane says: 'What is interesting and significant will emerge only under the conditions of our submission to, and examination of, the organic effects on us⁻of these [he is talking about skyscrapers, steam whistles and other surface phenomena of our time—F. S.] and other fundamental factors of our experience.' And in reading his poem you feel that he really has submitted; but in his attempt to establish his form he has begun from his concrete experience of all the material of the modern world that he could possibly come in contact with.

But what is the position in Mr Fairburn's *Dominion*?

It seems to me that Mr Fairburn does not (at any rate in the beginning of his poem) take his materials 'raw'. 'Utopia', the first section, is a sort of newspaper world; men aren't digging potatoes or getting coal out of mines; they are abstractions moving about among the abstractions of big business, finance, journalism, etc. And by bringing his reactions into the description of it all Mr Fairburn converts it into the waste land. In other words he produces a picture of men and women and their creations that is an abstraction from an abstraction.

In the next section, 'Album Leaves', he is rather more concrete. One episode, 'Back Street', is a Chekhovian vignette that is perfectly done. In the main, however, it is still a paper world that he is dealing with.

Then comes 'Elements'—the sun, the soil, rivers, trees, flowers, fruits. The poet has thrown the abstract modern world overboard and men and women have been emptied out with it. He has arrived, as it were, at the point at which Crane begins his poem. But there are differences. Crane begins by 'accepting' (i.e., 'submitting' to) the modern world. Mr Fairburn begins by making a temporary 'acceptance' of a much more abstract version of it, and then making a complete 're-jection'. The elements he is left with are those of a latter-day garden of Eden; but the garden is untenanted owing to his eviction proceedings.

Now we come to the last two sections, 'Dialogue' and 'Struggle In A Mirror', and these sections are to me the most interesting of the poem. The poetry, particularly in its imagery, is the finest, I think, that Mr Fairburn has so far achieved, yet in every review that I have seen quotations have been taken from the earlier parts where he is more or less doing what we have for some years known he can do so well.

In 'Dialogue' we are back in the modern world again. Two men are discussing the present and the future, and it is the use that is made of Christian metaphor which suggests to me that Mr Fairburn has been somewhat arbitrary in rounding off the form that he is seeking to establish. In 'Utopia' he has described a nightmare world in which all that is implied by the Christian mythology means nothing at all; in 'Elements' he has given no hint of Christian elements; but here are some of the lines in 'Dialogue':

> . . . . to maintain
> faith unimpaired, the image of divinity
> within our restless hearts.

> For something is, my brother,
> that may not be destroyed: faith is its vessel. . . .
> In us the Word endures, a seed in rock.

And in the final section after a powerful description of a world utterly wrecked and burnt up there is this conclusion:

> In the beginning was the Word:
> and in the beginning again shall be the Word:
> the seed shall spring in blackened earth
> and the Word be made flesh.

In view of the preceding sections of the poem how can Mr Fairburn justify this arbitrary use of the concept of the Word? His view of the modern world is (or I have endeavoured to show that it is) intensely abstract. I am not saying, however, that it is not valid. But surely the poem would require to be differently written to enable this final abstraction to be presented as a valid hope for the future.

As I said to begin with, I have no illusions about the adequacy of this brief enquiry. Nor do I feel competent to answer any question I may have raised. If I have stimulated readers to investigate for themselves a most important contribution to New Zealand letters I should be well satisfied.

Tomorrow, 22 June 1938 (v.4, no.17) pp.536-7. The essay is in response to a review of Fairburn's *Dominion*, signed A. C. (Allen Curnow) in *Tomorrow*, 11 May 1938.

A. P. GASKELL: The Big Game

It would hardly make sense, I think, to talk about a typical New Zealand short story—although it would make quite good sense to talk about a typical Australian short story. I don't know though, that our lack of a strongly marked out tradition in short story writing has been altogether to our disadvantage. Not in recent years, anyhow. I don't know that we should otherwise have had these stories by A. P. Gaskell. It seems to me that the absence of the local type story has had quite a lot to do with their range and variety. Not, of course, that Mr Gaskell is an isolated phenomenon. As a colonial writer he must derive, directly or indirectly, from an older tradition. But whatever his influences may have been, the great point is that he has nicely assimilated them, and produced something distinctly his own.

And what is this that is distinctly his own?

Well, if I were asked to indicate some of the characteristics of good story writing I should say something like this: first, that the writer should have the capacity to hear, see, feel, think, imagine, invent, and arrange; second, that his capacity for using words should be such as to make the reader feel that he had received an important communication—one that would be, among many other things, both moving and entertaining, and one that would be truthful above all other things; third, that directly or indirectly, everything that he wrote should reveal an attitude. (A faith or a belief?—not in these times, I'm afraid.)

And if I more or less apply these tests to Mr Gaskell's stories, I may be able to give some brief idea of what I think he has achieved in this book.

Throughout this collection there is wonderful observation: in 'School Picnic' for instance, there is the borer dust filtering down through the slab of sunlight, the rain falling and rolling, still globular, in the dust—touches of observation that make the alert reader immediately sit up and take notice. Nor do I find genuine feeling lacking in any of the stories. Sometimes indeed, the reader is led some distance along the garden path before he discovers exactly what and where the feeling is. To take instances: 'Tidings of Joy' is essentially a story about the war, yet on the surface it consists of hardly anything more than fragments of trivial, house-warming conversation. (I hope that only the casual sort of reader will be unaware how skilfully that conversation has been arranged and used.) On the other hand 'No Sound of Battle' uses the military camp scene only incidentally; the story isn't really, I think, about the war at all; what Mr Gaskell is doing here is communicating very powerfully some feelings about the human situation of all of us—the fact that as human beings we are sometimes ridiculous, and always and inevitably mortal. Then again, turn to 'The Picture in the Paper'. Apart from other qualities, it seems to me to be distinguished by a brief but brilliant imagining of a very particular individual in a very particular situation. How, the curious reader might ask, was Mr Gaskell able to disguise himself so completely in the character of an imprisoned Maori?—completely yes, though paradoxically you somehow realize that Mr Gaskell is there all the time. And that realization is important. That is where the attitude comes in, the attitude that is revealed to a greater or less degree in each one of the stories. I can define it only as a sort of humanism, though a rather special colonial variety, one that might possibly never have developed at all if the European had remained always on European soil.

But I don't want to pursue my test-formula too far. Like all good writers Mr Gaskell can't really be judged according to any formula—his versatility alone, I should say, enables him to escape any such judgement. He is quite at home with the Maori, or the wool-store worker, or the fanatical sectarian; and equally at home with the university student or the middle-class household. He can be tight and compact and economical, so that every word counts, as he is in 'The Picture in the Paper'; or he can loosen up and spread himself as he does in 'The Cave' or 'Holiday'. He can bring off the excellent piece of literary photography that he calls 'Purity Squad'. And in 'The Pig and Whistle' he

can get away with a rather forbidding story, by using moving and penetrating touches such as the bit about the young always being impatient
with the talk of the old. Not, of course that he is faultless, or always
successful. What writer is? I wouldn't, for example, place 'Holiday', the
longest piece in the collection, among the most successful stories; but
everybody, I imagine, will be held by the strange and rapid transitions,
backwards and forwards, from comic situations to tragic ones—until
both sorts are hopelessly and ridiculously mixed up together. And
anyhow, this story is important, because it quite probably points the
way towards work that we may reasonably hope to get from Mr Gaskell
in the future. Another thing is that, whatever its faults, it is, like everything that its author has written in this book, always and pre-eminently
readable:

It remains only to say that no literate New Zealander will have any
excuse for not reading the book.

Book review in *Landfall*, March 1947 (v.1, no.1), pp.68-70.

]5[

KATHERINE MANSFIELD

I'm afraid I find myself in a rather unhappy situation. The short stories of Katherine Mansfield are among the most famous stories of this century—or at any rate, some of them are. So I don't feel it to be altogether an advantage that I myself have written short stories. I imagine that many writers of fiction just don't read the work of many of their fellow craftsmen—let alone talk about it in public. And I think for a very good reason. Because if you are a writer you will probably find you have to be very careful about your influences. You may know that the stories of such and such a writer are generally reckoned to be very good stories indeed, but if they don't happen to be more or less in the tradition that you are working in yourself, you may feel it necessary not to expose yourself to their influence too much. Still, I fancy most of us take the risk pretty frequently. Reading books is much easier than writing them, and very much more pleasant and enjoyable.

Now, you will have noticed that I used the word 'tradition'. There are readers, and there are even professional critics, who imagine that if you have a story to tell you simply tell it, and don't concern yourself with any particular tradition, or style, or method of approach. With one or two important exceptions however, I'm afraid that this viewpoint is a mistake. And certainly it turns out to be a fallacy if you endeavour to apply it to Katherine Mansfield's stories.

There are, of course, many traditions, and many points to be considered about each one of them. For instance, many critics have referred to the influence of Russian short stories on Katherine Mansfield's work, particularly those by Anton Chekhov. And certain it is that if you read Chekhov you see the influence. I would like to show that Katherine Mansfield established herself in a tradition that hasn't a great deal to do with anything she may have derived from this Russian writer. No, what I think every reader must feel, and feel very strongly, is that she is in the *feminine* tradition.

And perhaps my saying that will make some listeners laugh and say, Why, of course, silly—she was a woman wasn't she?

But my reply is that it isn't nearly so clear-cut and straightforward as all that. Because what I have called the feminine tradition in fiction, was to a very great extent brought into being by a London printer and bookseller of the 18th century. His name was Samuel Richardson, and one of his novels he calls *Pamela*. The story is about a pretty servant girl whose impregnable virtue wears down her wicked master—until he turns virtuous himself and marries the girl. It is told in the form of letters, most of them signed by Pamela herself, and if the name, Samuel Richardson, were not on the title page, I imagine many readers might find it impossible to believe that a man could compose letters so saturated with what we call feminine sensibility. The book is, indeed, an astonishing performance, but you have only to think of some novel written in a more masculine tradition (one, say, by Richardson's great contemporary, Henry Fielding) to see how serious its shortcomings are. It is, in fact, what I would call a *minor* novel. And I think it is fair to go on and say that the feminine tradition is the *minor* tradition. That's not a reproach though, not necessarily—indeed it might very well be a compliment. Because it is in this feminine, this minor tradition of fiction-writing, that you find some of the best stories. Those of Jane Austen, for instance. And coming on to our own times, those of Mr E. M. Forster. And coming to our own *place*, some of those of Katherine Mansfield.

Because as you all know Katherine Mansfield was New Zealand born.

But before I try to explain just how I feel about some of her stories I must first answer this question: What is one of the outstanding characteristics of novels and stories in the feminine tradition? And the answer is this: A tendency to be concerned with the part rather than the whole—in other words a tendency to make your story depend for its effectiveness on the isolated details and moments of life. These details and moments can, of course, be very beautifully and significantly rendered; and when you have a writer of the stature of, say, Jane Austen, they nearly always are. But the point to remember is that if they are not, the story will not only fail, but fail very badly. Because everything is so very tenuous—everything is, as it were, hanging by the finest of threads.

Well, now that I have given you some brief idea of my line of approach to Katherine Mansfield's work, let me say something about two of her stories. First, one called 'The Voyage'. This, to me, is without question one of the finest things she wrote. It is about a child and her grandmother who are crossing by night boat from Picton to Wellington. All you are given are little details about the trip, and little scraps of conversation—but you gather that the child's mother has died, and her grandmother is taking her back home with her to live in Wellington. The child, Fenella, looks after a troublesome umbrella, and her grandmother says her prayers and deals with stewards and stewardesses. Here is Katherine Mansfield at her best. The old lady has seen a basket of ham sandwiches;

> She went up to them and touched the top one delicately with her finger.
> 'How much are the sandwiches?' she asked.
> 'Tuppence!' bawled a rude steward, slamming down a knife and fork.
> Grandma could hardly believe it.
> 'Twopence *each*?' she asked.
> 'That's right,' said the steward, and he winked at his companion.
> Grandma made a small, astonished face. Then she whispered primly to Fenella, 'What wickedness!'

Now a good story is like a good dinner—or a good anything else. If it satisfies you, there is nothing much to say about it—except perhaps murmur something rather vague that is intended to express your appreciation. But I would like you to note two points about this story. The first is that the characters tend to be somewhat larger than life. That is, they are not just *a* child and *a* grandmother. No, there is a sense in which it is true to say that the child is everybody's child, and the old lady everybody's grandmother. And when you feel something like that about a story, it is always a sign that it is a good story. A very good example would be that wonderful book, *Don Quixote*. We all know people who tend to try to live in an ideal dream world. They are summed up, perfectly, in the famous Don. And we know people who tend to be humdrum practical realists. They are Sancho Panzas. And the second point about the story I would like you to notice is this: towards the end

the child enters her grandpa's bedroom, and above the bed there is a
text: It reads:

> Lost! One Golden Hour
> Set with Sixty Diamond Minutes.
> *No* Reward Is offered
> For It Is GONE FOR EVER!

Now I think that text may have a significance the author hardly
intended it should. Because always, as I hinted a few minutes ago, it is
the moments (the diamond minutes and the golden hours) that are so
important in Katherine Mansfield's stories. And I think I can illustrate
this point by what I have to say about the second story I have chosen. It
is called 'Her First Ball'—and the title by itself almost tells the story. A
young country girl is staying with her town cousins who take her to a
drill-hall ball. It is all very much indeed in the feminine tradition.
Dresses, gloves, powder, flowers—and the similes come tumbling out:
*A girl's dark head pushes above her white fur like a flower through snow
. . . little satin shoes chase each other like birds. . . .* But later on we come
to the point of the story. The girl, Leila, bewildered and enchanted by it
all, is breathless with excitement. How heavenly, how simply heavenly!
she thinks. She dances with young men with glossy hair—and then with
an older man who is both bald and fat. He perceives that it is her first
dance and tells her that he has been doing this sort of thing for thirty
years. Then he goes on and pictures Leila herself in years to come. Her
pretty arms will have turned into short fat ones, he says. And she will be
sitting up on the stage with the chaperones while her daughter dances
down below. And his words destroy her happiness. The music suddenly
sounds sad. And she asks herself an agonizing question: Why doesn't
happiness last for ever? 'Deep inside her' we read, 'a little girl threw her
pinafore over her head and sobbed.' And of course she hates the bald fat
man.

Now I don't know how my listeners will feel about this story, but
for me it just doesn't come off. It is, no doubt, true enough of many
young girls, but for my part I'm afraid I can't help making some comparisons. For instance, had any of Shakespeare's young heroines
(wonderful ones, say, like Perdita in *The Winter's Tale*, or Marina in
Pericles)—had they encountered that elderly bald fat man, and had he
told them that shocking truth—well, I don't know, but I fancy they
would have just laughed and asked him why he wanted to say anything
so obvious. In other words, young female character can be made of

somewhat sterner stuff, and there is something in my make-up which refuses to accept the suggestion that that particular trying moment in the girl's life was really so important and significant as it is intended to be.

There is another story which is called, very simply, 'Bliss'. And again you have a young woman who experiences a few hours of intense happiness for no particular reason. She is just happy to be alive, that is all. But it all ends with the discovery that her husband is engaged in a love-affair with a woman they have been entertaining at dinner. But here's the point—if the mere fact of being alive will make you happy, then you must be careful, because being alive must always imply that you will have to be prepared to face disagreeable experiences. And so many of Katherine Mansfield's young women are unprepared. There is, indeed, a rather startling lack of variety in them, and Miss Kathleen Raine, an English critic, has gone so far as to say that she lacked the gift for inventing characters. And perhaps the explanation may be partly found in the fact that Katherine Mansfield, both as a woman and a writer, spent much of her life in a state of suspension between two hemispheres. As a young woman she hated New Zealand and longed to get away from it, yet it was Wellington she wrote about towards the end of her life when she was doing her finest work. But I don't think a state of suspension is a good state to be in when it is a question of inventing characters. You have to depend on yourself too much—and what you find *in* yourself. Suspension (or to use another word, freedom), always has its dangers, and it is particularly dangerous for a writer to be virtually free from any sense of social tradition. And up to a point it is true to say that is the situation Katherine Mansfield found herself in.

But I don't want to leave you with the impression that her work is nearly all shortcomings. Not at all. Perhaps it is still a little too soon to say for sure just how good a writer she was. But in the meantime one can at least say that there are, as there are with all good writers, certain of her stories that are 'musts'. I want just briefly to refer to five of them.

First, 'Prelude'. It is mainly about children, and it begins with a horse and cart journey which rather resembles the beginning of the chaise and pair journey in Chekhov's excellent story, 'The Steppe'. Next, 'At The Bay': the same children and adults appear, and among other things the story is notable for the wonderful evocation of the New Zealand seaside—that is, when the weather doesn't let you down. 'The Garden Party'—perhaps, taken all round, this is Katherine Mansfield's most accomplished and technically satisfying story. Again we meet the sensitive young girl who looks forward to a day of happiness, and finds it a day of tragedy instead. 'The Fly'. It all takes place in a businessman's office, but as it is really about World War no. I, it has perhaps more social implications than any other story. Last, 'The Life of Ma Parker'. It is a sketch of a London charwoman, and here again is a taste of Katherine Mansfield at her best. The old char is with her grandson:

> 'Gran, gi' us a penny!' he coaxed.
> 'Be off with you; Gran ain't got no pennies.'
> 'Yes, you 'ave.'
> 'No, I ain't.'
> 'Yes, you 'ave. Gi' us one!'
> Already she was feeling for the old, squashed, black leather purse.
> 'Well, what'll you give your gran?'
> He gave a shy little laugh and pressed closer. She felt his eyelid

quivering against her cheek. 'I ain't got nothing,' he murmured . . . .

A radio talk first broadcast in the 1YA session 'Mainly about Books' on 28 July 1948. A shorter version of the talk was published in the *New Zealand Listener* of 6 August 1948 (v.19, no.476) under the title 'The Feminine Tradition: a Talk about Katherine Mansfield'. This full text is taken from Sargeson's manuscripts in the Alexander Turnbull Library.

JAMES COURAGE: The Fifth Child

It appears to me that Mr Courage, who has all the technical skill necessary to write a first-rate novel, has been too much hampered by the intractable nature of his raw material. The people in *The Fifth Child* are South Island sheep-farming pukka sahibs—but you don't meet them on the farm. Mrs Warner, who has an income of her own, has rented a house in a city suburb, while her husband continues to 'mess' about the farm. For company she has her little boy and girl, and two servants— and shortly they are joined by her other two children, both in their later teens and fresh from boarding school. Mrs Warner is soon to have her fifth child: unfortunately her husband has been 'insisting on his rights'. She is bored and anxious, annoyed and depressed—and she wants to be away from her husband while she tries to decide whether she will leave him permanently or not. She has had much to put up with over the years, apparently. 'One of the habits she had never, never after what seemed a lifetime of trying, managed to break him into was that of eating punctual meals at a well-set table.' Mr Warner came out from England as a young man, and one infers that he must have quickly made up his mind that it was pointless to come so far only to be bored by the table manners of Hampstead. His wife doesn't have much of a time in her suburb, however. She takes her younger children into town and lets them eat themselves sick on cake; if one of them is having a bath she worries about whether the blind has been pulled down; her teen-age daughter makes dates with a boy-friend; her eldest son doesn't know what he wants to do; and her husband keeps coming down from the farm in his car to tell her he sees no reason why she shouldn't return to him. Finally, after the birth of her child, she does return. (Her husband undertakes to remain in his own bed for the future.) After all, both servants have given notice, her son is going off to England to become a doctor, and she has consented to her daughter's tentative three year engagement. Things are breaking up in fact, so she must be brave and take it and not let the whole show down.

The material of *The Fifth Child* is thoroughly banal: there aren't many suburban fatuities that Mr Courage has left out. But a writer should never be blamed for his choice of material. All that may fairly be said is that he must recognize that the limitations inherent in certain material may make it most unlikely that he will succeed in creating a major work of art. Mr Courage's material is of the sort that may yield very good minor art with the right handling. And it must be recorded right now that there are very beautiful passages in *The Fifth Child*, particularly some of those dealing with the two younger children. There is also, throughout the book, a really penetrating rendering of the character of the adolescent daughter, Barbara. Mr Courage's technique is rather like that of the Imagist poets, who try to make you see very clearly, and leave you to draw your own conclusions. Nevertheless, it is impossible for any serious novelist to finish his story without letting you know (at any rate, implicitly), that he has judged his characters. And much of your feeling about the quality of his work will depend upon whether or not you are convinced that his judgements are the right ones. I'm afraid I disagree with Mr Courage's main judgement. With somewhat more detachment from his material he might very well have avoided his tendency to side with the depressing Mrs Warner. Nor do I feel that the almost complete absence of any social context, except the pukka sahib one, is altogether to the novel's advantage. But I would emphasize that it is a distinguished contribution to the literature of our country. There isn't a single hint of the technical ineptitude, the earnest amateurishness, that has disfigured so many of our 'efforts'.

Book review in *Landfall*, March 1949 (v.3, no.1), pp.72-73.

DAN DAVIN: Roads From Home

It is probably worth noting that a review of a New Zealand novel may be as difficult to write as the novel itself. The labour will not, of course, be nearly so prolonged, but in each case the difficulties will be similar. And perhaps one may very briefly sum them up by saying that for the novelist the question will be: Where am I to derive my standards of excellence from? For the critic: What standards of judgement have I? Unlike the Australians we have no established tradition of our own, which we may choose either to accept and develop, or else take as a point of departure. Hence the somewhat haphazard variety of our novels and criticism. And although variety may appear not such a bad thing from the reader's viewpoint, it will not be an advantage to the writer if it appears unrelated and merely confusing, because much of his energy will be drained away in a difficult preliminary endeavour to discover his necessary bearings.

So much for the problems of the situation. They are not, however, problems that remain exactly the same year after year, since there is always the possibility that a new novel will make one think rather differently about them. And this is certainly what happens when one reads Dan Davin's *Roads From Home*. Not that Mr Davin has actually solved the problems; but neither is it true to say that they are evaded. Instead, one rather gets the impression that with the aid of his superabundant energy he has knocked them right and left. Nevertheless the plain and encouraging fact of the matter is simply this: that something very like New Zealand is to be found in astonishing abundance inside the covers of this novel.

In the story the reader finds his attention mainly directed to the two grown-up sons of an Irish Catholic railwayman. They are John, who also works on the railway; and Ned, who is to satisfy his mother's pious wish by becoming a priest. John has already set out on his own road from home, and discovered it to be an almost impossibly difficult one; he has married a Protestant girl, only to discover afterwards that he is not the man she was hoping to marry. But luckily his mother isn't aware of this situation; for her it is quite bad enough that his marriage is a mixed one, and that the child that has been born has not yet been baptized. Ned's situation is even more difficult. Not only is he deciding not to be a priest, he is on the point of losing his faith as well. Eventually his mother will have to know, but he cannot in the meantime face up to the suffering that his decision will cause her; and yet he can avoid inflicting it only by carrying out the religious duties which his mother expects from him, but in which he is ceasing to believe.

These apparently insoluble predicaments of John and Ned are disclosed in the early chapters; or rather, one should say, they gradually emerge from a wealth of relevant detail, which the author presents with an unusual degree of literary skill, restraint and discretion—though without any sacrifice of his natural vigour so far as this reviewer can discern. Moreover, in addition to the railway background, the story depends for its development on such typical features of New Zealand life as a football match, an afternoon's rabbiting, and a race meeting. And the solutions, when they are finally arrived at, are satisfying enough if one remembers the strong Irish Catholic feeling for the family and its continuity. There is, indeed, only one matter about which the reader may feel some uncertainty. Mr Davin has a brilliant gift for exposition, so it is hardly to be wondered at that he has used long expository passages in telling his story. There are occasions, however, when they seem to distract attention away from what is happening in the story, instead of concentrating attention on it—occasions when the reader tends to pause and think of the author as a gifted *mind* rather than a gifted *novelist*.

Finally it must be said that, apart from everything else, there is a really remarkable feature about *Roads From Home*; and one that appears quite contradictory at first sight. How is it one feels such an abundance of New Zealand in a story that draws its material from the Irish Catholic minority? The answer is simply that the book takes the puritan spirit for granted; it is saturated with it. One remembers G. K. Chesterton's complaint about H. G. Wells: that because *he* was born into little Bethel, he supposed everybody else was too. But in New Zealand the tradition that Chesterton represented has somehow become inextricably confused with that of little Bethel.

Book review in the *New Zealand Listener*, 10 June 1949 (v.21, no.520), pp.17-18, under the title 'Life Abounding'.

]8[

RODERICK FINLAYSON: Tidal Creek

It is one of the merits of Mr Finlayson's book that it will set many readers thinking about the impulses that brought their forefathers to New Zealand. When our country began to be settled scientific socialism wasn't heard of, but the humanitarian sentiments of utopian socialism were becoming widely known and felt. Many of the early immigrants had had painful experience of the disadvantageous side of the social and economic bargain so very admirably summarized by the Rev. Dr Folliott in Peacock's *Crotchet Castle*—'There are two great classes of men: those who produce much and consume little; and those who consume much and produce nothing.' Many of them must have emigrated with the hope that they would find a better order of things overseas; and their things-will-be-better-out-there feeling is probably connected with the present-day New Zealander's belief that things *are* better out here.

Mr Finlayson cannot, however, be said to share in this prevalent belief. As may be discovered from his interesting essay, *Our Life in This Land*, published in 1940, he believes the one clear advantage of settlement in New Zealand was the opportunity it gave men to acquire sufficient land for what might be described as mixed subsistence farming, and so establish themselves in a fruitful, but at the same time chastening, relation with the mysterious forces of Nature—and farming more or less of this kind did indeed become the foundation of our national life, until refrigerated shipping was introduced and began to destroy 'our soil, our health, and our social structure'.

In reading *Tidal Creek* it is an advantage, I think, to know something of this historical background, and Mr Finlayson's attitude to it—otherwise the reader may fail to see what the author is driving at, and feel inclined to dismiss the story as a mere piece of period reporting. *Tidal Creek* belongs to a quite different literary order; and a convenient parallel may be found in the short stories of Henry Lawson. What Lawson did for Australia, Mr Finlayson more self-consciously attempts to do for New Zealand. That is to say, he attempts to give literary body to what is for him essentially true and vital in the colonial spirit; and there is a further parallel with Lawson inasmuch as he does so at a time when the everyday manifestations of that spirit are becoming more and more rapidly extinguished.

Uncle Ted, then, the untidy bachelor farmer on his untidy little farm at Tidal Creek, is not just an eccentric whose idiosyncrasies were carefully observed by his young nephew, remembered, and are now faithfully documented by a nostalgic author in search of the odd and old-fashioned. There is, of course, something of that, and at the same time there is a great deal of something more. Everything that Uncle Ted says and does has a double function; it is what one expects from a character so indubitably flesh and blood; and it is perfectly in keeping with all that the author has ever felt, and passionately felt, about the country to which he belongs. Which is to say that Uncle Ted has not been copied from life, he has been created; and to a very great extent successfully created.

His adventures and misfortunes are never presented as mere anecdotes, detached and complete in themselves: instead they each of them go to make up a larger pattern of things—a pattern which, if you examine it closely enough may be found to reveal simple clues to the essentials of the good life for men upon this earth. For example: waste is bad; the ancient rites of hospitality and friendship must be observed; true well-being is in the labour of achieving, not in the leisure of achievement; men should be reconciled to each other, to Nature, and to God; the untidiness of the countryside is a sign of life, the tidiness of the city may be a sign of death.

It is possible that *Tidal Creek* may eventually come to be regarded as a sort of swan song of our country's comparative innocence. (Though 'song' may be hardly the right word, since Mr Finlayson's writing is visual rather than aural.) But in the meantime its transparent honesty will recommend itself to all readers who are prepared to appreciate something genuine if and when it comes their way. As those who know the best of the author's short stories may expect, all that is familiar and for the most part taken for granted in our environment, is accurately observed and deeply felt. Personally, I would disagree with Mr Finlayson in only one particular. Wouldn't the 'bees' that buzz around the cow-muck on page 203 really be hover flies?

Book review in the *New Zealand Listener*, 22 July 1949 (v.21, no.526), p.18. Printed under the title 'The Colonial Spirit'.

ROLF BOLDREWOOD: Robbery Under Arms

Until about forty years ago Boldrewood's novel was so well known that almost anybody in Australia or New Zealand could have told you who Starlight was, or Warrigal, or Rainbow. Not today though, at least not in New Zealand. With rare exceptions only the eyes of the old-timers light up.

The story first appeared as a serial in the *Sydney Mail* in 1881, and if some accounts are to be believed it attracted very little notice until it appeared as a book in 1888. *Huckleberry Finn* first appeared as a book in 1884, and there are times when one can't help wondering whether Mark Twain read Boldrewood's story in its serial form. Why did Twain decide on a 'first person' story, one that would allow Huckleberry to use his own language? I am no scholar in these matters and don't know, but it is possible to suppose that he *may* have been following Boldrewood's example. At least it seems clear that he was anticipated in his discovery of the wonderful uses that colonial vernacular could be put to.

This handsome Oxford edition is introduced by Dr Thomas Wood, the Englishman who fell in love with Australia in the 1930s, and wrote the book, *Cobbers*. Dr Wood's remarks are perceptive and generously enthusiastic, but it is impossible to agree when he says that Boldrewood 'went wrong at the start by deciding that the story should be told in reminiscence by a man of little schooling'. It isn't possible when a little previously it is said (in effect) that only Dad, a few minor characters, and Starlight's horse, Rainbow, come fully to life in a very long story. How can it possibly happen that such a book is now to be found among The World's Classics? Well, let me try to explain.

Robbery Under Arms is told in the first person by the young bushranger, Dick Marston. He writes his life story while he is in prison waiting to be hanged for killings incidental to stealing cattle and holding up coaches. But he doesn't hang. Instead he is released after twelve years, and marries the woman who has waited for him through all the years of his wickedness plus his prison term. The story, very briefly epitomized, is something like this. Dick's father is a Lincoln-shire man transported to New South Wales for poaching. After doing his time he marries and goes bush farming. His children are Dick, Jim and Aileen, and as they grow up they notice their father's mysterious disappearances. The two boys are gradually involved in his cattle-stealing and he reveals to them his hideout, the Hollow, where they meet Starlight and his *âme damnée*, Warrigal, the half-caste. No living person knows of the existence of the Hollow except these five, and so long as they remain or return there they are never discovered. Their many exciting adventures are frequently amusing and always profitable (they include a trip as far as Adelaide with stolen cattle, and a period of hard work on the goldfields); but when Starlight and the two brothers decide on honest lives beyond the sea, only Dick survives a battle with the police as they are attempting to reach the sea-coast.

Now all this, I know, must make the book sound like an out of date Australian 'western', one that very few adults can be expected to give their attention to these days. I must insist that it is nothing of the kind. You can say hard things about the story, and Dr Wood says some of them. There is the moralizing obviously: the narrator's tiresome insist-ence that he knows his life to be one of wrong-doing; his sentimental imagining of what it might, and worse, *ought* to be—and thank heaven never is until the story is over. And there are generous helpings of the spittoon philosophy that is so detested by those who fancy themselves as professional wiseacres. Worse again, there are the shadowy characters: Starlight for example. He is an Englishman of noble birth whose real name is never revealed. He is a slight dark handsome man, a cultivated generous courageous man, a quick strong man, a wonderful horseman, chivalrous and gentlemanly always, particularly towards women whose hands he usually kisses—and stops short at that. One never quite sees or believes in him, and yet one never forgets him. And the reason I am going to suggest is that he is not so much a man as a myth: more, a prophetic myth. His resemblance to that colonial figure of his own time, and later, the remittance man, is obvious; but as Captain Starlight he reaches all the way forward to such popular figures of our own day as Captain Marvel, or Superman. Or if you like to go backwards in time, Robin Hood, or King Arthur's knights. And once a point like this is perceived, then, I think, various hidden meanings begin to reveal themselves; meanings which are so very closely wrapped up with the quality of the book. Moreover Starlight isn't the only myth; and if you are interested in symbols you will find stacks of them to fascinate you not only in themselves, but because of what they imply.

But first there is the language, the Australian language of Dick Marston. To this day it is wonderfully fresh, alive and transfigured on the printed page, wonderfully immediate and animated, and except where it occasionally falls down, wonderfully employed to carry the weight of the story. (For contrast one has only to think of the literary dead wood from which Marcus Clarke fashioned a crutch for that limping novel—*For The Term Of His Natural Life*.) And there is something about this language that goes further still. The Sydney *Bulletin* was pretty well on into its decadence in the early 1920s, and yet D. H. Lawrence heard in its pages something that sounded to him like the voice of an enormous continent. 'It was not mere anecdotage. It was the sheer momentaneous life of the continent. There was no consecutive thread. Only the laconic courage of experience.' That also applies to Dick Marston's narrative, though it is inadequate in some ways. No doubt we can't all expect to have D. H. Lawrence's long ears; nevertheless Dick Marston, who speaks for himself, and at the same time unconsciously speaks for a whole continent, is a man well worth listening to.

For me, what it all adds up to is something like this. Starlight and the men of the Marston family are at war with the society of their day. They just can't take it. Starlight got out of England to escape it there, and Dad escaped it by being transported; but what they escaped from is waiting for them out in Australia in its colonial form. So they try to escape again, with the two boys following their lead. But now, having already arrived at the ends of the earth, there is the problem of discovering a fresh place to escape to. Somewhere there *must* be a place (it is the semi-conscious wish, the dream at the heart of all colonizing movements surely); and sure enough they discover the remote and idyllic Hollow, where there are good streams, good grass for their stolen horses and cattle, and a good convenient cave in which they can live and be secure. (And how familiar both Hollow and cave will be to those readers who know their colonial writers! See Twain, Dreiser and others in America; see Satchell, John Mulgan and at least one other in New Zealand.) Another point is that it seems to be an entirely male world that their more or less unconscious wish directs them towards. In the story there is much sentimental longing for the company of woman, of wife and family—but on two separate occasions the narrator is betrayed by a woman. Dick's brother Jim does in fact contrive to marry and have a child. Also Starlight becomes engaged to Dick's sister, but I'm afraid this must be counted an aberration on his part; the reader is sceptical, expecting nothing to come of it—which is as it turns out. On the contrary Starlight's most deeply felt relationship is with Warrigal, and there are some extraordinary passages about it. Warrigal, whose grief over his master's death is genuinely moving, 'would have made a bridge of his own body any time to let Starlight go safe'; and on an occasion when they meet after being separated, Warrigal 'throws himself at his feet, bursting out crying like a child'.

But at least one of the book's meanings becomes wonderfully clear in a passage towards the end of the story. Dick tells the reader that he 'came into prison a big, stout, brown-haired chap, full of life, and able to jump over a dray and bullocks almost'. And how does he go out? 'A man with a set kind of face, neither one thing or the other, as if he couldn't be glad or sorry, with a fixed staring look about the eyes, a half-yellowish skin . . .'. For 'prison' substitute 'office' or 'factory'—or just what you fancy. And if you still doubt my 'prophetic myth', just lean back in your chair a moment and think—think of the thick in a jiffy lather, the top speed soap powder, the half inch on the dry brush that creates a foam of penetrating bubbles, the vital juices (or losses), the body carpets, the daily bath, the daily blah blah of press and politics, radio and cinema, the daily blah blah chorus of the teeming middlemen who inhabit every place from the shop to the university college . . . . Yes, a moment's thought please, gentle reader.

One last symbol I must mention. During Dick's prison term the Hollow is discovered by a party of prospectors. Warrigal is there, dead, killed by Dad, who has afterwards killed himself.

> . . . continents suspected deep in the south . . .
> It was something different, something
> Nobody counted on.

Book review in *Landfall*, September 1950 (v.4, no.3), p.262-5.

D. H. LAWRENCE

It is good to see that many of D. H. Lawrence's books are becoming available again, but I don't know that I am the one to be writing this note on the man and his work. It is for the younger people to decide about him now. Most of my Lawrence I read in the 1920s; and since then I have read him very little. For the purposes of writing this note I began to re-read, but didn't continue when I found I hadn't the uninterrupted time to give to an exacting task. So I ask the reader (and D. H. Lawrence's shade) to forgive me for mainly relying on that imperfect faculty, my memory.

But first I must make another point clear. There is much of Lawrence's work that I have never read, and am never likely to now I'm afraid. *The Plumed Serpent*, for example: I never forget my attempts to read that novel before I abandoned them as hopeless. And the complete *Lady Chatterley's Lover* I know only as *L'Amant de Lady Chatterley*. How extraordinary that is! Nearly everything Lawrence wrote deserves as much attention as anything so far written this century—and yet I have been able to come by one of his novels only in translation. My copy has an introduction by André Malraux, and that too is significant. The English text is officially proscribed as a piece of obscenity; but if it were really that, how could it be anything but boring to an intelligent Frenchman? It is generous of M. Malraux in his introduction to speak of *bêtise humaine*, when the adjective more aptly might have been *anglaise*.

In his book Mr Aldington mentions that Lawrence's work, during his lifetime, was much better thought of almost anywhere abroad, and particularly in America, than it was in England. I think it is quite easy for the New Zealander to understand why this should be so in America: Americans, like New Zealanders, would tend to recognize Lawrence as one of themselves. What I mean is that we tend in many ways to think of Lawrence as a colonial writer; and I suggest the reason is that he was so well and truly tied up with something characteristic of all English-colonial settlement. I mean little Bethel; and the poisonous psychological and social effects that, hand in hand with nineteenth-century industrial and finance capitalism, it has produced. It was Lawrence's little Bethel aura that Mr Aldington, his personal friend during his lifetime, found so very irritating; and it is evident from his book that he is still irritated by it twenty years after the death of a 'genius, but . . .'. My point is that this aura would not have appeared odd, unexpected, or even particularly exasperating in an American or colonial writer; but you don't exactly find yourself launched on the mainstream of English life and literature, if you find yourself born into the sectarian home of a Nottinghamshire coal-miner.

But first let me try to say what sort of a writer it is that we may expect to come out of little Bethel. Frequently he will come from a home that is female-dominated and tend to be mother's boy; frequently he will be opinionative, theory-ridden, arrogant, priggish, tending to argue and preach in and out of season; his puritanism will not really admit compromise and he will want things one hundred per cent, demanding perfection in both life and literature, and setting up a howl when he doesn't get it; he will always tend to be a little upset at the sight of people taking their pleasure; and when he finds himself in the company of those whose background he recognizes as quite different from his own, he will tend to suffer abominably from feelings of inferiority and envy. And sometimes it will all bring him to the point where, instead of seeing himself in the modest role of self-liberator (and perhaps liberator of some of those who suffer under little Bethel), he will feel himself chosen to be the saviour of the entire world—in which case he will be fortunate if he has powerful qualities that may compensate and save him from becoming completely insane. But do let there be no mistake about it. Lawrence was hopelessly implicated in the complex I have sketched out—and so are most of the inhabitants of New Zealand. And do let me emphasize that what particular church you were born into or brought up in, or whether or not you have ever set foot in any church during your life, just doesn't affect the matter at all. You don't escape little Bethel—its ramifications are infinitely more far-reaching than those of any Gestapo; and perhaps those who imagine they escape them do so least of all.

The point about Lawrence is that besides being implicated, he was acutely and savagely aware that he was implicated; he knew the thing for what it was, and for the effects it had produced; and at the same time he knew there was no real or immediate escape for himself or anybody else. It was a double knowledge that you find running right through his ambivalent nature; the double knowledge of a situation so desperate, that it always seems quite miraculous when anybody closely involved succeeds in disentangling himself sufficiently to see it clearly and objectively. Yet that miracle Lawrence achieved. It must be granted that the aura is always there, but over and over again the devil is recognized, and defeated if only on the printed page; and if the devil has many disguises and succeeds in slipping back into a great number of the pages, without Lawrence's apparently being aware of what is happening—well, you mustn't expect too much of any one man.

There is an excellent illustration of my argument in 'Reflections on the Death of a Porcupine', written in 1925. It seems to me that something like the essence of nearly all Lawrence's work is concentrated into an essay of about seven thousand words. To begin with you get some of those wonderfully fresh and vivid evocations of human and animal life: it is Lawrence at his best: there isn't a hint of abstraction: it is all plus, not minus: life is more life, as some people say Cézanne's apples are more apple. But halfway through the essay there comes a change. The incantations begin: 'Life is more vivid in a snake than in a butterfly . . . . Life is more vivid in the Mexican who drives the wagon, than in the two horses in the wagon . . . . Life is more vivid in me, than in the Mexican . . .'. Much of it is quite wonderful, of course: 'Being is *not* ideal, as Plato would have it: nor spiritual. It is a transcendent form of existence, and as much material as existence is . . . . In the seeds of the dandelion, as it floats with its little umbrella of hairs, sits the Holy Ghost in tiny compass.' But eventually you reach this: 'You will know that any creature or race is still alive with the Holy Ghost, when it can subordinate the lower creature or races, and assimilate them into a new incarnation.'

Now I know that I am over-simplifying, but perhaps I'm not too wide of the mark when I say that the three stages that you find in this essay are more or less the stages of Lawrence's entire work. Who can ever forget those early novels, *The White Peacock* and *Sons and Lovers*? They are vivid with life, life plus, life made marvellously manifest in plant flower bird beast—and human beings despite the discouraging social environment. Lawrence was writing of what he knew, what he felt and what he understood. It had of course to be Lawrence to know feel and understand—and write. And it was. But in *Aaron's Rod* or *Women in Love* you immediately notice that there has been a disturbing change. The argumentativeness, which had been more or less a family affair, is now extended very much further; and Lawrence has acquired the habit of popping his aristocratic literary and bohemian friends into his novels—after only very brief and recent experience of them very often. It mightn't have been so bad if he had merely rendered them without comment just as he had perceived them—but not at all. He *had* to prove that he understood them, that he was better than they were, and that he could put them right by explaining all their short-comings. And the unhappy consequence is that they nearly all turn out to be caricatures. How for example could Lawrence really understand or appreciate the happy hedonism of Mr Norman Douglas? It was impossible. And it put him in an additional rage to see some of his own sacred impulses expressing themselves, through Douglas, in a round of Florentine fun and games. So he set to work to rage on paper; to argue preach rant and incant. Until he eventually arrived at the last stage of his development which shows in his Mexican writings; and is perhaps fully expressed in his story, 'The Man Who Died'. There is much to be said for this late work no doubt, but how does one overcome the awkward suspicion that his dark gods may be, secretly, close relations of the gods of little Bethel? That perhaps it is only the old devil in a new disguise after all?

But I hope I don't delude myself into thinking I am expounding the 'truth' about D. H. Lawrence. He and his work cut figures far too great for almost anybody to see in anything like their full stature and wonder: his pugnacious vitality, something that nothing and nobody could kill, by itself separates him out from all but a few of his contemporaries. (One can agree with Mr Aldington's 'genius, but . . .'; but disagree if the but is applied to Lawrence specially: all geniuses are geniuses but; and to suppose that they can be geniuses pure and undefiled, is to make a puritanical mistake.) Among the novels there is *Kangaroo*, which deserves a long note all to itself, and is particularly interesting to the New Zealand and colonial reader; and besides the novels there are the stories, the travel books, the poetry, essays, pamphlets, and letters. It is fine to see Mr Aldington's enthusiasm for that rarely seen book now, *Twilight in Italy*; and yet, who could be sure of preferring it to *Sea and Sardinia*? And about the poetry. I don't know that Lawrence's early poems can now be expected to give the young reader the feeling that he has been caught up in a new world, located somewhere between heaven and earth; but the later ones can certainly be depended upon to evoke that feeling, though with the difference perhaps that location is somewhat more difficult to define. In the best of the poems, sometimes in the very shortest, there is all of Lawrence in very tiny compass—like the Holy Ghost sitting in the seed of the dandelion. (And once again it is of particular interest to the colonial reader that this should be done in a free verse closely related to what Whitman gave us when he was at his best.) Sometimes in a love poem Lawrence seems to get so miraculously close to the never quite revealed truth of human experience, that he compels you to feel that human insight can go no further. It is a measure of his greatness. You have only to look at erotic Hindu carving to know that, after all, he may have been quite wide of the mark. Nevertheless one is inclined to suppose that in the long run the best of the poems will be preferred to the best of the novels and stories. In the novels Lawrence is prophetic, but perhaps not so destructive as he imagined himself to be; in the long run it may turn out that there is more dynamite concealed in the E. M. Forster novel.

I have seen it noted by an English reviewer that Mr Aldington's biography does not bring any fresh material to light. I don't know Lawrence sufficiently well to know whether this is so or not. It seems to me that you get as much of his story as you can reasonably expect: mining village, countryside, provincial town to begin with; Croydon and London; the extraordinary marriage, at one and the same time lucky and unlucky; the execrable persecutions; the escapes to Italy and Sicily; the fruitful blundering round the world. I ask pardon for continually referring to Lawrence's interest for colonials: his ability as a cook and a man about the house and place is something that comes very close to many of us.

Review of *Portrait of a Genius, but . . .* by Richard Aldington, *Landfall*, December 1950 (v.4, no.4), pp.357-61.

WRITING A NOVEL

I

When I was asked for a talk on this subject, at first I thought, No. Then I thought Yes—perhaps in a country like New Zealand, it is just as well if somebody who devotes much of his time to writing novels, should occasionally be permitted to say something about his problems. It is, of course, usually the reviewer whom the public hears—the man whose job it is to read novels as they are published, and try to give readers some idea of their value.

But why did I say 'in a country like New Zealand'? Let me try to explain. In England you have English reviewers dealing mainly with English novels: the parallel situation in New Zealand would be New Zealand reviewers dealing mainly with New Zealand novels. This is not so—the great majority of books dealt with are English, besides, of course, American, and translations from a number of foreign languages. Only a very tiny minority are New Zealand novels. Now this, I think, makes for a somewhat awkward situation, for both the New Zealand reviewer, and the New Zealand novelist. The reviewer is a man who spends much of his time seeing life through the printed pages of a book—and if he is a New Zealand reviewer, the life he sees is not very often New Zealand life. His reading may, indeed, have tended to isolate him from much of the life that is going on all around him. The novelist, on the other hand, knows that he can only write convincingly and well of what he knows best—and that, of course, is New Zealand life.

So much for a few general remarks—which, perhaps, should have come at the tail-end of my talk. Now I must begin all over again.

I hope I don't sound too high-flown, when I say that to write a novel is to perform a creative act. The urge to create, and the capacity to do so—these are two striking characteristics of human beings. You have only to look around you to see that this is so. There is, of course, a reverse side to our creativeness, an urge to destroy—and unfortunately a great capacity to do so these days. These characteristics are plainly visible in children. Watch a child making something, say a mud-pie—he becomes entirely concentrated on what he is doing, making something out of the material to hand, some shape or form, of a particular size colour and texture. And while he is concentrated, he is oblivious to the passing of time and all other interests. There is an implicit warning to everybody not to interfere. Finally he appears to achieve the effect he has been striving for—and then he may suddenly become indifferent to his own creation. It has absorbed him for the time being, and he has had his moment of satisfaction, but all that is past and done with now—and sometimes he will just as suddenly turn on his creation and destroy it. Now the mud-pie has no purpose which is easy to define. It was something the child *had* to make, probably it has exercised his imagination, and enabled him to express something of his own unique individuality—but there isn't a great deal you can say about it. At least for certain. When the child grows up, he doesn't continue to make mud-pies, but, if he is fortunate, much of his life's labour will be a sort of extension of that kind of activity. I say 'if he is fortunate' because in our present-day society, with its technological and commercial emphasis, a great proportion of the population is engaged in labour which is either non-creative, or else creative only in a routine sort of way: as likely as not the object created will be machine-made, and lack the imagination, the liveliness and the individuality, which we associate with hand-made objects: and the maker will be deprived of that intense satisfaction which comes from personal creative achievement—and which, like most human satisfactions, makes for a feeling of well-being and sanity. I am, I know, touching on a very big subject. The point is, however, that the novelist belongs to that minority group of people who have been able to retain, and extend into their adult lives, those impulses which drive children to make mud-pies—impulses which they are able to link to much larger, and much more highly developed creative purposes. Though naturally, I don't mean to suggest that everybody who does routine work, is necessarily quite uncreative in a personal way: the routine worker may have his creative hobbies, which he exercises in his leisure time.

I can remember, in my own case, that this transition, from the mud-pie to something more highly developed, took place when I was twelve years old. I read *Ivanhoe,* and immediately decided I wanted to be a novelist like Sir Walter Scott. But strangely enough, instead of setting to work to write a novel of my own, I began to copy out *Ivanhoe* into one of my school exercise books. My mother discovered what I was doing, and I was greatly humiliated when she ridiculed my labours as a waste of time. It was another twelve years before the impulse to write a novel returned to me—and by that time, I had discovered a great many novelists besides Walter Scott. There wasn't, this time, any question of merely copying out another man's book—nevertheless, the idea of copying must have been strongly implanted in my mind, because I supposed in my ignorance that some book that I admired, such as James Joyce's *A Portrait of the Artist as a Young Man,* for example, was a sort of accurate copy of what had actually happened in the author's life. So I set to work to write my own life story from its earliest beginnings, rigorously determined to admit nothing that was in any way imaginary. But I hadn't got very far before I decided the results were appalling. I told myself that nobody was going to be bothered to read this dull, lifeless stuff—and luckily nobody ever was bothered—except myself. But, in another couple of years I felt myself impelled to try again. I had, in the meantime, tried my hand at a few short stories—and although I was still dominated by the idea that I must endeavour to transcribe what had actually happened, I had at least made some advance in supposing that what had happened to other people might appear on paper as rather more interesting than what had happened to myself. Now I remembered a girl whom I had greatly admired at school, a beautiful talented creature whom everybody admired. Since I had left school I had lost sight of her. What had happened to her? I didn't know, and I wondered—and wondered until I decided my novel would be about what *had* happened to her, as I imagined it. The only thing I would copy would be the small-town background, which would be as familiar to her as it was to me. It took me more than a year to write the novel, and during the hours I worked on it, I was as completely absorbed as any child ever was over a mud-pie: and by the time I was finishing off the 70,000 words that the story seemed to require, I was in a state of exaltation. It was, perhaps, my first adult experience of the delights of creation—though of course many of its pains and penalties as well. The novel wasn't a success—nevertheless it was the most notable advance that I had made so far. By revealing to me my capacity to invent and imagine, to work at transforming the raw material of life, until it began to assume a more fresh and lively appearance, my novel had enabled me to rid myself finally of the notion of copying which had hampered me for so long. Nevertheless, I still had to admit the novel wasn't a success—and years passed before I could feel sure that I had discovered the reason why.

Up to that time I had read scarcely any New Zealand novels at all, and those that I *had* read I hadn't thought much of. I measured them against the standard of the great European novelists whom I most admired—and naturally, I found them falling short. Now, however, conscious that I had fallen extremely short in my own attempt, I began to read every New Zealand novel that I could lay my hands on. And it seemed to me that, in almost every case, language which did not differ a very great deal from that used by English novelists, was used to deal with the material of New Zealand life. My thoughts kept turning back to my own novel, and the Galsworthian prose style it was written in—and for the first time, so far as I can remember, I asked myself the question whether there might not be an appropriate New Zealand language to deal with the material of New Zealand life. I had got rid of my notion of copying *life*, but it seemed I still had to rid myself of another sort of copying. Copying language, as it were. The question, moreover, led on to a whole series of questions concerning language. Was language merely the tool that the novelist worked *with*? Or was it a part of the raw material of life which he worked *upon*? Or was it a complex and difficult combination of both? If language was merely a tool, then the less attention it attracted to itself the better—and all fine writing, and delight in words and sentences for their own sake, had better be done without. If, on the other hand, language was a part of the novelist's raw material, then things of that kind might well be permitted. Another important question that persisted in suggesting itself was this: should the aim of the novelist be to make the reader see?—as Joseph Conrad had suggested: or should one aim at writing sentences which appealed more to the reader's ear—making him hear voices as it were, the voice of the novelist perhaps, the voices of his characters certainly, each one with its own particular rhythm and cadence. Or should there be a combination of both seeing and hearing? So far as I can remember, none of these questions I had considered previously—at least consciously. And there were dozens of other questions, some of them even more difficult and complicated. I felt myself overwhelmed by their number and magnitude—so perhaps it is not to be wondered at that nearly ten years were to pass away before I felt confident enough to write another novel. Not, of course, that I didn't make a great number of attempts—and with my problems to solve, I had neither the time nor the inclination to be idle. I had decided there *was* a New Zealand language appropriate to the material of New Zealand life—or if there was not, then it was up to me to create such a language. Every time I wrote a short story, I was as much excited by the thought of the advance I had made towards bringing this New Zealand language to light, as I was by the substance of the story—and such is the isolation one feels in New Zealand, when working at such problems, I was for far too long ignorant of the fact that other writers were working along similar lines—writers whose work, when I got to know it, I could thoroughly respect and appreciate.

By the time I felt ready to write my novel, however, I suddenly seemed to run up against the most serious problem of all. For years it had seemed to me that the problems were mainly the technical ones I have been talking about—but confident at last that I could handle a language appropriate to the material of New Zealand life, I suddenly asked myself, What *was* this material of New Zealand life? What was it exactly? Previously I had thought I knew—I mean in this way: that I had a notebook full of jottings, ideas for more stories and novels than I could write in several lifetimes. It had, in other words, never occurred to me that I might be short of material to work upon: it had always somewhat amused me when I heard people say they would like to write, but had nothing to write about. Now it seemed to me that this question of what one could write about was much more serious and difficult than I had supposed. For one thing, like Byron at the beginning of his *Don Juan*, I felt the need of a suitable hero; and wanted if possible, to avoid any suggestion that the author himself was the hero, as is rather common in novels these days. I wondered whether my failure to find a suitable hero was a shortcoming of my own, or a shortcoming of this material of New Zealand life, that I was so determined to deal with. And this question, as had happened previously, led on to a series of questions. What was the European doing in this country? Had he the right to be here? What were the ideas and ways of life that he had brought with him, and how had they developed? Was a society being built up that could continue to flourish, or was the European's occupation of these islands a sort of tenancy, which would eventually be terminated? Did I, personally, agree with the prevailing sentiments about these questions? And if I did not, was I right or wrong? And so I felt I had to put off writing my novel until I had explored these matters much more thoroughly than I had ever done previously. After all, the

European had also established himself in such places as America, South Africa, and Australia. What sort of a fist had he made of his settlement there? I decided I had to try to find out—and found such wonderful things had at least been done in literature that I seemed to come within a hair's breadth of abandoning all further attempts to write my novel. I had never supposed myself capable of coming anywhere near the degree of excellence that I recognized in the great European novels, but I *had* thought I might do something noteworthy compared to what had been done in say, Australia or South Africa. But what could I say for myself, when I read Olive Schreiner's *Story of an African Farm*?—or rather I should say *re*-read—for I had read the novel when I was very young, when egotism and frustrated ambition had blinded me to its wonderful genius. And besides, the formal literary language that it was written in tended to upset many of the theories about language which I had carefully worked out over so many years. Further, I felt myself crushed by the thought that this book had been written by a girl scarcely out of her teens.

Perhaps, though, there was never any serious question of my abandoning my attempts. I said earlier on in my talk that a man might have a creative hobby, but I had never thought of my dealings with literature as in any sense a hobby. Right from the word go, I had known that what I was setting out to do must be the central aim and purpose of my life. Like the child with its mud-pie, it was my own particular kind of creation that I was determined to achieve, and everything else must be secondary. I must contrive to live as I could, paying attention to the daily necessities of life—food, clothing, shelter, money and such-like—only insofar as they pressed urgently upon me. After all, the shifts I might be put to, to meet these necessities, would enrich my experience of life, and hence the work I was engaged on. And now, after so many years, I felt I should be left with scarcely any aim or purpose in life at all, if I abandoned my writing. So I persisted, and seemed eventually to find more or less satisfactory solutions to all my problems. If my novel had never been written, I suppose I should never have been asked for this talk. It was, I thought, well in advance of anything I had previously achieved—nevertheless I felt some dissatisfaction when I reflected I was in my thirty-ninth year. Nor did I find that the novel itself satisfied me for very long. Very soon I had set to work again, trying to write another novel, finding myself with a whole set of fresh problems to work out.

II

Some time ago, I was speaking to you about some of the problems a New Zealander is likely to meet with if he tries to write a New Zealand novel. On that occasion I was mainly concerned with some of the technical problems—for instance, the question of the sort of language that would be appropriate to the material of New Zealand life: and my account of the difficulties involved was largely drawn from my own personal experience. Now I would like to speak more generally, this time taking for granted a great deal that I felt I had to try to explain last time—for example, that the novelist's job tends to be linked to those primary creative impulses which may drive small children to make mud-pies. It isn't all that sort of thing that need concern us now: instead, let me try to simplify matters by supposing that somebody has had the necessary qualifications to write a New Zealand novel: the novel is already there, written—so let us see it in two ways if we can—before and after, as it were. First there was the New Zealand scene which all who live in New Zealand can more or less see for themselves: now that scene has been represented or recreated on paper. How many people are going to agree that the novelist has seen it accurately? How much of it has been left out?—how much put in?—and for what reasons? Are the characters in the story truly representative New Zealanders? These are the sort of questions I want to consider. But, by the way, please note that what I have said, assumes that our novel will be what is loosely called a naturalistic or realistic one: there are other kinds of novels, but they are usually produced by writers who belong to a more highly civilized society than ours—they aren't the ones that New Zealand novelists are likely to write—not, at any rate, at our present stage of development.

Our novel then, represents or recreates the local scene—and we are expected to recognize the characters as true New Zealanders. Yes, *but*—and almost the first thing that springs to my mind is the difficulty of place-names. It's a small country we live in, and thinly populated. No doubt any of the larger cities may be named in the story—one might even name a slightly false address in Freeman's Bay, or Sydenham—or, in a different sort of novel—Remuera or Fendalton—but I'm afraid one would be taking a grave risk by openly identifying one's story with any of the smaller towns: very few people get through their lives without having a number of friends acquaintances enemies and relations—and the writer is not without his share. It is well-established that people are very ready to identify themselves with characters in fiction—or if they are not, then their friends will oblige them by pointing out the resemblance. And very often, of course, there *is* some resemblance—after all, the novelist must find his material somewhere: there is the old saying, that there can be nothing in the mind that hasn't previously been in the senses: it is very unlikely that anybody unfortunate enough to be born blind and deaf would ever write a novel—and still more unlikely if the other senses, touch taste and smell, were also absent. What it all amounts to, is that the novelist is unlikely to interest us unless he has exercised his capacity for invention and imagination—but the material he begins with must, of necessity, be the human beings that he knows best. It is probably true to say that whenever a novel is published, somebody, somewhere, is bound to feel flattered or honoured, offended or ridiculed: it has been said of James Joyce that he defended with drawn sword the right of the artist to use his own life, and the lives of those around him, as material for his art without consideration for people, and without regard for public opinion. The latter part of the statement does seem to carry things rather a long way—nevertheless, it seems quite likely that, without the principle that Joyce rather extravagantly asserted, we should have very few novels of enduring value. There is another old saying—about life being short and art being long: there is, indeed, very little that does endure over the centuries except works of art: and good novels if they appear in New Zealand are seen to be particularly valuable, if you reflect that we Europeans, we New Zealanders, as we call ourselves nowadays, may not always keep our hold on these islands: time dispenses with us as individuals, and for all we know, may eventually dispense with us as a people—but time may have a harder job dispensing with our novels if we can produce good ones—at least if past history is anything to judge by. I won't say they should be written without regard for public opinion and people's wounded feelings—but without *too much* regard . . . . let us be presumptuous enough to modify James Joyce's principle to that extent. And even with the modification, New Zealand novelists who attempt to make honest use of the material to hand aren't going to have an easy time: but unless the attempt is made, how can we expect to have truly representative New Zealanders in our fiction?

Well, so much for openly identifying your novel with any particular locality—and the difficulties I have sketched out are just as likely to be headaches to the English novelist, or the American, or Australian. I come now to a disadvantage which seems to be rather special to the New Zealand novelist. Many readers, the world over, must conceive what Englishmen are like from reading English novels: in New Zealand, for example, one still meets people who will say that they have

been brought up on Dickens: and of course there is an immense number
of English novels to select from. But how does anybody who has never
visited New Zealand conceive what a New Zealander is like?—you just
don't, anywhere in the English-speaking world, reach out your hand in
a bookshop or library for a New Zealand novel—and you don't do it
even in our own country. Now the English novel as we understand it
began its extraordinary development in the eighteenth century: certain
main lines were established: you have, for instance, the robust novel
with the robust hero, in Fielding and Smollett: the novel of feminine
sensibility, in Richardson: adventure, in Defoe: and fantasy, in Swift. I
am, of course, only generalizing—and very broadly at that. These
novelists I have mentioned were beginners in a sense, but some of them,
I would say Fielding, Defoe and Swift, were so immensely gifted that
their work has never been bettered: succeeding novelists may be
measured against them, and found not quite to measure up: thus they
have had a remarkable stabilizing influence on the English novel: most
English novelists write, as it were, in their shadow—or in the shadow of
one or other of them. Hence you find a certain kind of consistency in
the English novel—readers the world over more or less know what to
expect—certain types of character will appear again and again, and so
on. Now it would be too much to say that the New Zealand novelist has
to get completely out from under the shadow of these great men—nevertheless it is true that he must endeavour to throw off their influence,
insofar as it may hinder him from attempting to grapple with the New
Zealand scene. This throwing-off of hindering English influences has
been done previously—in novels written in the English language, but
not on English soil, and not concerning themselves with the English
scene: it was done by Mark Twain—and the occasion marked the
appearance of two extremely interesting and important characters, quite
new to fiction: I mean Huckleberry Finn and Tom Sawyer—and we see
now that Tom was a marvellous anticipation of the sort of person that
vast numbers of Americans in our century have become. And another
throwing-off, much closer to hand, was done in Australia in the last
years of last century—by Henry Lawson: and once again, something
quite new in the history of literature emerged. The important thing to
notice about both Twain and Lawson is, that they have had a great
public influence. Australia, these days, is by no means the Australia of
Lawson's stories—nevertheless great numbers of Australians still read
them, and are thus enabled to picture their own lives, and their own
times, against a stable and clearly defined background. And Australian
novelists read him, and decide to continue on from where he left off—or

attempt a somewhat different line of their own, if they feel no further development is possible. Unfortunately, nothing comparable to Twain or Lawson has happened in New Zealand. Attempts by a number of writers have been made to throw off the English influences, insofar as it is a hindering one, but the response from the reading public has not been very encouraging—which means, among a number of other things, that the young New Zealand novelist hasn't the advantage of being able to start off by assuming that previous novels about his own country have had an attentive and receptive reading public—a public that would be eager to read fresh novels as they came along. In spite of American and other influences, the English influence is still too strong—and its strength was well demonstrated a few years ago, when New Zealand novelists and short story writers were scolded by a local critic for slavishly following a variety of overseas fashions: but it apparently did not occur to the author of these strictures, that his entire critical principle was lifted, *en bloc*, from critical writing that happened to be fashionable in England at the time.

How, then, should I begin to sum up my argument? I think, somehow like this: we New Zealanders are European, and the great majority of us have our more recent origins in some part of the British Isles—but we live at the other end of the world. I imagine I can hear listeners saying, How obvious! and, How tedious to listen to what is so obvious! Yet it must be repeated again and again—a sort of mental pinch as it were, to wake ourselves up—otherwise we shall go on to the end of time, representing snow-storms in our shop-windows at Christmas, when the sun outside is melting the asphalt pavement: and how disconcerting it is, to suppose that the reading public, or a large percentage, expects our novelists to disregard the realities of our lives in similar fashion—or at any rate to distort them. And perhaps this is a view that is logical in its way—because I fancy that one of the very first things the New Zealand novelist must be aware of, is the large number of distortions which he has to deal with. If you are a New Zealander, and have at the same time some experience of other ways of life, it doesn't need much perception to see that what is pervadingly characteristic of New Zealand is its own particular variety of puritanism. It is, for example, an illuminating fact that great numbers of New Zealanders tend to think of the Christian religion not as something that is good, but as something that is goody-goody—surely a very serious distortion, if ever there was one. But it isn't positive puritanism that pervades New Zealand, so much as its negative manifestations: not so much the 'shalts', as the 'shalt nots'—and everything that flows from attempts to regulate human conduct by a system of rigid prohibitions. If you attempt to deal with the natural inclinations of human beings in the wrong way, then certain results are inevitable—something that is clearly understood by those whose job it is to deal with children, by the way—and in New Zealand, you have the results staring you in the face. How frequently one feels that the emphasis is all wrong!—natural human exuberance, denied its natural human outlet in spontaneous gaiety and enjoyment, seeks instead for calculated excitement and sensation: instead of the open and humorous appreciation of human existence in its entirety, you have the sly telling of the bawdy story, which depends for its effect on severely restricting itself to only a portion of that entirety: instead of the leisurely civilized pleasures of alcohol, you have vast quantities of beer consumed in a very short space of time: you have an almost universal craving for the relief afforded by the imported film—and over all, you have the assumption that commercial values must precede human ones, on all but the most disastrous occasions. These are generalizations, one must admit, and no doubt many people would disagree—and perhaps it might be asked, what has it all got to do with the novelist anyway?—mustn't he take his material as he finds it? Certainly he must—and he does—and the result, very often, is that he has to listen to bitter complaints from his readers because he has done so. But another reply to the question would be, that surely the novelist may legitimately concern himself with the *quality* of his material —because, after all, the quality of his novel is going to depend, in some measure at least, upon the quality of the material which is available for him to work on: and if he proves his ability by doing good work, then, I suggest, we should be willing to pay some attention, if he has qualifications about the indifferent quality of his material—though what he has to say will usually be implicit in his novel—which, besides representing and recreating the New Zealand scene, will at the same time be a criticism of it. But please note that I am not trying to suggest that the novelist is a superior sort of person, free from human weakness, and independent of the weaknesses he may discern in human society. He is deeply involved, both as an individual and as a part of the society to which he belongs. And being involved, he is as much entitled to his say as anybody else—and like anybody else, he may be mistaken in his judgement.

And now, to return to the questions I began my talk with—or at any rate two of them—about how much of the New Zealand scene has been left out of our supposed novel? and how much left in? It seems to me that the novelist will select and emphasize what is most common to us New Zealanders, whether we live in the town or country, and whatever may be the social class to which we belong: there are very great differences in us taken as individuals, but besides our common humanity, we all, or nearly all of us, have our view of life slanted by certain common ideas—and one of these is, I think unquestionably, the puritanism which I have been talking about: it is the novelist's business to seek out the threads of our lives, and show us where they all lead to if he can. There is just one other point, though: a good novel that might gather up all the threads, might not necessarily be a novel about contemporary life: it might be an historical novel: perhaps the thing to remember about historical novels, is that you don't have them, or at any rate you don't have good ones, until the events the novelist wishes to focus on have been far enough removed by time: I mean far enough removed so that they may be seen in clear relation to what has succeeded them: it is, I imagine, partly the function of the historical novel to light up the times it is written in, in addition to the times it is written about. So far the time hasn't been ripe for the historical novel in New Zealand: so far we have been too much tied to the event, to think of an imaginative interpretation of the event: there have been too many old-timers about, only too ready to trip up the novelist on points of historical detail. Eventually, it seems to me, the detail doesn't matter a very great deal—or at any rate, only inasmuch as it will stimulate the novelist's imagination. Of course he will need many resources, besides an imagination capable of responding to the right stimulus: but if the right time hasn't arrived yet, then I suggest it may not be very far off, and in any case, one must always except the honest, and sometimes very interesting, attempts that have already been made at imaginative interpretation.

First broadcast as two radio talks in 1950. Not previously published, though extracts appear in H. Winston Rhodes's *Frank Sargeson* (New York, Twayne, 1969).

12

NEW ZEALAND FARM AND STATION VERSE

One takes up this book and feels grateful to Mrs Woodhouse: with masses of good bad and indifferent material to choose from, she seems to have done an excellent job of work. But reading, one begins to doubt: there are extraordinary omissions. Where are Mr Denis Glover's magpies for example? and where is Mr Allen Curnow's old Miss Wilson? In a volume which Mr L. J. Wild refers to in his introduction as 'a mirror of our rural history and development', it is difficult to understand how Mrs Woodhouse could justify the exclusion of these two pieces—remarkably fine poems certainly, but farm and station verse if you like. And how, on the other hand, would she excuse the presence of scenic verse (Francis Hutchinson's 'The Forceful Quiet of the Dawn' e.g.), which would appear to fit her category only by stretching courtesy to its extreme limits? Further, it troubles me that Mrs Woodhouse in her preface should speak of New Zealand farmers who 'feel a deep love for their land', and that Mr Wild should commend the book as a guide to what politicians call 'the New Zealand way of life'. Surely both these remarks require strict qualification—which they don't receive from the verse presented (although Professor Arnold Wall's 'Colours of New Zealand' is an exception). Much of the verse attempts to deal lightly with the trials and troubles of a way of life that, on the face of it at least, may eventually transform vast areas of our countryside into a desert: the best of it (again with some exceptions), is in the Australian popular ballad tradition that began with Adam Lindsay Gordon: and assuming for the moment that I am right in my judgement, perhaps I can say something about that tradition which may help to elucidate my point of view.

At the root of the Australian popular ballad there is, I imagine, something of this nature: it takes for granted vast land masses which intimidate the human spirit. 'What is the dominant note of Australian scenery?' Marcus Clarke inquires in his remarkable preface to Adam Lindsay Gordon's poems: and he answers, 'Weird Melancholy'. He says: 'The Australian mountain forests are funereal, secret, stern. Their solitude is desolation. They seem to stifle, in their black gorges, a story of sullen despair. No tender sentiment is nourished in their shade. In other lands the dying year is mourned, the falling leaves drop lightly on his bier. In the Australian forests no leaves fall. The savage winds shout among the rock clefts. From the melancholy gum strips of white bark hang and rustle. The very animal life of these frowning hills is either grotesque or ghostly. Great grey kangaroos hop noiselessly over the coarse grass. Flights of white cockatoos stream out, shrieking like evil souls. The sun suddenly sinks, and the mopokes burst out into horrible peals of semi-human laughter . . . . All is fear-inspiring and gloomy. No bright fancies are linked with the memories of mountains. Hopeless explorers have named them out of their sufferings—Mount Misery, Mount Dreadful, Mount Despair'—and in one of Banjo Paterson's ballads there is even a pub which is called The Shadow of Death Hotel. All this is a very different proposition from 'historic Europe, where every rood of ground is hallowed in legend and in song'; it was too much for Gordon ('intensely nervous, and feeling much of that shame at the exercise of the higher intelligence which besets those who are known to be renowned in field sports . . . .'), the Melancholy got him in the end and he killed himself—but until he did he wrote his best verse when he could forget about the scenery, and concentrate most of his love upon horses. Love of horses is as strong in Paterson: in Henry Lawson it becomes love of men, 'men whom the elements could not beat but the Banks could and did', as Jack Lindsay says. ('Droving songs are very pretty, but they merit little thanks/From the people of a country in possession of the Banks.') Lindsay points out that Lawson was not merely collecting the current songs: 'he was using their method to utter a whole vision of life, to raise to a new level of intensity the attitudes and affirmations of the pioneers, the diggers and drovers and small-farmers, who tamed a continent . . . . He re-creates the popular tradition of Australia. At the moment of its dissolution he transmutes it into art.'

Now one more quotation: in his preface to one of Paterson's volumes Rolf Boldrewood says: 'It is not so easy to write ballads descriptive of the bushland of Australia as on light consideration would appear. Reasonably good verse on the subject has been supplied in sufficient quantity. But the maker of folksongs for our newborn nation requires a somewhat rare combination of gifts and experiences.' Exactly; and in Mrs Woodhouse's collection, among those who are working in the Australian ballad tradition, it is virtually only David McKee Wright who makes the grade: the rest, almost without exception, are writers of what might be described as occasional verse, produced on altogether too 'light consideration', and lacking that deep-felt sense of a strange savage and hostile environment. As for the singers of the trials and tribulations, the humours, of farm and station life, too often they give us too much of the too too whimsical jingles that begin in the Children's Corner of the daily newspapers, but unfortunately do not always end there. Nevertheless, it must be pointed out that there is a fine selection of verses from the work of Donald McDonald: and here and there among the fifty odd writers represented (in addition to those I have named), one finds some things that are truly moving and arresting.

The book is typographically competent and interesting, but a little dull: and that goes for the illustrations as well. On p.38 a line has not been indented: and it is anybody's guess who is responsible for the eccentric line-division of George Meek's 'Ballad of Benmore', beginning on p.60.

Review of *New Zealand Farm and Station Verse, 1850-1950,* collected by A. E. Woodhouse; *Landfall,* September 1951 (v.5, no.3), pp.233-5.

13

JANET FRAME: The Lagoon

It is probably quite right that this book, beautifully produced by the Caxton Press, should appear without a blurb on the dust-jacket; stories of such rare quality can be their own recommendation: the reviewer who is confronted by them may very well risk following the publishers' lead, and limit himself to saying no more than will serve to emphasize their merits.

There is very little of what is common experience for every New Zealander that hasn't found its way into the twenty-four stories: it is all there—soil, sea and sky, bird and beast, plant and flower, all seen and felt as though with dazzled wonder and delight for the first time in human history. But it is from the New Zealanders themselves, or some of them, that the stories mainly derive their piercing flavour of anguish and suffering.

Perhaps one may say that in their entirety they seem to pose a momentous question: Can people ever be said to be truly at home when they can never quite decide whether it mightn't be an advantage to be somewhere else? But in the meantime there is the brick bungalow to camp in—and beneath its tiles love grows timid and fearful, faith and hope eventually become pinned to the ticket in Tatts, the children develop the nervous tensions that may never be resolved in a lifetime, and the adults either sleep the mental sleep from which there is no awakening, or suffer the emotional strangulation that is slow but sure, and as deadly as death . . . . It is, I repeat, all there, all clearly rendered in language which, despite its simplicity of statement and rhythm, is the author's own special creation. From now on our literature is the richer, and the author, Janet Frame, becomes one more light to help diminish the vast region of darkness by which we are all surrounded.

Book review, under the title 'A New Light', in the *New Zealand Listener,* 18 April 1952 (v.26, no.667), pp.12-13.

]14[

RODERICK FINLAYSON: The Schooner Came to Atia

The central figure in Mr Finlayson's novel is an Australian missionary at work among the natives of a South Sea island, where he represents the New Believers who have their headquarters in Woshtosh, California. This middle-aged sectarian is presented as a drab-minded mediocrity, so it is somewhat against odds that Mr Finlayson succeeds in engaging for him the reader's sympathy. It is my purpose in this review to suggest that the author's success may be explained, in part at any rate, by his missionary's being a tragic epitome of a way of life which many New Zealanders are in the habit of taking for granted.

Taken at its face value the story has something in common with Mr Somerset Maugham's *Sadie Thompson*. The missionary, Hartman, is endeavouring to control the desires which have been excited in him by a native servant-girl, when there turns up on the island a young war-shocked New Zealander who engages the girl's interest: Hartman comes across the pair of them one night when he has a gun in his hand, and cannot resist his impulse to shoot the young man.

But that is only the bare outline of the story. It is by his filling out of detail that Mr Finlayson removes his story from the Maugham category (Mr Maugham has only an urbane shrug of the shoulders for the beliefs which have determined *his* missionary's character), and, if I may be permitted another literary comparison, brings it much closer to Mr W. H. Auden's *Victor*—a ballad which horrifies because of its penetration and understanding. Mr Finlayson's understanding of Hartman and his situation is to me thoroughly convincing. He has a wife who has never attracted him except as a fellow-worker engaged in bringing 'light to the unenlightened', and yet two children have somehow contrived to get themselves born of a marriage in which physical distaste is mutual: his thoughts about the native girl are a hopeless mixture of quotations from the *Song of Solomon* and the proposal-of-a-certain-nature-indecency-then-took-place sort of thing: he cannot bear to think of an 'innocent' girl being 'ruined' by a young 'blackguard'. At this familiar level, however, the reader is still not so far beneath the surface of the story. It is by probing into the vast area of yawning vacancy which somehow manages to support the walking shell called Hartman that Mr Finlayson fully demonstrates his capacity for dealing in horrors. Hartman is inhibited from any pleasure that he might have derived from films, radio, alcohol, horses—all that usually serves to plug this vast hole so that it may be pretended it isn't really there. He has literally nothing except his religion, which in theory should fill him to over-flowing, and in fact is so 'practical' that it avoids any emphasis on the 'supernatural'. 'The Maoris are superstitious enough as it is', he says. When he addresses his congregation he is reluctant to consider 'both carnal love and true charity', and so fails to make himself clear about the 'love' on which he preaches. The men and women think how good it is to be told to love one another—and the girls giggle and hide their eyes from the boys' glances.

I think it is the word 'practical', with its suggestion of a code of conventional and good tradesman-like living, which provides as good a clue as any, if we want to discover what Mr Finlayson is trying to say. Before being converted at a mission rally in Sydney as a young man, Hartman has been a motor mechanic. The reader is not told anything about his life at the time, but one assumes him to be a sort of end-product of the Protestant Reformation: that is to say, a person depending entirely on his own meagre spiritual resources, and without any sort of guidance except what is secular. The fold that he is brought into, a latter-day sectarian version of Reformed Christianity, which apparently insists upon unceasing practical activity, fails to remedy his sense of isolation—and this point is made clear at the end of the novel when the reader discovers, somewhat to his surprise, that there are people established on the island whom Hartman thinks of as 'papists'. In despair over the murder which he has committed but which he is not obliged to face up to according to the law, since it has been hushed up as an 'accident', he has an impulse towards 'confession': but it is an impulse he recoils from with lonely horror: his spiritual isolation is complete: his immediate practical activity has failed him, and the God he believes in seems to him incredibly remote.

I don't however wish to suggest that the novel convinces me as a whole. It is perhaps some disadvantage that one is held and moved by Hartman to such a degree that the other characters seem a little flat by comparison. And although Mr Finlayson may be quite right in suggesting the Catholics as a possible solution for Hartman, merely to bring them in as he does is to rely considerably too much on a sort of *deus ex machina* device—a minor misfortune for the novel perhaps, and one that is paralleled by some off-moments when Mr Finlayson appears to be influenced by Hartman's habits of language: 'excited every fibre of his being', for example, would be acceptable only if it were made clear that it is to be attributed entirely to Hartman.

Review in *Here and Now*, November-December 1953 (v.4, no.2), p.32.

ONE HUNDRED YEARS OF STORY-TELLING

First of all, just a few more or less formal observations. I remember when this book was proposed by Mr Davin, nearly three years ago, somebody remarked that it would be premature—and to me it was a disturbing remark. As we all know, these Oxford books are intended to provide the reader with Literature—and whatever else Literature may be, it is usually thought of as something which has stood up to what we may conveniently call the test of time. I could however, console myself by thinking that the volume would probably start off with Lady Barker, who was contemporary with people such as George Eliot and Anthony Trollope, and many other distinguished figures of last century: and in addition to Lady Barker, there would of course be Katherine Mansfield. But I am afraid that beyond those two, my thoughts tended somewhat to run out. Naturally I had, and have, my own ideas about what is Literature—and no doubt I am sometimes conceited enough to suppose that I can decide what is Literature, without any reference to the time-test. But however all that may be, and no matter how different the ideas of Mr Davin, Mr McCormick and myself may have been, there was I think one thing perfectly clear: Mr Davin must endeavour to present Mr Cumberlege, of the Oxford University Press, with a number of stories which he might feel like publishing, without too much risk of bringing disgrace upon his Library of World Classics: the difficulty was, that he would have to be confronted by a list of authors, whose names would be quite unknown to him with very few exceptions.

Well, as I have said, all that was nearly three years ago: and now that we are celebrating the appearance of the book, there is no point in my going into the delays misunderstandings and disagreements, which sometimes attended its progress towards publication: nor do I want to emphasize the amount of work it has meant for everybody concerned: all such matters must be taken for granted—and although thanks are due to many people, they are no doubt primarily due to the many authors whose work is represented. But the book is over to the reviewer now—who we hope will be generous enough to take us up without pre-supposing that he is going to be bored: and it is over to the reader, who we hope won't get us confused with the endless range of Bibles offered by the Oxford Press, and for pious reasons only, think of us as something that should be in every home.

And having said that much, I suppose that according to the rules I should have nothing further to say. After all, the reader has Mr Davin's introduction before him, and any remarks of my own might be inter-preted as a sort of special pleading: in addition, the reviewer might resent my trespassing on territory which he would want to claim as his own. I intend nevertheless to break the rules and offer you a few remarks—but they will be concerned more with some general ideas which appear to me to be connected with the book, rather than with the literary material itself.

I daresay many of you will be familiar with a paper by Mr Robert Chapman, which appeared in *Landfall* this year. Mr Chapman endeav-oured to show that the social pattern which prevails in New Zealand is mainly derived from the Evangelicalism which many of the settlers brought with them last century. Perhaps there was nothing so very original in this argument, which had previously been touched upon, at least, by a number of New Zealand writers—and, indeed, it is pretty obvious to anybody with the intelligence and curiosity to wonder how on earth our social set-up came to be what it is. There was however an unusual feature about Mr Chapman's argument; it was strongly suppor-ted by evidence, which he had derived from a very thorough investi-gation into the particular kind of fiction which many New Zealanders have been writing in recent years.

Now it interested me, when I had read what Mr Chapman had to say, to try if I could discover some sort of test for his argument. If Mr Chapman could demonstrate a significant relationship between New

Zealand Evangelical belief and much New Zealand fiction, then it would probably be possible to demonstrate a somewhat similar relationship between English Evangelical belief and some English fiction at least. The New Zealand fiction which most aptly supported Mr Chapman's argument did not appear until quite recently: that is to say, it did not appear until New Zealand Evangelicalism had become thoroughly secularized—so it would seem probable that the English fiction which might clearly exhibit the relationship would be likely to appear some time during the latter half of last century: that is, it would appear soon after English Evangelicalism had declined into puritanical worldliness—more or less the sort of thing which we in New Zealand tend to associate with the people whom we eloquently call wowsers.

So with thoughts of this kind in my head, perhaps it was more or less to be expected that I should think of the novels and life of a writer I have already mentioned. I mean George Eliot.

George Eliot was a novelist who, during the twenty odd years in which she was writing fiction, progressed from the pastoral sort of thing which she gives you in *Adam Bede* (published in 1859), to the penetrating explorations of human character and relations which you get in the finest parts of *Daniel Deronda* (published in 1876). I think if you read *Daniel Deronda*, you may sometimes find yourself turning back to the title-page—just for re-assurance that you haven't picked up one of Henry James's later novels by mistake. Four years previous to *Daniel Deronda*, there was *Middlemarch*—an impressive piece of fiction if ever there was one, with its searching investigation into the social life of a large provincial town and its adjoining countryside, and its entirely convincing description of a complicated marriage relationship between an earnest young woman and a scholarly old man. Surely there is no Victorian novel that quite compares with *Middlemarch*, if we expect a novel to be unromantic, and, without being commonplace, to contrive to make us feel that we are participating in the experience of life as we know it actually to be. It is the sort of thing which Tolstoy did with such staggering perfection. Now who was the author of these massive novels, which in part at least are thoroughly mature, and objectively accurate—in other words, well in advance of the usual run of novels of their day?

George Eliot grew up in the Midlands, the daughter of a working-class man, who eventually became a kind of land-agent: she was influenced by the Evangelical movement as a girl, and at the age of twenty felt seriously troubled about whether it was proper to read novels: two years later she lost her faith: she was at that time a plain sickly-looking girl, who suffered from frightful headaches: so far as I can remember, she had no particular advantages of schooling, and she was certainly without the benefit of a University education; but she was gifted with an extraordinarily powerful intellect, which she cultivated until she became one of the most intelligently learned people of her day: she was nevertheless unhappy, dissatisfied and restless, until her mid-thirties, when, without concealment, she began to live with G. H. Lewes, who could not marry her owing to there being a wife somewhere in the background: the relationship was a happy one, and within a few years she had begun her career as a novelist, with the first of her *Scenes from Clerical Life*, which appeared in 1858. If we keep in mind the bitter strength of mid-Victorian puritanism, perhaps we may sum it all up in a sentence—in George Eliot we are presented with the extraordinary phenomenon of a Victorian blue-stocking, which actually came off.

Now doesn't all this, or some of it, rather begin to remind you of something? George Eliot discovered that she was unable to fit into the social pattern which prevailed in her day, and although she eventually discovered her true vocation as an artist, and achieved a tremendous success, it is extremely likely that she was impelled to her persistent and patient examination of society, and the human relations which it implies, by the unhappiness and dissatisfaction which she experienced in the first thirty or so years of her life; and by her situation as a sort of social outsider, which she had to put up with when she began to live with Lewes. But what is remarkable about her examination of society, is the absence of rancour; instead there is a scrupulous honesty, and a rarely failing sympathy and fairness. She herself broke the rules only on grounds of high moral principle, but her intelligence, sympathetic, rational, and extremely powerful, ruled out the notion that human beings can ever be divided up into the goodies and the baddies. She astonishes us by her sympathetic insight into people she does not agree with, does not like, and indeed, disapproves of very much. Further it is the *range* of her insight which is perhaps the most remarkable feature of all: she can, without prejudice, and without a hint of condescension, depict a poor but honest and blameless Methodist preacher, as convincingly as she can depict a rich aristocrat, who is having a spot of bother over endeavouring to rid himself of a mistress he no longer requires. Throughout her novels there are few exceptions to this rule of sympathetic insight—though it must be admitted that one of them is quite outstanding, and has frequently been noted: she is more than somewhat of the opinion, that a pretty face on a girl will be a fair enough indication of a lack of brains and character. Perhaps all the reader can do is shrug his shoulders, and reflect that it is probably quite natural for a plain blue-stocking to show an Achilles heel.

But I hope I don't sound as though I am making a stupid attempt to guy George Eliot. In any case, her very formidable genius places her well beyond the range of any piddling pea-shooting on my part. Note, however, that there were attempts to guy her last century. Ruskin said that the characters in her novels were like the sweepings from a prison omnibus: and Swinburne, disliking intensely the verse she wrote, was rude enough to say that as a poetess she presented the distressing spectacle of an Amazon, sprawling across the crupper of her spavined and spur-galled Pegasus. It is, of course, not so difficult to understand the Ruskin-Swinburne point of view: it pined for the aesthetic qualities which George Eliot seemed to lack completely. How *could* you make works of art out of such unpromising material?—heavy provincial business men, Bible-banging preachers of both sexes, sincere but bone-headed country politicians, beautiful but dreary village girls who come to grief and get themselves transported, and so forth. If only George Eliot would be the reader's guide to what is beautiful, and pay rather less attention to what is sordid ugly and dull! And it must of course be admitted that there is a very great deal to be said for this viewpoint, which was later on brilliantly argued by Oscar Wilde, in his Dialogue called *The Decay of Lying*. But even so, so far as George Eliot was concerned, we can see today that much of this type of criticism was quite mistaken: the aesthetic qualities of her novels are highly developed, and essentially her own.

You now see the point I am sure. Given a certain kind of society, you may reasonably expect a certain kind of novelist. George Eliot, with her pervading seriousness, and her veracity, was exactly the right kind to appear in mid-Victorian times. Please note that I have lifted 'veracity' and 'pervading seriousness' from Mr Davin's introduction to the Oxford book of stories. But he is not speaking of George Eliot. Mr Davin also uses the phrase, 'rarity of humour'—but again he is not speaking of George Eliot, even though what he says would fit to perfection. So what I am suggesting is this: that insofar as there may be a large and formidable ghost haunting many of the pages of this book, it is not the sort of composite ghost, with an American trademark, which so many critics have said they can discover, fluttering among the vocabulary and phrasing of much latter-day New Zealand writing. Of course, it is a long way from England to New Zealand, even for ghosts—so the one I am suggesting may very well have come via America, and have had a little grim fun there, haunting the pages of writers such as

Anderson Hemingway and Farrell, before moving on to New Zealand. After all, the stories of one writer in this Oxford book have recently been referred to as 'drizzly', by a young New Zealand critic, who also insisted that New Zealand is a very drizzly kind of country. Well, maybe—but one can't help being reminded of Ruskin's sweepings from a prison omnibus.

But it is time now for me to take a brief look at the stories, or some of them. I have outlined my view that George Eliot's novels are closely connected with her having been a considerably isolated figure in mid-Victorian society: but obviously I cannot take each New Zealand author in turn, and show that he or she is, or was, similarly isolated in New Zealand society: many of the authors are living authors, and they might strongly object—and might *particularly* object, to any gratuitous suggestion of irregularity in their sentimental arrangements. But it is fortunate, for the purpose of my theory, that I can point to another kind of isolation—one that it was George Eliot's personal good fortune not to experience. As a creative artist, at any rate, there was a place for her in English life: on the other hand, by far the greater number of these New Zealand stories were written in an environment which is for the most part sceptical and indifferent—if allowance is made for those rare and precious individuals whose main test for a work of art is not that it should have been created somewhere overseas, but that it should stimulate and delight the imagination. Until and unless this book gets about New Zealand—how unlikely that more than a handful of living people will ever have enjoyed Henry Lapham's story of the Otago goldfields (the one entitled 'A Member of the Force', and published in 1880)—an astonishingly well-written story, and very remarkable for its heroine, a girl who is rather more human than one would expect to find in New Zealand goldfields' fiction, though doubtless not at all uncommon in New Zealand goldfields' fact. Turn to Miss B. E. Baughan's country-side idyll, which she calls 'An Active Family': I hope Miss Baughan won't be offended if I say that it is pure and delightful George Eliot of the early pastoral period. Or take Miss Alice Webb's story entitled 'The Patriot': what is to be said for readers who have never before discovered a story of such moving simple sincerity, mainly because it has been written right under their noses?

But it would take me far too long to run through the entire list. The reader will notice for himself the tightening up of the prose, as the stories approach our present decade (although there are some notable, interesting, and to me exciting exceptions—Mr A. P. Gaskell and Mr Anton Vogt being good examples perhaps)—a tightening which, in my view, is closely connected with writers becoming more and more defensively over-conscious of their isolation. And yet, as always, there is no certain formula for writing a good story. It is, for example, easy to single out, 'The Day of the Sheep', by Miss Janet Frame, as a superb piece of artistry: without the faintest hint of unfair prejudice, or personal complaint, Miss Frame irretrievably damns the New Zealand social set-up—but I am not prepared to say whether or not I prefer her story to Mr Ballantyne's, called 'And the Glory', which miraculously retrieves us after all. All I say is, that I am as astonished and delighted by Mr Ballantyne's ten-and-a-half-page epic of urban man, as I am by Miss Frame's local *Inferno*, which she convincingly warms up for us in less than seven pages. I should however finish with a word for Lady Barker. There she is at the beginning, as she forever will be, giving us all a lead: admonishing us as it were, to write prose that is clear simple and lively. How surpassingly well she handles the language of her inset shepherd's story!—and incidentally, with what surpassing tactfulness the shepherd himself handles it! We must remember that just a few years earlier Samuel Butler was counting the number of times that the word bloody turned up in the conversation of Canterbury shepherds.

But I return now to my opening remarks: the book is over to the reader and the reviewer: perhaps in the years to come it will be over to the archaeologist who digs up the ruins of Mr Parsons' shop in Woodward Street. Who knows?—perhaps he may think us worth a place on the dicky-seat, when he re-embarks on his flying saucer.

An address at the launching in Wakefield House, Wellington, of *New Zealand Short Stories*, edited by D. M. Davin, Oxford, World's Classics, 1953. The manuscript of the talk is in Sargeson's manuscripts in the Alexander Turnbull Library. An abbreviated version was published in *Landfall*, March 1954 (v.8, no.1), pp.22-26, under the title 'A Book of Stories'.

The essay by Robert Chapman which Sargeson refers to is 'Fiction and the Social Pattern' (*Landfall*, March 1953, v.7, no.1, pp.26-58: reprinted in *Essays on New Zealand Literature*, edited by Wystan Curnow, Heinemann, 1973).

Sargeson offered more thoughts on Chapman's essay in a letter to *Landfall*: September 1953 (v.7, no.5), pp.227-8.

]16[

WHAT IS THE QUESTION?

Let me begin by drawing your attention to the deathbed utterances of three distinguished figures of this century. Samuel Butler does not of course really belong to this century—he died in the year 1902: it is said, however, that just before he died he called for his cheque book. Arnold Bennett died somewhere about three decades later: it is said that he called for his hotel bill. It is said of King George V that he asked, 'How is the Empire?' Now I well know that I am being quite unfair—very many excellent things might be said about these three people, and particularly about Samuel Butler. Nevertheless, if you have read his published work, and if you have read a few of Arnold Bennett's novels, and if you were born about the beginning of the century as I was, and lived throughout the reign of King George V—you will know that these three reported sayings are remarkably consistent with what one knows about the characters of the people concerned. You would not be at all unfair in supposing that Butler really did feel there was no situation which might not be met with a cheque book. Bennett would have been most unhappy to be confronted with any account that might be due in the next world, without first having settled what was due in this one. It goes without saying that the King was quite keen on the Empire as the solution for quite a number of British problems—besides, I think, a number of foreign ones as well.

Very well. We may smile at these anecdotes—we may even assure ourselves that we may expect something quite different from Mr Graham Greene, or Mr Evelyn Waugh, when the appropriate time comes. But for my part, I find they leave a rather unpleasant taste in my mouth. I seem to miss something—or perhaps I may say that I seem to stumble up against something I would rather have missed. Let me see if I can explain.

Just a few years ago there died another distinguished figure; Gertrude Stein. Gertrude Stein, as I am sure you all know, was an American woman of German-Jewish origins, who has had a remarkable influence on modern literature. You may, by stretching things a little if you like, think of her in relation to Ernest Hemingway, as you might perhaps think of Marlowe in relation to Shakespeare. We are told that just before Gertrude Stein died, she asked: 'What is the answer?' And since no answer came, she laughed (it is, I think, rather important to notice that she laughed), and then she said: 'In that case, what is the question?'

Now I want to hang my talk on this peg—I mean these few extra-ordinary words that Gertrude Stein left us with when she was dying. If I can, I want to demonstrate to you that I was moved by what she said for at least two important and connected reasons. One, because the words have a profound meaning: two, because they came from a person who was not so much a European as an American: that is to say, a New World rather than an Old World person. I must admit that these terms are somewhat out of fashion these days, and many New Zealanders would probably dislike being described as belonging to a part of the New World. If we glance at the end pages of the Oxford Atlas, however, we see that our country just barely escaped being a blank on the map 250 years ago. Let us then, take it for granted that we in New Zealand are New World people—and yet it is equally clear that, quite early in our lives, we begin to turn back in the direction of the Old World. At school in my day, I was taught something about English history, but next to nothing about New Zealand history: as a young man I read Gibbon's *History of the Decline and Fall of the Roman Empire*, without ever thinking that it might be as well if I advanced my knowledge of my own country's history. I was grateful for my opportunity to visit the country my people were in the habit of calling Home—a habit which I often copied without thinking what I was saying.

But you will be saying to yourselves that this is tedious old stuff—and I agree. Particularly if we are interested in literature, music, paint-ing, history, philosophy—almost anything beyond the bare necessities of a livelihood, it is obvious that we would remain unsatisfied if we

depended on what has been produced in New Zealand. It is inevitable
that we should turn in various directions overseas, and any bare mention of the fact is quite without interest. There is however something
closely related to this turning overseas which is wonderfully interesting;
what I mean is that because of it, all of us must have our minds filled
with notions about human life on many other parts of the earth's
surface. Let us for the purpose of simplicity agree to call these notions
pictures. Surely one never ceases to wonder what these pictures look
like.

For the great majority of New Zealanders, there are of course
newspaper photographs and cable news items six days a week: there are
films, popular magazines, and novels, and there is the radio—and we are
probably quite right in supposing that it is from these odds and ends
that the majority derive the material for the mental pictures I have
referred to. But I want to put to you a suggestion which you may not
find palatable. I suggest that the minority of New Zealanders, who are
more alert and sensitive, also make their pictures from a collection of
odds and ends. Substitute the *New Statesman* for the cable news, the
New Yorker for the popular magazine, the novel by Mauriac and the
French film for popular novel and the Hollywood film, the BBC feature
for the ZB serial. You certainly have a difference, but not, I think, one
that is quite so important as we sometimes suppose. We may be
strongly inclined to dismiss the mental pictures of the majority as
spurious, but we should think carefully before we make any serious
claim that those of the minority are valid. It might be objected that
many of the more alert and sensitive members of our society have had
the benefit of a New Zealand university education—and therefore have
the advantage of knowledge and understanding (and particularly knowledge and understanding of the past), which is highly valuable to them
in making their mental pictures. But again, it seems to me, we find only
a sort of rag-bag collection of odds and ends. It is, for example, possible
in New Zealand to meet with history lecturers who have never read
Gibbon. I expect that quite a good case could be made out for them
—perhaps on some grounds of specialization, which would however
imply that the university is envisaged not as a place of learning, but as a
sort of super technical college: but in one of these instances I have
discovered that this omission to read our greatest historian implies an
almost complete ignorance of the history of the Christian church—I
mean even the negative history that can be derived from Gibbon. Yet
even though we admit the necessity for specialization, it seems to me
that we still don't avoid ending up with a collection of odds and ends.

Who, for example, could hope to remain in New Zealand and become a distinguished Shakespearean scholar? Only a fraction of the materials for research exist here. Or take some branch of modern science, and you immediately admit that there exists here only a fraction of the necessary technical equipment.

So it is at this point that my drift brings me again to Gertrude Stein. It seems to me very remarkable that, being I think a New World person like ourselves, despite the fact that she spent so much of her time in Europe, she could by her words at the end of her life make us feel that she had dominated the entire vast junk-heap of odds and ends, and reduced it to the simplicity of her question and answer. I suggest to you that there isn't a single one of us (I mean particularly if we are New World people), who can honestly say that he doesn't catch on to her meaning. Perhaps nobody has ever put it quite like that before, but I suggest that there is a sense in which it is true to say that we all know what the question is, even though it can't be formulated. And I will even risk the additional suggestion that *if* we could formulate the question we should have the answer to it as well . . . .

Now I hope I don't sound as though I am trying to mystify you with some muddle of my own: perhaps things will be a little clearer by the time I have finished: but at least I imagine that you begin to see why the three anecdotes I began with should leave an unpleasant taste in my mouth. It is because they are all evasions—they evade the question. Or put it another way: they appear to treat a small part of the question as though it were the entire question. And this is particularly distressing to me as a New Zealander, because I can recognize without much difficulty that we in New Zealand are particularly susceptible to evasions—to an unfortunate habit of mistaking a part of the question for the entire question: or, if you like, a habit of mistaking any one of the numerous odds and ends we are confronted by, for something much more important than it is.

But perhaps if I become rather more concrete I can make my point clear, and illustrate it. So I will examine some aspects of our life in New Zealand, to see how we face up to the all-important perennial yet admittedly unformulated question. Though some prevalent aspects need hardly concern us here. Sport, for example—the speed of highly bred horses, human skill in controlling the flight of balls of various kinds, a young Dunedin woman who can jump twenty feet or thereabouts: all such activities can be wonderful and fascinating, I know: all may be said to be part of the question, and provided it is agreed that they are only a part there is no harm done. It is only when they become inflated that they become dangerous. The man who lives to eat is, I should say, a rarity; but the man who lives not even to engage himself in athletics, but to watch others doing so, is unfortunately not so rare. But instead of condemning him, we should look carefully into his social-economic environment. It is this environment which I want first to examine—though of course very briefly.

I think that most people take their social-economic environment very much for granted: it is part of Nature which they question only in their day-dreams: to question it seriously would bring to mind too many disturbing thoughts—no job, no pay, nothing to eat, clothes wearing out, and so forth. Insofar as people who are terrified by these spectres feel themselves to be unjustly treated, or see injustice done to others, they tend to fall back on some sort of homespun philosophy: the devil you know is better than the devil you don't know. But if the majority refuses to question the social-economic set-up, the minority must certainly be prepared to do so: the minority must refuse to believe that the distribution of material necessities need be the disorderly and complicated business that it is: and that the making of a personal profit from it should be the central purpose of any man's life.

But the distribution of material necessities is only the top half of the social-economic environment—or should I call it the topsy-turvy half? At any rate it is the predominantly urban half: distribution (and you may add exchange if you like) depends upon production, which in New Zealand is mainly rural—which means in its turn that production in New Zealand mainly depends upon the yielding capacities of the soil. It is only about a hundred years ago that the New Zealand countryside began to be farmed, but it appears to be certain that vast areas of it cannot be farmed for another hundred years—and the reason is, that what we call farming should more properly be called mining. It goes without saying that if you make your country your mine, you have a wasting asset on your hands.

Now this voracious mining of the soil is a world-wide phenomenon, but it has proceeded at such a rate in the countries of the New World, that thirty to fifty per cent of the fertility of the entire American continent has been calculated to have been destroyed. It is, of course, a consequence of the industrial revolution and the sensational expansion of nineteenth-century capitalism. I hardly need mention the fantastic increase in population: but I think it should be emphasized that the present-day demand for more and more production, because of the increased population, has some very dishonest features about it.

It is true, for example, that New Zealand farm products are needed to feed English urban workers, but if those workers can be allowed only about two shillings' worth of meat a week, while they are engaged in producing highly-priced motor-cars which they haven't a hope of ever owning—then you have the spectacle of a vast social-economic system headed for disaster. What is dishonest about the demand for more and more production is this: that it conceals the real demand—which is for more and more consumption. A young person who is led to believe that his main purpose in life is to get on in the world, is not, I think, being told to get on and produce whatever will add to the common wealth: he is, I think, being told to get himself into the position of being able to consume—to be able to afford, for example, those motor-cars, which in addition to being highly-priced, are likely to be excruciatingly ostentatious and vulgar in appearance, and almost certainly of shoddy mechanized workmanship.

And similarly, if you are an older person, and are reproached for not having got on in the world, it is no answer to say that you have contributed to the common wealth: the test is whether or not you are in a position to receive from the common wealth. And since the common wealth in our present-day society depends upon the waste of the resources of the soil, we are being merely frivolous if we congratulate ourselves on our present-day prosperity.

But I have, I think, said enough about the social-economic environment to serve my purpose. If I say that it evades Gertrude Stein's question, I hope you may have some idea of what I mean: at least you will see how closely it ties up with those three death-bed utterances I began with: and if you smiled at those anecdotes, and thought, 'Oh well, poor Butler, poor Bennett, poor King George V, they are quite out of date now'—then I hope you will feel the same way about the particular social-economic environment to which all of us are accustomed: because it too is quite out of date.

Now I'm afraid I have tended to speak of the social-economic environment as though it were a thing in itself—a sort of abstraction, which is constructed by reducing human beings to social-economic units. Actually of course it is not like this at all: the human material is much too refractory for one thing: but apart from that there is always a number of conditioning influences: one of the most potent of these influences in New Zealand is the Christian religion: and it is the Christian religion as it manifests itself here in New Zealand that I want to take a brief look at.

I doubt very much whether the majority of people these days think of the society they live in as a Christian one, but I think it is probably true to say that they did so last century: after all, any off-shoot of Victorian England would tend to. A marked characteristic of Victorian society was its belief in missions of various kinds, and particularly missions for the conversion of the heathen. I remember when I was a small boy playing one morning on a neighbour's back verandah. A Chinese market-gardener who hawked his vegetables came to the door, bringing with him a stone jar of preserved ginger as a Christmas present for the lady of the house. She went inside for something to give in return, and handed him a coloured card on which Christ was depicted carrying in his arms the sheep which had been lost: she tried to explain by gestures the significance of the picture to John—as she called him. She pointed up for heaven, and down for another place: she stretched out her arms, turned up her eyes, and made her face look as though she was suffering pain: she pointed to the lost sheep and then to John, identifying each with each. But although I was entranced by the entire performance, I could not help noticing that she contrived throughout to hold in her hand the pot of ginger she had received—and certainly I hoped that she would hold to this material advantage, because she was always generous with any sweets that she had. Of course I can see now that it all might have been a sort of tableau, wickedly staged as a satire by some advanced group of sceptics: I need hardly remark that it was the sort of thing which is not nearly so likely to occur these days.

Now it is regrettable, I know, but it is a fact that anecdotes of this kind tend to recur to my mind whenever I hear about the wonderful possibilities of a Christian revival. I tend to ask myself what exactly it is that is being revived, or is going to be. Perhaps I tend to ask myself whether an old heresy is going to re-appear, or whether a new one is about to be created. There are, of course, many positive signs of the Christian religion in New Zealand: there is no need for me to enumerate them here. But there are also many strongly negative signs: there are, for example, our atrocious and deplorable licensing laws and our barbarous drinking habits.

But take another example: the man who leads you to believe that the main purpose of your life is to get on in the world may not think of himself as a Christian, or a member of a Christian society—but perhaps you would be running some risk if you were to inform him, quite plainly, that neither he nor the society he lives in is Christian. In other words, it is the negative test you apply to get a reaction. And if I am right about this, we can infer that a great deal of importance is attributed to the label.

But I suggest that there has always been in New Zealand a rather shocking amount of uncertainty about what it is that we label Christian. Let me illustrate in this way: ever since I can remember I have been accustomed to a substance which in New Zealand is called cheese, a substance which I ate for years without much enthusiasm until I went overseas, and made the exciting discovery of a substance which Frenchmen call cheese. You see what I mean, I hope: if I had never eaten anything but New Zealand cheese, I might have supposed all cheese to be as unattractive, besides being an obstruction to digestion instead of an aid to it. I am sure there are hundreds of thousands of New Zealanders, for whom the Christian religion may be any one of the numerous and possibly heretical and schismatical groups, which are to be found all over the country. Heresy implies orthodoxy, of course; but you will hardly, I am sure, expect me to go into theological differences—and I should in any case feel far from competent to do so. Nevertheless, there are one or two matters I must touch on.

First, I want you to imagine for a moment that we are all disbelievers who have willingly suspended our disbelief, and agreed to identify the Christian religion with the Catholic Church. I mean by the Catholic Church what many in New Zealand would call the Roman Catholic Church—and some, I am afraid, the Irish Catholic Church. Now extend your imaginings a little: imagine that the Reformation never happened, or that if it did the Church promptly and effectively reformed itself and cut the ground away from beneath the Reformers' feet. All right: you now envisage the spectacle in New Zealand of a unified instead of a fragmented Christian religion. Now I don't ask you to take anything more for granted: I ask only that you listen carefully to my argument, no matter how much you may disagree with it. For my part, I would suppose that two very important points could be inferred from the situation we are envisaging: one, that the Bible would not be readily available for anybody to read: and two, that the Mass would be celebrated in pretty much the same way as it is in fact celebrated.

The first point is somewhat obvious—private interpretation of the Scriptures can be dangerous to the individual and to the unity of the Church, and there would no doubt be the additional argument that the Bible came out of the Church, and not the Church out of the Bible—an argument which must be admitted to be a very powerful one.

But it is point two which is, I think, more interesting to us here in New Zealand. Any intelligent person who has attended Mass knows where the secret of the strength of the Catholic Church is to be discovered: it is to be discovered in the mystery that lies at the heart of the

Mass. For contrast, you have only to note how attention is likely to become dispersed during the sermon: feet are shuffled, coughs are not checked. But attention during the supreme moments of the celebration is as concentrated as you are ever likely to find it when you have a large gathering of people. I think it is because the sermon will very often deal with matters of simple piety that you have the loss of attention: I think most people more or less understand what the Christian virtues are, but because it seems to them insuperably difficult to carry over these virtues into their daily lives, they tend not to take them too seriously.

But there is no questioning the seriousness with which they take the central mystery which I have referred to: and I suggest the reason is this: what is done by the priest, what happens on the altar, it is all an extraordinary development and refinement of a mystery which can be traced back through countless centuries before Christian virtues were ever thought of. Or put it another way: the Mass is traditional far beyond the limits of what people usually think of as Christian—and those of you, I am sure, who besides reading your Bibles, have read works of anthropology, such as Frazer's *Golden Bough*, will have a pretty good idea of what I mean.

Then, besides the daily Mass, you have the great yearly or seasonal Festivals of the Church: the Nativity, for example, and Easter. And these Festivals, besides being closely connected with the Mass, and indeed inseparable from it, are also traditional far beyond the limits of what we tend to think of as Christian. Will anybody seriously suggest that Easter is not a springtime celebration? Or that the Nativity has no connection with the winter solstice? But in New Zealand we are apparently expected by the Church to accept a serious break in tradition without question: personally, I can only say that I have never been able to reconcile myself to the fact that the great springtime festival of resurrection is followed by the melancholy of autumn, and the gloom of winter.

So what it all amounts to is this: that it is difficult to see that the Christian religion has been successfully extended to New Zealand, when there is an apparent failure to take into account the serious break in tradition, which the extension implies.... Of course this break in tradition has been frequently noted, and frequently, I am afraid, it has been dismissed as of no importance. I doubt very much whether you could hope to convince people, who tend all the time to become more and more urbanized, that it *is* of any importance. But if we take a quick look at South America, a continent which is mainly in our own geographical situation in terms of latitude, I think we see, if we are perceptive enough, something which may perhaps throw some light on our own religious situation. A very great proportion of the Indian population in South America has for many generations adhered to the Christian religion. Nevertheless, these people insist on mixing in with their Christian observances a variety of observances derived from their own religious traditions. I am making only a guess of my own, but perhaps the reason is something like this: these people feel quite unable to accept the new religion as a satisfying entirety, when the great Festivals that it keeps are so hopelessly out of keeping with the seasons of the year.

But by this time, you may well be thinking that Gertrude Stein has been completely lost sight of. Not a bit of it, however. It is true that she belonged to a part of the New World more closely connected to the Old World than our own country is connected. Mr T. S. Eliot and Mr W. H. Auden, for example, can change places with each other, without having to face up to the serious break in religious tradition which I have been talking about. But remember that, for the purposes of my argument, I asked you to imagine a unified Christian religion: in fact, the spectacle is one of fragmentation—and Gertrude Stein, as a New World person, was confronted by a disorderly collection of odds and ends, not very different from the collection which we in New Zealand are familiar with. Think in addition of those odds and ends which I previously touched upon, the bits and pieces of our social-economic environment, of our higher and lower education—of indeed almost any aspect of our life in New Zealand: and you have, I think, much the sort of scene you may expect to find in almost any place where the European has attempted to settle himself down. It is the sort of scene which it pleases me to think that Gertrude Stein was able to dominate with her famous question and answer . . . .

It pleases me, too, to think that Gertrude Stein was an artist. It has been suggested by her biographer, Mr Donald Sutherland, that her last words say what she was always saying in her work. I am not altogether sure about that—but for some of us, I am sure, it is certainly true that her last words help us a very great deal to understand something about the astonishing power of her work to stimulate our sensibilities. I am far from being a propagandist for Gertrude Stein's work in its entirety, but whenever I take up some early and easily comprehensible piece, such as *Melanctha,* the story about a negro girl in the volume entitled *Three Lives,* I always feel that I am powerless to resist being caught up and gathered into the marvellous rhythm of the story. But there is a lot more to it than that: there is in addition a rhythm quite beyond my powers to describe, and I can only attempt to do so by saying that perhaps it is something like Beethoven at his best: or if you like, think of it as some vast interlocking system of rhythm which, besides including you and me, can easily include as well the soil and the sun and the seasons of the year. I suggest that if we have never had any intimations of this rhythm, then of course we will be as unconcerned about the mining out of the earth's resources, which I referred to earlier, as we will be about the dislocation of the Christian year.

But question and answer, rhythm—I am aware that I shall probably be charged with being elusive, so let me anticipate the charge. I mentioned just now Beethoven, and for my purposes I might just as well have mentioned such names as Bach and Mozart. These names represent for us some of the achievements which we can easily recognize to be among the highest and noblest of the last five hundred years. Yet what could be more elusive than the rhythmical patterns of sound created by these men? If we are unable to understand the system of notation which enables the achievements to become permanent, we must depend upon the temporary impact of performance, and in between whiles upon our memories.

And yet who will be prepared to say that I am talking nonsense if I claim that we may listen to a performance of one of Beethoven's last quartets (I am thinking in particular of the one in C sharp minor), and may afterwards discover that our lives have been transformed and enriched far beyond our expectations? How can we explain the transforming power of these sound-patterns? So far as I know, no satisfactory philosophy of music has ever been worked out—but however that may be, a Christian might perhaps say that Beethoven was a Christian, and his music transforms us because it has been created to the glory of God: on the other hand a Marxist might say that Beethoven was an artist in a bourgeois society, and his music has all the characteristic limitations of bourgeois art. Perhaps there is truth to be discovered in both these viewpoints—but I should be inclined to think there is more truth in the view that Beethoven was Beethoven, because he transcended both the religious and social limitations of the times in which he lived: like Gertrude Stein, he was concerned with the question that goes far beyond the more usual sort of question: I mean, if I may be permitted for a moment to deviate into a sort of Steinish language, the question of the question and the answer. For me, it will always be to Gertrude Stein's immense credit that her last words reveal her as completely undismayed by the religious and social breakdown of the times she lived in. Please remember that she laughed—a fair enough indication, I think, that she was game to the last.

And that remark brings me to the end of my talk. I must say now, that my subject was supposed to have some connection with contemporary New Zealand writing. Well, I haven't mentioned any New Zealand names, but I think the connection is fairly clear. It is indeed quite clear if you think particularly of some of the finest work of some of the finest of our New Zealand poets.

First given as an address to the Otago University Literary Society, then published in *Here and Now*, March 1954 (v.4, no.4), pp.22-26.

JAMES COURAGE: The Young Have Secrets

I suggest that Mr Courage should now include with each novel he writes a sketch plan of Canterbury as he has imaginatively remapped it. I make this suggestion seriously, and in good faith. Is there anything in New Zealand fiction to compare with Mr Courage's consistent working over of a particular area? Neither William Satchell nor Jane Mander stuck consistently to the gum lands, but Mr Courage's Canterbury allegiances appear to be unbreakable if we except two or three of his short stories. In this new novel, however, on page sixty-three, there is a good indication of one reason why New Zealand novelists are unlikely to receive their due from New Zealand readers of their own generation. Two pre-world-war-one boys are discussing Tobler chocolate cards, and lamenting the fact that some of them are very rare. The rare card mentioned is number five of Animals. Now my memory readily agrees about the number, but just as readily substitutes Beauties for Animals. Of course I may be wrong, and what does it matter anyway? But there is something about the prosaic fact-obsessed New Zealand mind, which does not take kindly to factual lapses: facts are sacred truth, and the imagination is a shocking liar.

All the same, it is doubtful whether the average New Zealand reader can be expected to face up to facts of a somewhat different order, which Mr Courage confronts us with. He is obsessed by the facts of pain and suffering which every individual must endure—and if the sufferer happens to be a child, or a person who cannot conform to the socially acceptable patterns, so much the worse. (Pain, suffering? Take an aspirin, call in a doctor, let's go along to the pub for a drink. Children? give them a taste of the stick, make it Mt Eden in extreme cases.)

In this novel a ten-year-old boy is mentally and emotionally plagued by having seen a dog run over by a tram, and then thrown over a bridge to drown. Yet he is unable to refrain from blurting out a piece of information, which is a link in a chain of cause and effect leading to the death of an adult human being. Another way of indicating what the novel is about, is to say that Mr Courage more or less conceives of the child world being circumscribed by a circle, and the adult world by another. The two circles constantly overlap, but because of the nature of things, they can never be made to coincide. A geometrical metaphor, however, and it does little justice to the human complications which the novelist handles with a very considerable degree of skill.

The child world is so excellently rendered, one feels that Mr Courage tends to fall in love with his own skill. The detail tends to proliferate, and to be cherished for its own sake, with the consequence that the balance of the novel as a whole is somewhat upset. Perhaps this would not matter quite so much if the novelist were contriving to render the adult world entirely from the child's point of view. But this is not quite the case, though even as things are, there sometimes has to be the device of overheard conversations to inform the reader of what is going on in the adult world. (On this point however, it would be unjust not to say that Mr Courage, besides making use of a technical device, is quite effectively indicating the frightening abysses which separate the two worlds.) And towards the end of the story there is a scene in which a young woman tells the boy (remember he is only ten years old), about her affair with her brother-in-law. 'All that passion we had . . . it was wonderful to both of us, dreadful and wonderful . . . .' We know that emotional strain will prompt young women to confide sometimes in the most unlikely people; but what happens in life may take some getting away with in fiction, and I am afraid I was not entirely convinced. (That word 'passion' by the way: isn't it about time that some people in fiction were prompted by their creators into a better use of language? 'Passion', that is to say 'suffering', is real and common enough God knows, but why use the word on an occasion when 'pleasure' would be a more accurate description? Is it just part of our ingrained puritanism? Is 'pleasure' a quite unsuitable word for children's ears? Surely it is absurdity of this kind that leads to the tragic absurdity of a recent report on children's behaviour.)

But perhaps I am carping. All I intend to say is that the story as Mr Courage has conceived it should be told, does not always move along as smoothly as one could wish. Considered as a work of art, this is to me the least satisfying of Mr Courage's novels. But as against all that, he has widened his range. Besides the boy and his friends, there is a 'low life' character, a Mrs Nelson, who is a notably rich addition to the more usual gallery of characters. And the òld schoolmaster is another. The novel is conversational, and distinguished by the lightness of touch we have come to expect: the scene is mainly Sumner, but there are glimpses of Christchurch, and two high country sheep farms.

Book review in *Parsons Packet*, January-February 1955 (no.32), p.11, under the title 'Courage Country'.

]18[

CAN A NEW ZEALAND WRITER
LIVE BY HIS WRITING?

I hope you won't feel tricked, if I say that the more obvious meaning of my title is not the one with which I propose to deal. Can a New Zealand writer live by his writing?—in the sense that his writing will bring him sufficient income to meet the daily necessities of his life. From my experience I can only say no, but it is quite possible that some other writer would give a different answer, and I would agree, that in theory anyhow, there is no insuperable reason why a New Zealand writer should not make an income sufficient to pay his way.

But the meaning of the title I want to explore is something quite different. Can a New Zealand writer live by his writing?—that is to say, is it possible for writing, for literature if I may call it that, and all that it implies, to constitute a kind of faith by which one can live one's life? And I would emphasize that I mean the word 'live' in the sense of being more alive than just performing those routine motions with which we are all familiar, and at times painfully familiar. I think you will agree that what I am saying opens up some biggish questions, so difficult to answer that I haven't a hope of satisfying you. But if I throw out a number of suggestions, I can at least hope that I may stimulate you into having a shot at your own answers.

First of all, let us take a look at some rather cold facts about the local literary situation. We all know about the millions of pounds spent annually on education, and quite a proportion of the amount is required for teaching English literature. Am I being too optimistic, if I say that some young people will take their teaching seriously? What I mean is that they will wake up to the wonderful achievements of English poetry and prose. Or to put it another way, they will become aware that besides having a name for exporting textiles, machinery, and whatnot, England has an even more famous and enduring name for exporting her literature—a commodity by the way which any country can export, and at the same time keep; and furthermore, keep for ever.

Now I suggest that some young people will go one step further, and ask themselves what imperishable commodity New Zealand can export, in exchange for what we have received. In trading matters it is taken for granted that a fair exchange is very necessary—or at any rate it should be: but so far there aren't many signs that we in New Zealand understand the realities of our situation in this matter of literature. What I mean is that we don't realize we are hopelessly in debt, and so fail to see the need of building up a contra account.

Those are the cold facts of the situation as I see them. It is true that we have at least the beginnings of a contra account—thanks to the initiative and devotion of a handful of writers. But what is one to think when this handful, whose work may penetrate to many odd readers scattered about the earth's surface, can count on the devotion of only a handful of New Zealand readers? How does that tie up with so much money spent on education and the teaching of literature? And in the light of my remark about an account and a contra account, can one take seriously the suggestion that the New Zealand writer should settle overseas if he wishes to reach a wider public? I think if we care about our literature we will aim at exporting our best literary achievements, but not our best literary brains. After all, that is England's way of doing things, and so much in New Zealand is devoutly imitated from what is done in England. But in any case, if we make a practice of exporting our best literary brains, surely we are heading in the direction of something really disastrous. I mean we are inviting people with second and third best literary brains to step forward, and act a part for which they are not fitted, by their gifts or their achievements. I need hardly say we could never remedy our deficiencies in literature by such a masquerade—nor, for that matter, in any of the other arts.

But to get back to those difficult questions, implied by my remark about writing being a possible faith to live by. Faith. That is a big word, and I think for many of us it suggests religious faith generally, and faith in the Christian religion more particularly. In 1953, when I was invited to speak to some Otago University students, I tried to say something to the point about the Christian religion as we find it in New Zealand, and I don't wish to repeat myself. I merely remark that anybody who happens to be interested will find the talk printed in the Otago students' paper. For my purposes this evening however, I must say that any hopes I have of convincing you that writing does constitute a kind of faith by which a writer can live, depend to a great extent upon our agreeing about the non-Christian character of present-day society. In his Reith lectures recently, Professor Arnold Toynbee referred to European society as ex-Christian, and this view of the matter strikes me as quite objectively accurate, besides courageous and sincere when you take into account that Professor Toynbee is himself a professing Christian. All of you, I am sure, will have some general ideas about the development of this calamitous European situation. The Christian religion spread through Europe during the early centuries of the Christian era, reached its high tide mark in the Middle Ages, and since has suffered the setbacks of the Renaissance, the Reformation, and more lately, and perhaps most seriously, the Industrial Revolution. It should, of course, go without saying that New Zealand wasn't heard of when Europe was as Christian as it is ever likely to be; and it requires a pretty high degree of innocence and inexperience before anybody can take very seriously the fragmented Christianity which we have inherited from our beginnings less than a century and a half ago. In a town with a population of a mere handful, there may be half a dozen or so denominations, all adding up, not to anything so coherent as a Christian community, but merely to that aggregation of human beings which is one of the most characteristic features of present-day society.

Now it is surely not to be wondered at that where you have an aggregation of people in the modern sense, you will find many substitutes, which compensate for the absence of a central core of belief—a core to which people might fruitfully refer in times of doubt about the purpose and meaning of their lives. It is common knowledge that in New Zealand you can find quite a range of these substitutes. There is football, for example, and horse-racing, and the cinema—and at times one hears all of them spoken about as religions in themselves. What does it mean to speak of football as a religion? It means that a human activity, which is marginal to the daily and seasonal activities upon which human lives depend, has moved in from the margin to a much more central position. It could not have done so, of course, if that central position had already been firmly occupied—but the distressing fact of the matter is that central positions in New Zealand are usually discovered to be vacant, or else they are already tenanted by some substitute, which is always more or less under the threat of being ousted by pressure from some up and coming rival substitute.

Where and how does the writer figure in all this?

I remember, in my primary school days, I was moved and fascinated by a story which was printed in one of our school reading books. A cathedral was being built, and a stone-carver turned up and asked for a job. After he had demonstrated his skill, he was led up a scaffolding to a remote high corner inside the building, and shown what to do. Out of the way there, he worked year after year. He came early and he worked late: he was scarcely ever seen, but he was always known to be at work from the sound of his chisel, which as the years went by was taken for granted like the rising and the setting of the sun. Until at last there came a day when everyone was astonished by an unnatural silence from that remote high corner. I hardly need tell you the rest. It was found that the carver, an old man by this time, had died at his work—and, quite needless to say, his work, which nobody apart from himself had ever seen, was discovered to be of the most surpassing and imperishable beauty. Please don't laugh. I was quite right to find the story moving, and I suggest that we don't think of artists as being stamped with quite such a nobility of character these days. By comparison the modern artist is a substitute artist, and his work is likely to be substitute art. What I mean is, that instead of its being taken for granted by the artist, and his public, that his work has of necessity been created to the greater glory of God, a conscious effort of the mind will be required before it can be thought of in those terms. That is to say, if it can be thought of in those terms at all. Remember what I said about a central core of belief. The old man of the schoolbook story could be the artist he was, because he could take a central core of belief for granted. When that central core of belief is absent, you must expect to find bewildered artists, and bewildering works of art—and both are characteristic features of our present-day society.

But I see now, that I have been sidetracked into considering the writer as artist. He is and must be an artist, but let me for the moment put the emphasis on the characteristic I have just mentioned: bewilderment. It goes without saying that we are all bewildered these days, what with hydrogen bombs, flying saucers, and what have you. What can the lone and lonely individual man do to alleviate his sense of bewilderment? And remember that individual loneliness, combined with a barren sense of emptiness, is one of the most common and distressing features we meet with today. I suggest that in the absence of that central core of belief, which you will plainly see is an obsession to me, the individual man won't be able to do very much—apart from joining a football club, going to the races, and turning in at the nearest cinema. I suggest, however, that it is bewilderment on which the present-day writer thrives. Nobody lightly puts up with bewilderment, and writer least of all. And so he is impelled by the exigencies of the times in which he lives to combine with his calling as artist the additional callings of philosopher, sociologist, critic, psychologist—and the list could be extended indefinitely; to include by the way many odd jobs of manual labour. In all, or at least in many of these activities, the writer will be very much the amateur no doubt, but perhaps the amateur in the better sense of the word. I mean he will be absorbingly interested in questions about the meaning and purpose of his work: that is to say, he will be determined to seek out the reality beneath the appearance, which I am afraid will very often be the false appearance; and he will be absorbingly determined to seek it out for its own sake: he will in other words combine an absorbing interest with a disinterestedness which may be even more absorbing—if I am not too hopelessly contradicting myself: he will be entirely convinced that it is better to discover the reality than to remain ignorant of it upon any grounds at all—and particularly upon any grounds of narrow self-interest. He won't be like the footballer or the football fan, whose football has become a religion, but a religious sense will never be lacking in his approach to all his activities. Inevitably so, because his search for reality will take him beyond the world of appearances, with all its beguiling variety of sensual delights. I have yet to hear of a religion (I mean a true as opposed to a false religion) which doesn't aim at revealing or discovering reality; and at this time of religious breakdown, it is inevitable that the writer, along with a number of people in other vocations, will have a shot at discovering reality more or less off his own bat. He will frequently be disconcerted, and it is very possible that he will be completely defeated; it is, indeed, very probable that he will be: but at least he can be sure of one thing: because of his insatiable interest in his search, he will never be bored.

Now I am a little afraid that some of you will have found me somewhat high-falutin'. So to finish with I shall try to be rather more down to earth. I mentioned just now the writer's insatiable interest in his search for reality, so if you will accept the proposition that there may be many subdivisions in the reality estate, perhaps I can sell you a section. A few years ago an Auckland artist, a painter, was prosecuted for working at his occupation for money in view of the public on a Sunday. He was in fact painting a mural on the interior wall of a bicycle shop. There is, by the way, a tie-up here with the old stone-carver of my schoolbook story—but I leave you to work out the implications for yourselves. Now this painter was convicted of an offence against the law of the land, and fined, though I think not very heavily. Very well then, in some circumstances, you may not work for money at your regular occupation on a Sunday. I personally know that the artist was quite hard-up at the time he painted the mural, and Sunday, without the inconvenience of trade in bicycles going on about him, was the most suitable day of the week for the job, with the possible exception of Saturday—but it is perhaps a point of some importance that the pubs are officially open on Saturday. At least one Church sermon was creditably preached on the moral iniquity of the conviction, but, generally speaking, public indignation was not very violent. How can anyone who is concerned about reality, be content to dismiss the matter at that point? There is the fairly obvious possibility that two members of the Northern Club might sit at a Club window on a Sunday, and by pursuing in conversation their regular occupations, benefit themselves financially by a larger amount than our New Zealand painter could hope to make in a lifetime. But take the matter deeper than that. If you are in debt to a Bank you must pay interest, and interest on Bank over-drafts is calculated from day to day. Have you ever heard of any Bank knocking off fifty-two days' interest a year, because of fifty-two Sundays? You may find yourself a convicted person if you work on a Sunday, but you may find it necessary to work on a Sunday in order to pay your Sunday interest. Well, I leave you to work it out for yourselves. And by the way, did *I* think of that brilliantly subversive bit about Sunday interest? No. Did I then find it somewhere in the works of Karl Marx, Engels, or Lenin? No, I did not. I found it in an essay by Francis Bacon—who, I think, hasn't so far been frowned upon as a writer of subversive literature.

First delivered as an address to the Auckland University College Literary Club then published in *Kiwi*, 1955, pp.13-17.

19

OLIVE SCHREINER

I

I expect that everyone who knows anything about books, will at least have heard of Olive Schreiner, and her novel called *The Story of an African Farm*. Olive Schreiner was born in 1855 at a mission station on the borders of Basutoland, South Africa. The daughter of a German missionary father, and an English mother, she began during her late teens to write the novel for which she is famous, and she finished it in her early twenties, in the time she could spare from working as a governess, on various Dutch South African farms. Olive Schreiner was twenty-eight when her novel was published. She was at the time in England, where she spent much of her later life, and before she died at Cape Town in the year 1920 she had published some shorter works of fiction, and also some books on social questions.

I have purposely skipped over the details of Olive Schreiner's life—not that they are dull, or uneventful, and indeed everything is fascinating about her, to those who have felt the compelling strength of her best writing. But I have skipped the details, because I want to concentrate on her great novel. In these talks I want to see if I can discover some reasons, why a slip of a South African girl, living in what would appear to be the most unpropitious circumstances, could set to work, and contrary to all rules and expectations, produce a literary masterpiece.

But why do I say contrary to all rules and expectations? You may ask yourselves, Are there any rules and expectations in these matters? Well, for answer, I should like to mention some remarks which appeared in a recent number of the New Zealand magazine, *Landfall*. In his editor's notes, Mr Charles Brasch wrote about the strangely limited relations between the countries of the British Commonwealth. Mr Brasch says, speaking of Canada, South Africa, Australia, and New Zealand, 'between each colony and the mother country, ties of many kinds have been maintained, but the four colonies have noticed one another only for some passing advantage of politics or trade . . . and in the arts they have generally ignored one another's existence'. Now that is a general statement, which strikes me as being mainly true. But Mr Brasch goes on to say that, in the countries mentioned, developments in the arts have been roughly parallel, writers and painters having had the same kind of spade-work to do. Spade-work. That means work which has to be done, but work which cannot be expected to command a great deal of public interest. A small minority of the public will always be appreciative of the labouring work necessary in the field of the arts, but general interest will be aroused only by what comes to flower there. Here again, Mr Brasch provides us with a handy general rule—but the fact that Olive Schreiner's novel immediately suggests itself to our minds as a striking exception, is surely the kind of fact that demands some investigation. *The Story of an African Farm* was soon recognized as a great novel, and in addition to that, it rapidly became well-known all over the English-speaking world.

Perhaps, at this point, it might be as well if I assisted listeners who have never read *The Story of an African Farm*, by saying briefly what it is about—I mean taken as the story it purports to be in its title. And from this point of view it is quite simple and clear. The characters are quite severely limited in number, and in part one they remain always on the farm. In part two, the scene does shift away from the farm upon occasions, but never for very long. Presiding over the farm, a dry and sandy plain, is Aunt Sannie, a twice-widowed Boer-woman who weighs eighteen stone. She has two children living with her in the farmhouse, girls—one of them Aunt Sannie's plain, not very bright step-daughter, Em, and the other Em's beautiful and brilliant orphan cousin, whose name is Lyndall. Living in an outbuilding is the widowed German overseer, and also his young son, Waldo. Now that is the sum total of the European inhabitants of the farm—Aunt Sannie, Em, Lyndall, the overseer, and Waldo: there is quite a number of native workers and servants, but they are scarcely noticed. The early part of the story is much taken up with an elderly rogue, who turns up at the farm and ingratiates himself with Aunt Sannie. He bears the somewhat improbable name of Bonaparte Blenkins, and it must be admitted, I think, that he is something of a caricature. He is pitiful and penniless, but at the same time dangerously malicious and cunning. He torments the two girls, and also the overseer's lad, he repays the overseer's kindness by having him dismissed from the farm—and he nearly succeeds in his plan to marry Aunt Sannie. But finally he over-reaches himself, and his dismissal from the farm in disgrace marks the end of part one. And now for part two. At first there are only three Europeans on the farm—Aunt Sannie, and the two younger people, Em and Waldo, who are now in their later teens. The overseer is dead, and Lyndall is away at school—and before she returns, Em becomes engaged to a man called Gregory Rose who has leased a portion of the farm—which, in its entirety, shortly becomes Em's property, when Aunt Sannie departs with the young Dutch farmer she has made her third marriage to. Unfortunately for Em, however, Gregory Rose immediately transfers his affections to Lyndall when she turns up from school. But Lyndall rejects his advances, and leaves the farm with a lover whom she has met during the years she has been absent. She bears a child, which dies, and slowly dying herself, while she is quite alone in country township lodgings after having sent her lover away, she is nursed in the extremity of her illness by Gregory Rose—who has discovered her whereabouts, and disguised himself as a woman in order to be near her. In the meantime, Waldo has left the farm to try and find a niche for himself in the world at large, and when he returns to the farm, sick and sore from the blows the world has dealt him, he learns about Lyndall's death. Before long Gregory Rose also returns to the farm, and he and Em are about to be married, when the story ends with Waldo's sudden death, one hot afternoon while he is sitting drowsy in the sun.

So much for the bare outline of the story—and I should add, that told in Olive Schreiner's own words, in all its detail, it is a story which will hold a wide variety of readers, and particularly those whose main concern when reading a story is to find out what happens next. I must emphasize, however, that Olive Schreiner reveals herself in *The Story of an African Farm* as a novelist of a particular kind. She was not the kind of novelist who is content to let the story speak entirely for itself. On the contrary, she was constantly impelled to weave her own comments into her narrative, and if she sometimes held up her narrative while she set down her comments at quite considerable length, she apparently did not consider she was breaking any rules about novel-writing. Any such rules would, I think, have been most irksome to her, because we may reasonably infer that one of her reasons for writing the novel was that it provided her with an excellent excuse for expressing all she had thought and felt, about her very personal and vivid experience of life as a young woman. If she had been a somewhat ordinary young woman, with a gift for narrative, it seems to me that her impulse to comment would have resulted in a second-rate novel, with a temporary interest only. But the fact of the matter is quite different. Olive Schreiner was gifted with such precocious insight, and her intellectual powers were so highly developed, that despite her limited experience of time and place, she not only understood the wide variety of problems which contemporary people were faced with, but foresaw many of the problems we find ourselves puzzled by today.

First let me take her opening chapter—a chapter which I confess I have had to read a great number of times during my life, so that I might grasp its full importance to the book as a whole. I remember, that when I first read the chapter as a young man, I was mainly struck by Waldo's bewildered sufferings as a child, when he tries to fit such large matters as death, or God's apparent lack of omnipotence, into his picture of human life. But I can see now, that besides concentrating on Waldo in her first few pages, the author is depicting the dry and sandy wilderness, which is so supremely important to the book as a whole. No doubt it is quite like what we can readily imagine some parts of South Africa to be—but how do we explain the fact that somewhere at the back of our minds there is the notion that this landscape has already been our own personal experience? The reason, I think, is this. The landscape is familiar, because as children we were introduced to something remarkably similar in the pages of the Bible. Now from this important point, we quickly pass on to another of equal importance. The landscape is Biblical, but the people who inhabit it are Europeans—that is to say, apart from the natives, who, as I said previously, are scarcely mentioned. Both the older Europeans however, namely, Aunt Sannie, and Otto, the huge German overseer, are by no means out of place in the landscape. They are Europeans who are not living in their natural environment, yet there is a sense in which it is quite true to say that they are Biblical characters who fit perfectly into the Biblical landscape.

First let me take Aunt Sannie, to see if I can illustrate my point. She is the female counterpart to the Old Testament patriarch. A huge woman, she rules over her manservants and her maidservants, her sheep and other animals, and over her wilderness farm. She has a great liking for husbands, of whom she has had two, and she shortly marries a third time. She has a fundamentalist belief in the Jehovah of the Old Testament, and she has a profound distrust of new inventions, which can only invite the wrath of God. The Lord, she says, knew what he was about when he gave horses and oxen legs—that is to say, she disapproves of railway trains. If the Lord had meant soda to be put into soap, she says, what would He have made milk-bushes for, and stuck them about the land as thick as lambs in the lambing season? The land, with all its plants and animals, is the Lord's—and she too is the Lord's chosen. What more is there to be said about anything? And she is so inflexible in all these matters, that we think of her character as the kind we intend to describe, when we use the word 'hard'.

The almost equally huge Otto, the German overseer, is the very reverse of 'hard'—but I don't mean to imply that he is in any way 'soft'. He respects Aunt Sannie's beliefs, and indeed he shares them. But at the same time he extends them. He is an Old Testament character, but a New Testament one in addition. His belief in God, and God's commandments, finds perfect expression in his practice of charity. And Olive Schreiner's rendering of his charity in operation makes Otto one of the finest and most moving characters anywhere to be found in fiction. No one, I imagine, can read the passages devoted to him without emotion. He is that rarity—the thoroughly good man of fiction, with whom we are never bored, and about whom we cannot remain unconvinced. A closely related and shining example, if you should wish me to supply one, is Joe Gargery, in the Dickens novel, *Great Expectations.*

Very well then. I have indicated the Biblical setting, and two Biblical characters. What of the younger people? And can the contemporary century, which is such a strange contrast—can it be prevented from breaking in upon a tiny community, where the rule of the Bible is the be-all and end-all of life in its entirety? These are the questions I shall take up in my next talk.

II

In my first talk about Olive Schreiner, I said that I intended to try to discover some reasons why, in the latter part of last century, a South African country girl could set to work and produce a literary masterpiece. And with that end in view I summarized Olive Schreiner's famous novel, called *The Story of an African Farm*, and then I pointed out that both Aunt Sannie, who presides over the farm, and Otto the German overseer, are Biblical characters who fit perfectly into a landscape which is also remarkably Biblical. For this present talk, I left the

question of the younger people in the novel. Will they grow up to be
like their elders? Or will the contemporary world of the nineteenth century break in upon the little watertight community of the farm, where
the rules laid down in the Bible are invoked to cover all the affairs of
life?

There are three young people in the early parts of *The Story of an
African Farm*. There is Em, who is Aunt Sannie's step-daughter, there
is Em's girl-cousin, Lyndall, and there is Waldo, the German overseer's
son. First, let me take Em. A good-natured girl, plain and not very
bright, she is from one point of view a minor character, who plays no
great part in the story as such. But from another point of view she is
supremely important—because the meaning of the book as a whole is
bound up with the fact that, by nature, Em tends to resemble Aunt
Sannie; that she eventually replaces Aunt Sannie as the mistress of the
farm; and that she is the only one of the three young people who is still
alive when the story closes. Em, in other words, is the kind of person
whom Olive Schreiner intends us to recognize as always with us. Like
Aunt Sannie, she is what many people would call a sensible person—
that is to say, she is down to earth, reliable, and not ill-natured provided
she is not ill-used: she tends to reject innovations, particularly when it is
a matter of new rules for the conduct of her life: she prefers the rules
handed down to her from her elders, and at heart she agrees that no better rules can be devised than those the Bible provides. And she hopes as
the years pass that she will eventually be replaced by sons and daughters
whose natures will closely resemble her own. One could assert, no
doubt, that the Ems and the Aunt Sannies are the salt of the earth, but
before doing so, perhaps it would be as well to take a look at Em's two
companions, the girl Lyndall, and the boy Waldo.

At first sight, Waldo, with his black eyes, and his great head of
silky black curls, appears to be another Biblical character. Like David,
the shepherd boy who became King of Israel, he minds the sheep, his
ragged appearance fitting his desert surroundings exactly. Will he
become a great leader like the Biblical David? Or like Em, will he too
eventually turn out a sensible down-to-earth person? But very soon after
we meet Waldo, we know that his experience of life is going to be harsh
and bitter. He is sensitive and visionary. In the very first chapter we see
him unbearably plagued by visionary doubts concerning the Bible God,
whom he has learned from his father to believe in. And by the end of
the chapter, alone in the wilderness, with the wind and the stones and
the prickly-pear, he has arrived at the point where he can say out loud
that he hates God, but he loves Jesus Christ. And the author herself is

ready with her comment. 'The barb in the arrow of childhood's suffering is this,' she says—'its intense loneliness, its intense ignorance.'

As the years pass, however, it is Waldo's association with the brilliant and beautiful Lyndall that brings him his full experience of suffering. There is nothing at all Biblical about Lyndall—or if there is, it is entirely in the negative sense. She is the kind of girl who would find herself roundly condemned, and dealt with for her sins in the pages of the Old Testament; and stand in need of a vast amount of forgiveness from the pages of the New. Lyndall can match Waldo in her powers of imagination, and in her vulnerability when it is a question of feeling. But, intellectually, she is much more highly developed. Lyndall has, indeed, an intellect which is so precocious, that we should refuse to believe, if it were not for the author's skilful persuasion. In saying that, however, I am leaving out of account the well-documented facts about Olive Schreiner's own precocious intellectual powers.

Lyndall unceasingly tries to dominate her experience of life by her powerful intellect, which she promptly applies to every fresh situation she is confronted with. Thus, when she hears that somebody called Bonaparte Blenkins has turned up at the farm, she immediately tells the other two children about Napoleon Bonaparte, who, she says, because he was only one man, yet made all people fear him, was the greatest man who ever lived. This particular Bonaparte however, surnamed Blenkins, proves to be a sorry but at the same time dangerously cunning and malicious rogue, who torments the three children, and is responsible, though perhaps a little indirectly, for the death of Waldo's father, the wholly admirable German overseer. And all this painful experience forces Lyndall to alter her judgement about great men. 'When the day comes,' she says, 'and I am strong, I will hate everything that has power, and help everything that is weak.' There are of course difficult contradictions implicit in this new view, and Lyndall cannot resolve them—but at least one thing is clear: this child, endeavouring to make what she can of the world, and her relation to it, will never accept without question the rules handed on to her by her elders: instead, she will insist on rationally examining them, with reference to her own experience.

In the scheme of the novel, Bonaparte Blenkins represents the first clear and concrete impact which the outside world makes upon the little closed community of the farm. He is eventually got rid of, but much of the havoc he has caused is quite irreparable. When the children have grown into their later teens, there are three more significant invasions by outsiders, and each time something is contributed towards the breaking up of the community. The first of these outsiders is a stranger, an anonymous man on horseback, who interprets what Waldo has been endeavouring to express, in some carvings he has made on a wooden post. The stranger's interpretation takes form as a fable, a story about a hunter, who can never be satisfied until he has captured a great white bird. If Olive Schreiner had never written one line during her lifetime, except this fable, we would still be compelled to place her among the best of modern prose writers. All that she incessantly endeavoured to aim at in her own life, and all that her Waldo and her Lyndall were groping towards in *The Story of an African Farm*—all is wonderfully expressed in the few pages that contain the story about the hunter, and what he suffers in searching for the wild bird of Truth—which he never captures, though he dies holding one of its feathers. But placed as it is in the novel, the fable, apart from what it tells us as an inset story, has an additional, and indeed rather terrible significance. It is told to Waldo, who feels himself moved to his profoundest depths, and for two very good reasons. He can identify himself with the figure of the hunter, and thus foresee in his visionary imagination his own death. But in addition to that, he feels a personal fascination for the anonymous stranger on horseback, whom he afterwards remembers as a kind of living proof that those who inhabit the great outside world are not entirely a host of Bonaparte Blenkinses. It is largely owing to the stranger and his fable that Waldo shortly afterwards ventures out into the world. But what he suffers there drives him back to the farm, where he returns only to die.

Soon after the appearance of Waldo's stranger, however, another outsider turns up and leases a portion of the farm from Aunt Sannie. He is a man called Gregory Rose, and, Lyndall being away at boarding-school at the time, he promptly falls in love with Em. But when Lyndall returns, Gregory attempts to win her affections in a scene which is remarkable for its wry comedy. Gregory is at first sight a nonentity—a man who completely lacks the gift of insight, whether applied to his own nature, or anyone else's. His assumptions are staggeringly naive. He is a man, and he loves Lyndall who is a woman. The matter is that simple, and there are all the evidences of appearance to confirm it—so surely there cannot be any obstacle in the way of their being united in matrimony. There are, however, many obstacles in the way, and I must mention two of them. First, there is Gregory's own nature, and the author's understanding of it is a good example of how far she was in advance of most novelists of her day. Far from being a nonentity, Gregory is in fact a very complicated person, even though he innocently supposes himself to be quite otherwise. Lyndall discerns that he lacks all conscious knowledge of the large dose of femininity in his composition—and it is not until later on in the story that he painfully remedies his lack of self-knowledge, when he finds himself impelled to disguise himself as a woman, in order to nurse Lyndall in her fatal illness. But another obstacle to Gregory's plans for himself and Lyndall, is that the latter already has a lover.

In the scheme of the novel, Lyndall's lover is the last invader from the outside world. Like the man on horseback, who interpreted the carvings on Waldo's wooden post, he is another stranger—or rather, he remains anonymous to the reader, and also to everyone in the book, except Lyndall, who has met him during the years between childhood and young womanhood, when she has been away at school. When he arrives at the farm, she has to make her momentous decision. She is an attractive, highly intelligent young woman without any money, and her lover who offers her marriage is strong handsome intelligent—and he has money into the bargain. But Lyndall is by now very self-conscious about her situation as a nineteenth-century young woman. She has, as people say, 'a mind of her own', and she is constantly impelled to use it. Her feelings about her lover are as overwhelming as such feelings can be, but her mind supplies her with what she considers to be excellent contrary reasons. She envisages marriage as an equality, and if she marries within the present set of circumstances there will be no equality. On the contrary, she will have been a party to an affair of buying and selling, and the result will be male domination. And so she refuses the marriage offer, yet leaves the farm in her lover's company—and her decision to do so is a very momentous gesture from several points of view. For example, what she decides to do is sinful according to the rules of her upbringing—but she has long since decided that her worst sin of all is one which cannot be remedied: that is to say, it is the sin of having been born a woman at a particular time in the world's history. But her decision is even more momentous, inasmuch as it shortly results in her own death.

I think in my present talk I have said sufficient to make it clear, that two of the young people in *The Story of an African Farm*, Waldo and Lyndall, can neither stay on indefinitely within the little community of the farm, nor survive for very long after they have ventured out into the world. What significant meaning can be attached to the respective fates of these two young people? And is it a meaning which is significant for us in our day? I shall try to give you all my answers, in my next and final talk.

III

Now that I come to the final talk in my series about Olive Schreiner, and her novel *The Story of an African Farm*, listeners may perhaps remember my promise to answer certain questions. How was it possible, I asked, for a South African country girl to set to work in the latter part of last century, and produce a literary masterpiece? But before I answer that question, or try to, first let me refer to some other questions I raised. You may remember that after I had summarized *The Story of an African Farm*, I spoke first about Aunt Sannie, the matriarch who presides over the farm, and then about Otto, the huge German overseer—and both, I pointed out, are Biblical characters who fit perfectly into a landscape which we can readily think of as also remarkably Biblical. As mistress of the farm, Aunt Sannie is eventually replaced by her step-daughter, Em—who is by nature well suited to carrying on the farm, more or less on the lines laid down by Aunt Sannie. But the other two young people in the novel, the girl Lyndall, who is brilliantly intelligent, and the boy Waldo, who is a visionary dreamer—*they* don't fit readily into the life of the little shut-off community, and neither can endure to live on the farm indefinitely. But when Lyndall and Waldo break away, intending to find some place in the great outside world, where they may hope to be welcomed as individuals, each with his or her own particular gifts, they meet with such overwhelming disaster that neither survives for very long. What significant meanings can be attached to the respective fates of these two young people? And is it a meaning which is significant for us in our day? These are the other questions I raised.

All the answers are quite clear, and also quite obvious I think, if we don't forget that Olive Schreiner was the daughter of a missionary father, and was born at a South African mission station in the year 1855. Her parents were European-born, her mother English, and her father German, but Olive Schreiner came into the world as a mid-nineteenth-century colonial—and surely I am right if I say that children who grow up to become the first generation of colonizing parents are likely to find themselves in a rather special situation. For example, they are likely, at a very early age, to be confused about the meaning of the word 'home'—a word which, it should go without saying, is a very important one for a child. To all children (though with some exceptions of course), home very naturally means a house and its surroundings where they live with their parents. And a particular house, a particular landscape with its particular sky above—it is all something never entirely forgotten, something which certainly has its large share in determining the kind of people children will grow up to be. But children of colonizing parents, some of them at any rate, may be in some doubt about the matter—because from their earliest years, they will have to grapple with the strange notion that home is not altogether what they suppose. There is another home, located in some faraway place, only to be reached by weeks of improbable sea-travel. And in the case of Olive Schreiner there was the additional complication, that the remote overseas home was sub-divided.

I think it is true to say that in Olive Schreiner this particular contradiction existed in a state of unique tension. I don't know that she was ever known to say that South Africa was in her bones (as Katherine Mansfield said about New Zealand)—but she was vividly aware of her surroundings, and she profoundly sympathized with her missionizing father—as she demonstrated when she drew upon so many of his characteristics, with such a wealth of love and understanding, in order to create the character of the German overseer in *The Story of an African Farm*. It was her father's aim to preach in South Africa the good news about the coming of the Kingdom of God—and all the circumstances appeared to be quite promising. There was the landscape, which resembled the scene wherein the Israelitish religion began to develop. There were the black people, whose apparent simple-mindedness made them ripe for conversion. And there was the predominantly Dutch farming community, with its reputation for orderly and godly living. But in the nature of things, Olive Schreiner had a mother as well as a father—and her mother was a cultivated woman. That meant a mother whose thoughts persistently returned to her homeland for the kind of intellectual nourishment which South Africa could not be expected to provide. How then could a child who promised to grow up both beautiful and brilliantly intelligent, who combined a fiery vitality with an addiction to voracious reading—how could she be expected to fit into the South Africa that her father envisaged?—or alternatively, into the community at large, where extravagances of all kinds would be looked upon with disfavour as freakish? It is, I think, quite obvious that Olive Schreiner, being the kind of person she later on proved herself to be, had to find some sort of a solution for the tensions involved—and so, a girl in her teens, she set to work to write, attempting other works before she brought *The Story of an African Farm* finally to completion, by the time she was twenty-three or twenty-four years old. And besides dealing in her novel with the immediate personal problems that are always particularly distressing to young people, she endeavoured to deal with the large problems which she saw contemporary society confronted with, even though the particular society she belonged to might seem to be hardly aware that any such problems existed. As we read and re-read *The Story of an African Farm*, we perceive that all the problems that were tied up with nineteenth-century colonial settlement are being touched upon—and that is an important part of Olive Schreiner's achievement. But perhaps a further part is even more important. We are also aware that many of the most difficult problems posed for nineteenth-century Man are also being touched upon—and I should add, for twentieth-century Man, because these problems aren't solved yet.

Perhaps if we take another look at the novel, I may be able to illustrate what I mean by these rather large statements.

If we take the farm and its tiny community as representing what nineteenth-century colonalism was aiming at, that is to say orderly and godly prosperity, we soon see that this stability is not going to remain unchallenged for very long. First, there is the threat from outside. There is, for example, nothing the least bit orderly or godly or prosperous about Bonaparte Blenkins, the adventurer who arrives on the farm, and causes such irreparable havoc before he is finally got rid of. And when Waldo investigates the world that surrounds the farm, he finds that Bonaparte Blenkins has by no means been its false representative. But secondly, there is the threat to the farm's stability from within—that is to say, the tiny community has reared two individuals, the girl Lyndall, and the boy Waldo, who do not fit its notions of what is unquestionably right and proper. In my previous talks I spoke in detail about Waldo and Lyndall, so now I will roughly generalize, and say that Lyndall can be taken to represent Mind, and Waldo can be taken to represent Imagination—and note that Olive Schreiner, very self-conscious about her situation as a nineteenth-century intellectual woman, chooses a woman instead of a man to represent Mind. What she is saying, and saying no doubt with some exaggeration, since all that she experienced as a young woman was experienced at such a high pitch of intensity—what she is saying, is that she can see no place for Mind or Imagination, in the kind of society which nineteenth-century colonialism was aiming at. But she goes further, and in effect says that she can see no place for Mind and Imagination in the nineteenth-century world generally—the world which, at the time she was writing, was in a state of disorder, owing to the social and other changes brought about by the Industrial Revolution. Gifted with precocious insight, Olive Schreiner contemplated the wordly world, and she decided that it was immensely powerful. It had no place for the Lyndalls and the Waldos, and could be quite indifferent whether they lived or died. And it could penetrate to remote places where orderly and godly living was established, and kill off such wholly admirable people as old Otto. Some people, however, the worldly world would leave untouched—the Aunt Sannies, the so-called practical people, who do not admit to dreaming any troubling dreams, or to thinking any dangerous thoughts.

Now all that, I think, indicates one clear reason why Olive Schreiner's novel is still so fascinating to read. It is still quite topical—indeed, right up to the minute in many of the questions it raises. It also fascinates by its transparent, and at the same time, rather fierce and terrible sincerity. Olive Schreiner was that sometimes inconvenient person, the kind of person who insists that you look steadily at the facts without any flinching. (There is a story that, when in England, she insisted on living for some time in the east end of London, because she considered it the only place where people didn't wear masks on their faces.) Also, she tended to ask the most awkward questions. She was the kind of person who will ask the question Why?—or, What for?—when it is pretty generally agreed there is no satisfactory answer. One can imagine her appreciating that dismaying story by Oscar Wilde—which tells how Christ came to a city, and saw an old man lying weeping on the ground. And when asked for his reason, the old man replied, 'Lord, I was dead, and You raised me into life, what else can I do but weep?' Olive Schreiner would appreciate that story—yes—she would agree that all at times we must lie on the ground and weep, because life has turned out barren and empty, when we hoped it might have been splendid and grand. But she would never have agreed that anyone should lie on the ground and weep for very long. It must be granted that *The Story of an African Farm* is not at all an optimistic novel. The good man is shamefully misused and defeated, the Imagination must submit to having its wings cruelly clipped, and the thoughtful person isn't particularly wanted, in a world full of practical jobs. But even so, the novel with Olive Schreiner's name attached to it is not entirely negative—because it is shot through and through with the author's personal affirmation. We put it down knowing that despite all the odds, something can be achieved, because in the case of Olive Schreiner something *was* achieved—something which is entitled *The Story of an African Farm*.

Let me finish with a quotation from her fable about the hunter, which she inserts in the novel, and which I referred to in a previous talk. Remember that the hunter has spent his life endeavouring to capture the wild bird of Truth.

The old hunter folded his tired hands and lay down by the precipice where he had worked away his life. It was the sleeping time at last. Below him over the valleys rolled the thick white mist. Once it broke; and through the gap the dying eyes looked down on the trees and fields of their childhood. From afar seemed borne to him the cry of his own wild birds, and he heard the noise of people singing as they danced. And he thought he heard among them the voices of his old comrades; and he saw far off the sunlight shine on his early home. And great tears gathered in the hunter's eyes.

Ah! they who die there do not die alone, he cried.

Then the mists rolled together again; and he turned his eyes away.

I have sought, he said, for long years I have laboured; but I have not found her. I have not rested, I have not repined, and I have not seen her; now my strength is gone. Where I lie down worn out other men will stand, young and fresh. By the steps that I have cut they will climb; by the stairs that I have built they will mount. They will never know the name of the man who made them. At the clumsy work they will laugh; when the stones roll they will curse me. But they will mount, and on *my* work; they will climb, and by *my* stair! They will find her, and through me! And no man liveth to himself, and no man dieth to himself.

These three talks were given on radio in 1956. They have not been previously published. The manuscripts are among Sargeson's papers in the Alexander Turnbull Library.

20

SHAKESPEARE AND THE KIWI

I try to put aside the paralysing thought that as a published writer my name is probably better known than Shakespeare's was in his lifetime, and tell myself the date I am keeping is with the Complete Works in three Everymans which, after thirty-five years, begin to look too unfit to be disposed of secondhand at sixpence each. But what I have more in mind is the one volume copy printed in double columns which used to be a common object in many New Zealand homes. Sometimes there might also be a Tennyson, but he was a mark of refinement and not at all in serious competition with Shakespeare—for the decisive reason that Shakespeare was raised high above questions of social standing by powers attaching to his name which were as mysterious as they were undefined. Even his admitted reputation for indecency did him no damage; Tennyson on the contrary could not have survived the discovery of one dubious word.

At a time when the supremacy of the printed word was yet to be challenged by films and radio, Shakespeare (or so it seems to me now), was believed by many New Zealanders to be the man, and indeed the *English* man, who had come the closest to writing a book which might challenge the supremacy of the family Bible. Only a dull person would fail to see that distinction could go no higher, for it could be assumed that only an unimportant minority would refuse to admit that the Bible was written by God.

Did the Complete Works help to create an interest and a taste? The Bible background was supplemented by Sunday observances, and Shakespeare about the house was a preliminary to Shakespeare in school; also, play-reading circles for adults were usually known as Shakespeare Clubs—but for myself I can only say I was in my mid-twenties before I was fortunate enough to be shocked into recognizing that I had missed out on Shakespeare; and yet for years I had been devoted to Bernard Shaw, whose lively but derogatory views on Shakespeare I had been delighted to read and accept without question. I did not understand that my devotion was no anomaly—that Shaw happened accidentally to be a playwright with an apparent relation to Shakespeare, and was much more bound to turn up somewhere along the line of direction almost any curious and dissatisfied young New Zealander would be likely to take from a more or less average background. From Scripture it was only a short step to all the relevant and numerous scriptures of every variety of social and socialist thinking. It is not my present business to argue whether much in New Zealand which has since emerged is to be reckoned a benefit or a disadvantage—the point I am making is that the entire complex of results is related to the *moralizing* for which the family Bible provided a basis which was believed to be eternal, and an impetus which still remains astonishingly powerful.

What are the implications of the neglect of a possible line of development from that area of family background where the Complete Works occupied a niche? Moralizing has produced results, or at any rate has greatly influenced them—but what does one look for and not find in surroundings for which my own generation must be held largely responsible? It may with luck turn out that these questions have been answered, if I say how I at last discovered my need of Shakespeare and touch upon the consequences.

In 1928 I returned from England where I had seen some of the worst Shakespeare staged this century; or so at least I am told by somebody whose knowledge in these matters is superior to my own. For my part I had no complaints about Sybil Thorndike and Lewis Casson, but I lacked the opportunity to see them in anything beyond two of the comedies (for some reason Shakespeare was hardly to be seen anywhere at all in London during the 1927-28 season), and I confess I was a good deal more attracted by what Robert Lorraine could do for Strindberg, and Edith Evans for Congreve and Farquhar. Also, fascinated by the techniques of acting and speech for the stage, I frequented evenings run by a Compton street group known as Playroom Six where the skilful work of players who were unemployed could be observed at very close quarters (one of them I remember was Michael Sherbrooke, an actor of menacing power who had appeared as Dr Schutzmacher in the first performance of *The Doctor's Dilemma* in 1906).

In New Zealand it was good news that Alan Wilkie would soon be over from Australia for another Shakespeare tour; but he was presently snubbed by meagre audiences and a smug refusal from the New Zealand Government to assist with a subsidy. It should be kept in mind that by this time the talking film had arrived to deal the stage a series of knock-out blows, from which there were only feeble and mainly false signs of recovery for more than a decade and a half—but the dismaying thing about Mr Wilkie's theatrical knight errantry was his apparent failure to realize that his personal limitations could hardly have survived a lighter challenge. It was certainly not the economy of his properties, nor the particular kind of Shakespearean actor he happened to be (there is traditional ground for many kinds)—it was a curious delivery of his lines which had become more extravagant with his years. Words began as prolonged rumblings in the depth of his chest, and would finally be passed to the audience as a series of squeaks: but to conclude a period he would be likely to go into reverse, so that what began on the piccolo would finish as a kind of organ bass. (And incidentally, in the thirties it used to be one of Rex Fairburn's party jests to imitate Mr Wilkie's diction.) And yet, how am I to pay my debt to Alan Wilkie? Nobody else has since provided me with a prolonged and comprehensive season of Shakespeare: and it was the sudden impact of a few lines beautifully spoken by the company's Romeo, while he bent over Juliet (played by Mr Wilkie's wife, Miss Hunter-Watts), which ensured that during thirty-five years I would be marvellously compensated by the printed page for what I would have to do without on stage. The lines began, *Death that hath sucked the honey of thy breath* . . . .

It was as though that young man had wiped a window clean with his words—providing me with a view which, previously obscure, was now seen to be radiantly clear. Also, it was a double view—or rather I should say it was a view I could on the one hand comprehend as a positive invitation to enter the enchanted landscape of the poet's imagination; and on the other as a complete denial of every confident and complacent assertion to which, as a New Zealander, I was so very much accustomed. But above all, I returned that night to my lodgings drunk with the understanding that the totality of splendour which attached to the world of Shakespeare's imagination was inseparably rooted in *words*: it was an infinite comfort to know that I could be separated from it only by being separated from the printed page. Nor have I since wavered in my belief that Shakespeare's primary attraction, and indeed his primary value, resides in the range and variety of his verbal images and their incomparable splendour. Spenser before him and Milton afterwards have only in patches what he has in abundance.

But by now, with such stress upon verbal image, and so little regard for the ear, it may be inferred that I am putting forward the Complete Works as a kind of vastly extended 'Kubla Khan', from which the sound has been removed. And perhaps so—it is heresy no doubt, but if there is any such thing as pure poetry, that is to say rhythmic sound which is picked up by the ear, and comprehended as a kind of dance into which every movement that one has ever been aware of has been resolved, then I will risk saying that the two poets I have just mentioned are at their best superior to Shakespeare (*to hear the charms of his enchanting skill*: and *myself my sepulchre*). Probably what I am trying to say is that for me poetry is for the better part a matter of listening; and that if I am asked whether those parts of Shakespeare which are to be comprehended through the ear give me the finest satisfaction, I find myself obliged to hedge and ànswer yes and no.

It may however be objected that Shakespeare wrote for the stage, so plays are primarily what we should ask him to provide—and the obvious comment is that familiarity with the texts puts us at a disadvantage unknown to those who saw the plays when they were first performed. My meaning is clear if I say that any person thoroughly familiar with a Shakespeare text has never seen the play he derives from it performed on stage. It may be Olivier or it may be Mr Campion's players (with Mr Tim Eliott making an embarrassing hash of Romeo despite the gift of his fine voice); it may be Gielgud or Olivier on the films (with Sir Laurence Olivier in *Richard III* sagging to his unspoken but nonetheless deplorable *look at me, Laurence Olivier*); it may be marvels of radio speaking and acting by known and unknown names (not forgetting novelties such as M. Jean-Louis Barrault, with his *bon voyage* to accompany Hamlet's inspection of the remains of Polonius behind the arras; or the sad bleat of his *maman, maman, maman,* as a refreshing change from the *mater, mater, mater,* which an English actor may only just by good fortune manage to avoid); it may be what you will—except that it will never be the play that escapes from a charge of vandalism without a stain on its character by remaining faithful to the verbal document from which it is derived. And in any case, all this is to beg the question whether *anyone* knows how to speak Shakespeare on stage. And then again, it is well to remember that Shaw's views on

Shakespeare are not all nonsense: certainly it may be argued that if you present figures upon the stage who with hardly any exception speak language of unparalleled splendour, then it should not surprise if a profusion of verbal images will tend to hinder the dramatic conflict and tension which it is your purpose to create. To listen to Shakespeare is often to be reminded of those epic similes which may be prolonged until a detailed new landscape and a fresh set of figures have been projected across one's field of vision. It seems that my answer to Shakespeare proposed as a playwright is another equivocal yes and no.

I said above 'figures upon the stage . . . .' Should I have said characters? And the answer is no, with one literally tremendous exception named Falstaff. As for Hamlet Lear and the rest, they are more to be thought of as generalizations—and here I must insist I am not making unfair comparisons with the achievements which many novelists and some poets have since made us familiar with: I have no need to, for there was created in Shakespeare's own day that most wonderful of all literary characters Don Quixote (*'Tis his virtue makes him mad*) who, if he is taken along with Sancho his complement, additionally becomes a generalization which will cover every single item of importance implied by our use of terms such as 'life' and 'human nature'. About Falstaff there can be no possible doubt whatsoever; he is totally there in the round as irremovably as Dr Johnson—and yet without the doctor's advantage of being able to produce a certificate of existence quite apart from the pages of Boswell. And who could calculate his influence as a character on God knows how many writers, who have since endeavoured with dialogue to search the private hells common to every human psyche? I can imagine myself tiring at last of much that I read, but to admit that I no longer cared to turn to those terrifying pages where Falstaff and the prince pretend each in turn to be the prince's father, would be a frank admission that I had tired of life. But to write down Shakespeare's people as figures is by no means to write them off. Nobody can ever forget those very lovely very feminine young women, so lost and forlorn, whose charming names will sometimes underline their sad conditions—Marina, Perdita, Imogen; or the more resourceful Viola and Rosalind, who can make us wish they will never change back from the Ganymedes they have made themselves out to be; or that forward creature Portia, whose disguise is simply an excuse to indulge a remarkable talent for drawing room elocution.

It is because we associate Shakespeare with such a vast autonomous world of his own creation, that the kind of question I have been asking could be indefinitely extended—without ever any chance of an answer that would not be ambiguous. Confident answers can be expected only if you direct your inquiries away from the Complete Works. Problems of scholarship may be solved if you are willing to cover a few yards of the miles and miles of exposition; consult Eric Partridge (an ex-New Zealander) if you are interested in the question why all the great wits were bawdy; for revelations of wisdom and religious truth look up all the relevant words in a Concordance; to become knowledgeable about the limits of knowledge about ultimate reality try almost any page of the *Critique of Pure Reason.* What has Shakespeare to do with all these matters? Everything and nothing. All questions resolve themselves into one which is over-riding and enormous; are there permanent values embedded in the Complete Works? Nobody knows. But in the mean-time we do know that . . . *they have taken away my Lord, and I know not where they have laid him* is one way with words, and *Time hath, my lord, a wallet at his back . . .* is another; and that both ways are to be valued beyond reckoning quite apart from what is communicated in both instances. Particularly for a New Zealander, the serious disadvantage of Shakespeare's way with words is that there is no easy and obvious relation with everyday speech and affairs. The Complete Works can be read in six months by anyone who will consistently get up in the morning one half to three quarters of an hour before his or her usual time—but the snag is that if you have not had the good luck to become accustomed to words and idiom early in your lifetime, it is doubtful whether you will persist until you have overcome their initial difficulty. It is just one of the sad facts of New Zealand life—take note of your surroundings, and you are in no doubt that moralizing has had its point and value; but one possibility of another kind of world was ditched when the Complete Works, too mysteriously semi-sacred to be entirely overlooked, were nevertheless neglected as of no practical importance.

Landfall, March 1964 (v.18, no.1), pp.44-54. 'Shakespeare and the Kiwi' was one of four essays published in that issue of *Landfall* to mark the four-hundredth anniversary of Shakespeare's birth.

21

HENRY LAWSON: Some Notes after Re-reading

From Lawson's own account of his childhood it seems clear that he suffered a precocious sense of interior desolation. There were reasons—poverty, disagreements and disputes between parents, besides the boy's own peculiarities of temperament. ('My aunts said it was a pity I hadn't been born a girl.') But an inquiry into the nature of Lawson's great literary achievement could be better served by emphasizing the permanence of this sense, than by any probing for its whys and wherefores.

In a letter to a friend serving in the 1914-18 war, Lawson, then in his later forties, said:

> I'll tell you this, Benno, old chap, and you can tell the nurse if you like, married or single, 'happy' home or not—*there's such a thing as home-home-sickness* [the italics are Lawson's] as well as the foreign kind; and when the hero welcome—or prodigal son welcome; it doesn't matter which—is over, you'll feel in your bowels that awful, sinking world-emptiness which is infinitely worse than any home-sickness abroad, because it is born of the hoary father of all disillusions, and is, or will seem to be, the End—the Limit. It's a mighty reaction of course—the same as on the first night in a Promised Land. . . . I've felt *that* kind of home-sickness for the last place I came from, or for anywhere. . . .

Is there anyone to deny that to be afflicted by that kind of sickness is to experience the worst of human ills? Is there any remedy? No doubt some would reply, yes, in religious belief (but Lawson was agnostic). Or must one make do with a sequence of distractions—of high or low quality according to capacity and taste? Again from his own account it is clear that Lawson in his childhood found some alleviation in his love for his father. 'I slept in a cot beside the bed, and I used to hold his horny hand until I went to sleep.'

In the stories and sketches I have counted somewhere about a dozen passages where this hand-holding situation, no matter how much 're-created', is reproduced. Its closest approximation is in a story called 'A Child in the Dark'—and there is an important detail added. 'The father . . . lit the candle at the kitchen fire, put it where it shouldn't light the boy's face, and watched him. And the child knew he was watching him, and pretended to sleep, and, so pretending, he slept.'

This situation, two people endeavouring to cope with the terrors of aloneness, is fundamental to Henry Lawson's creed of mateship—upon which a good deal of his best work is explicitly founded. Note especially 'The Hero of Redclay'. The title suggests Bret Harte, and the piece does indeed depend for its full success upon a longish inset story which strongly reminds one of the American writer. The enclosing story is however very much Lawson's own—and the final effect has depended upon his borrowing and re-creating to his own advantage.

Two mates, Jack and Joe, are away out working in a shearing shed and one is sacked a few days before cut-out. Joe waits for his mate—'I camped at the head of the Billabong where the track branched, one branch running to Bourke, up the river, and the other out towards the Paroo—and hell.' But when Jack turns up 'with his cheque, and his swag, and a new sheep-pup, and his quiet grin,' he is accompanied by a third man who is disliked by Joe. A triangular situation is now touched upon with great literary skill: the reader is made to feel that Joe is jealous and deeply hurt. The stranger leaves them at sunset however, and Jack accompanies him some way into the plain until Joe sees them leave one another after a prolonged handshake: the third man 'began to dwindle down to a black peg and then to a dot on the sandy plain, that had just a hint of dusk and dreamy far away gloaming on it between the change from glaring day to hard broad moonlight'. The two mates are together again, but Jack is sullen; and Joe suffering the crisis of his jealousy says a few words which threaten a showdown. But Jack redeems the situation by telling the inset story. (It concerns the third man; he has unjustly done a five-years lagging for attempted bank robbery: in fact he had been on the bank premises because of an affair with the bank-manager's house-keeping niece: the girl dies of shock, but her lover keeps his mouth shut—and after he has received a note from the accused man so also does Jack, who knows the facts of the situation. The note reads, 'We were mates on the track. If you know anything of my affair don't give it away.')

The telling of this story produces its cathartic effect, and Joe and Jack are reconciled: both have sympathetic thoughts for the third man tramping his 'lonely track'. But in the night Joe wakes from a nightmare to note again a couple of boughs hanging over the Billabong (these have previously been noted during a half-time episode for tea during the telling of the inset story, when he has thought them 'the perfect shapes of two men hanging side by side'). It now seems to him that he has dreamed the third man hadn't gone after all, or had come back, and that he and Jack 'had hanged themselves sociably'—his mate 'for sympathy and the sake of mateship'.

The story ends with Joe watching Jack's sleeping face which a path of moonlight crosses.

Now apart from the important suggestions (jealousy suggests the death of love; and sleep with its nightmare stands for the final separation of mates in physical death), there are a number of significant details to be noted about this story: for one thing there is the pup, and the tender regard of the two men for it (as well as being about the relations of people, the story is about the relations of people and animals); and there is the use of the expression 'a white man' (throughout Lawson a sign of approbation—and its pejorative use on this occasion is unique in his prose work so far as I know). But what is to be noted above all is the landscape. With some of Lawson's critics it is an open question whether he loved or hated the bush. In my view the question is not well put. He looked at the desolation of the Australian inland, and he saw his own interior desolation. He is not a 'realist' writer in the journalistic sense of the word: the 'realism' he is concerned with is to be found inside himself. It is true that he uses naturalistic phenomena to express his inward-looking vision; and the very thing that suited him admirably was all around him. It has been slickly said that he learned about the bush in the Sydney pubs. This is nonsense. The bush was desolation (and wasn't it certain from the accounts of the Explorers that it was?), and he knew all about that. As a growing boy, and again as a young man, he had had his look at the bush—and that was sufficient. What it essentially was was inside him, and known to him inside out.

But what should finally be said about 'The Hero of Redclay' is that readers have the unique advantage of reading about the origins of the enclosing story in a sketch called 'Mateship'. And among other things this sketch is invaluable for reinforcing one's intuitions about Lawson's skill and judgement as a literary artist. Nobody can miss the jealousy which is so important in 'The Hero of Redclay', but it is never once mentioned as such: and yet in the sketch Lawson speaks plainly about the jealousy which can be such a deadly business between mates.

In second place to mateship as fundamentally important to Lawson's prose work, is booze. Perhaps one could risk saying that mateship, as his practical and indeed his only solution to the enigma of life, entailed a further problem. To say that Lawson (who was deaf from childhood), discovered in booze 'a way to communication with his fellow-men' is probably fair enough; but apart from the sad fact that the end-result of alcohol is a heightened sense of isolation, it is clear from many passages that Lawson used alcohol as a consolation with an unfortunate tendency to get completely out of hand. Some of the stories about drunkenness, and many incidental passages, are to be ranked with his best work. Before him there was Zola (*L'Assommoir* was published in 1879), who combined clinical observation and imaginative understanding to produce a splendid work of art; but it is with Jack London (*John Barleycorn* appeared in 1913), a slightly younger contemporary, that Lawson has more in common: both men were writing about a subjective problem, but Lawson's range is the more impressive. 'Johnson's Jag' is a delight, a comedy about what is likely to happen when a city-man is strongly tempted and falls from sober grace; but away at the far end of the scale are scenes of 'shanty' drinking in the remote outback which it is not extravagant to describe as ghastly: the setting is likely to be an arid drought-stricken area of sparse vegetation, weird and ghostly in moonlight: in the early stifling hours of the morning everybody is soaked, lying sprawled and dead to the world about the verandah—and that includes the shanty-keeper, who will be asleep across the doorway of the room where his wife is in bed.

(At Mallacoota, a coastal place almost on the dividing line between Victoria and New South Wales, a friend of mine now in his mid-seventies had some acquaintance with Henry Lawson in the year 1910. He was then aged forty-three years—and had been persuaded to take a holiday from Sydney, where he was drinking and risking prosecution by his wife for failure to pay maintenance. At Mallacoota he was with the balladist, E. J. Brady, and T. D. Mutch (afterwards Minister of

Education for the N.S.W. Government); and according to my friend
this pair were unable or unwilling to deprive him of his booze. Eventually my friend saw him suffer an attack of dt's. He remembers a 'tall
dark skeleton', very reserved and morose.)

Lawson was one of those writers who appear to begin by springing into
full maturity: there appears to have been no apprenticeship—but unfortunately too, sometimes, there is no further development. In place of
development in Lawson there is much variation of style (how many
writers of his stature have suffered so badly from sub-editing?); and
although the more simple-seeming writing is his better part, we would
be the poorer if it were not for a number of occasions which depend
upon a denser, more elaborated prose. The style varies, but there
remains a remarkable consistency of subject-matter. An astonishing
feature about this large lavish edition is that the matter in the third
volume has had to be dredged for, and is now presented between hard
covers for the first time. (Henry Lawson died in 1922.) This has meant
more than eighty stories and sketches previously unknown to me. They
include 'A Child in the Dark' (not a good story, but crucially important
for readers who care about Lawson); many good Sydney stories,
including much of the best writing about drunkenness; some beautifully appreciative and tender stories about Australian Chinese (these
despite Lawson's commitment to the White Australia of his day). But
what has remarkedly and quite unexplainedly been withheld from hard
covers for so long is a series of six stories which are evidently a final
working-out of the theme of mateship: these thirty-three pages about a
man called Previous Convictions and his mate Dotty (he is short of the
full pound, say about fifteen shillings), suggest that Lawson by design
or accident had hit upon the device of Morality figures for one last concrete expression of his creed. The two men have met in prison. They
are ultimates in social rejection, helpless beyond minimum requirements for survival. All that is left to them is their mutual loyalty (what
is basically the watching-over-hand-holding situation turns up when
Previous Convictions wakes from a nightmare to find that his face has
been shielded from the sun by a screen of boughs rigged by the ever-
solicitous Dotty). It is significant that the first story begins with the two
men appearing to the narrator out of a dust-storm; and at the end of the
fifth they disappear into another. But it is as though by now Lawson
cannot bear to end in negation and despair; so he writes a sixth story
which ends with the narrator in bed on his verandah 'covered up warm',
but watching a fire among the trees in the distance where the two men,

now returned, are camped. The fire is like 'a star of Hope and Peace'. The men have surprisingly returned with somewhat mended fortunes.

What difficulties would a present-day writer be likely to encounter if he attempted to write of male friendship in terms of the mateship code? The question is teasingly relevant, because an answer might help to explain Lawson's 'lack of development'. Was the man naive? Did he for example know that Montaigne had written a very famous essay on friendship, which is all the more interesting for springing from his relations with his friend Etienne de La Boétie?—('If you press me to tell why I loved him, I feel that this cannot be expressed, except by answering: Because it was he, because it was I'). Montaigne is careful to let us know that although in his own case the close union of friendship was achieved free from any sensual ingredient, he is well aware that only a fine line may sometimes divide friends from friends who are also lovers: he cites the 'salutary loves' of Harmodius and Aristogeiton, an historical pair admired as heroes by generations of Athenians.

It is remarkable that although there are comparatively few pages in Lawson where some question of drink can be completely ruled out, you can read everything in these three huge volumes and find only one passing reference to anything that might be described as sexually unorthodox. (The term used is 'sexyil pivits'—and it relates merely to Dotty's having thieved some worn-out women's under-clothing.) Lawson's exhaustive treatment of drunkenness suggests that he felt no constraint at all about exploring its possibilities as literary material. The frownings of conventional society appear to have meant nothing to him. May one not suppose then, that there were other areas of human experience which a man with his genius for observation (it should not be forgotten that he was about the Sydney streets and pubs for the greater part of his life, and that the people he is graphically knowledgeable about are those who have 'loved suffered and felt') was sensitively aware of?—but which he felt himself powerfully interdicted from even mentioning. The extreme scarcity of references to the convicts and the convict tradition would appear to support this view: books like *Geoffry Hamlyn, For the Term of his Natural Life,* and *Robbery Under Arms* were part of the climate of the times; but they beg so many questions it is easy to imagine that Henry Lawson would have been somewhat more at home with James Tucker, whose *Ralph Rashleigh* had been written before his life began, but was never published until after it had ended. Himself a convict, Tucker leaves nobody in ignorance of what it was like to be socially rejected by the Australia of his day.

From my reading of these three volumes I judge Lawson's stature to have heightened with the years. The man endears as much by the recurring personal glimpses (his delight in the consolation of a freshly washed body and clean clothes turns up again and again: he likes to smell sweet: also there is his pleasure in contemplating any finished piece of work which has demanded his craftsmanship), as he does by what he writes. It is impossible to forget some of his images: custard marrows 'like the knee frills of a clown'. By far the greater part of his prose work is marvellously easy to read; and yet it demands the closest attention, as I think many a Lawson critic must have discovered to his cost. It is time to forget about his being a 'national' writer, certainly time to cease thinking of him as a 'realist'. Think instead of affinities with another 'colonial' writer—Theocritus. Like the Sicilian Greek, Lawson was completely at home with pastoral characters who lived not very far above the survival line. It is a curiously dour sardonic pastoral celebration of life that he engages himself with. Put cabbage-tree hats on Theocritus's goat-herds and call them shearers or rouseabouts; wipe the smiles off their faces and replace them with grins—and you are in Lawson's world. The sunlight and the aridity are already there: not too far below the surface is all the pain and terror of existence. It was Theocritus's Roman imitator who put it all into one line—loaded with a resonance beyond the resources of Lawson and the Australian language:

Sunt lacrimae rerum et mentem mortalia tangunt.

Landfall, June 1966 (v.20, no.2), pp.156-62. The occasion of the essay was the publication of *The Stories of Henry Lawson,* edited by Cecil Mann (Sydney, Angus & Robertson, 1964, 3v.).

22

AN IMAGINARY CONVERSATION:
William Yate and Samuel Butler

BUTLER. Mr Yate?

YATE. As it pleases you, Mr Butler. May I remind you of my years as a clerk in Holy Orders?

BUTLER. I intended no discourtesy. To me you are a clergyman—without any suggestion of reproach or satire. May that not be thought perhaps a little singular?—I mean in relation to what I write.

YATE. Now you comfort me. When there are grave matters to disturb me I am grateful for words that put me at my ease.

BUTLER. Ah, words! Yes indeed, words. If I am not wholly mistaken it is mainly words which are to be reckoned at the root of our mutual fortunes. Or perhaps I had better say, misfortunes.

YATE. I am not sure about your meaning, Mr Butler. We have our individual roots in our common humanity—and these roots are no doubt closely related to our fortunes and misfortunes. But what is there of fortune worth considering except in relation to Almighty God? Our only misfortune is to miss the re-union with our maker which he so ardently desires.

BUTLER. I can respect your faith. That's to say, insofar as it may relate to what is behind the Church of England—or perhaps better say, behind the Christian religion. Remember Mr Yate, that same Force (I am not prepared to say Almighty God. I yearn for definitions which I cannot supply, and have never been satisfactorily supplied with—and certainly not by our illustrious Mr Darwin)—that same Force, I say, is also behind every religion. But let it pass—in relation to these large matters your fortunes and my own must of necessity appear infinitesimally restricted. I say only that these same fortunes have touched us in our humanity—touched us sufficiently indeed to fill our humanity's entire horizon. It is these mutual fortunes that engage my attention. I endeavour to handle them with words, and it is my belief that they are themselves rooted in words.

YATE. You embarrass me by your hints, Mr Butler.

BUTLER. You will agree that it was our common fortune as young men to sail out to the Antipodes.

YATE. Ah!

BUTLER. Or misfortune.

YATE. I don't know that in my book about New Zealand I spoke of misfortune. There is much among my recollections of that country for which I am grateful.

BUTLER. In a book which I begin to write but perhaps will not finish, and do not expect to publish, leastways not in my lifetime—in this book I remark upon the human unhappiness which might be avoided if people would speak honestly to each other without reserve, if—

YATE. Pardon my interrupting, but I infer from your drift that you are aware of scandal concerning me. Very well. All that was a long time ago. May I ask if you have sought out an opportunity for troubling an old man? If so, Mr Butler, say so frankly—without reserve. And I will call in my beloved sister—to leave you in no doubt that our interview is terminated.

BUTLER. What is the worth of frank speaking unless it is mutual? It is not much likely that scandal which touches myself has reached you. I will repair that omission. That is to say, if you will permit me.

YATE. As you must be aware, I am padre of our mariners' church here in Dover. A moment ago I referred to matters that disturb me—my reference was to the ravages of sin here among my congregation. Sin and its suffering, Mr Butler. You will readily understand that I am accustomed to frank speech—it is my habit to encourage it. But I do not see that I am in any relation to yourself which would make me happy to dispense with all reserve.

BUTLER. There are times when all of us must envy the confessional of the Roman church. Daily life is no doubt made to appear simpler by the habit of that ritual and unquestioning submission to church authority. The troubled spirit may be soothed. But the price of this comfort is that we must be content with what I would call an approximation. I think there are signs that the Church recognizes this principle of approximation. For the unquestioning Christian the creed may be clear and final—but there were those church fathers who spoke of the creed as the *symbol.* That's to say, perhaps, as the approximation—a thing *faute de mieux.* If—

YATE. I again interrupt. I am not receiving you to hear your confession, Mr Butler.

BUTLER. Not in the church sense.

YATE. Unless I choose—not in any sense.

BUTLER. I have mentioned a book I write but do not finish—Mr Yate, in this book I try to depict myself truly without reserve. I did not come here to discuss with you books I *have* finished—my *Erewhon,* for example. But I would say that in my published writings I present myself to the world as a man for whom the intellectual life is dominant. To you, Mr Yate, I say that what I try to reveal in my unfinished book is a man stripped . . . solitary, naked, shrinking . . . the *animula vagula* of the emperor-poet. It is in the character of that man I have approached you today—a man who perhaps is little known to anyone except myself. . . .

YATE. You were saying, Mr Butler?

BUTLER. If one does not submit to church authority, there is so far as I know only one recourse available to the man who seeks to sanctify his private and personal life. I mean as a substitute for what the church claims to provide. . . .

YATE. Well?

BUTLER. We may privately invoke charity—I should hope with humility. You will agree that to say *agape* is probably an improvement. . . . It may well be that I am invoking your charity, Mr Yate.

YATE. But invoke? That word has to me a portentous sound. Had you not better say you *appeal* to my charity? And do you as well appeal to my pride? Your humility may be the occasion for my pride, Mr Butler. I see danger there. And your aim is that I might assist you consecrate your private and personal life? That is a very tall order. Again I warn you, Mr Butler—the church claims to be supra-personal, supra-human. You appeal to me personally—your appeal is to someone who is wholly unworthy.

BUTLER. Oh yes, yes. Pardon my impatience—if we stick to the human facts—

YATE. Facts seen under the form of eternity may cease to be human and and become divine.

BUTLER. For the purposes of what I have to say I agree. Consider. It is as one who as a young man sailed out to the Antipodes to encounter his fate that I invoke your charity. . . .

YATE. Was your . . . fate, as you put it—was your fate so severe?

BUTLER. In its incidentals, yes. To love is to suffer. It was for me written that I should voyage half way round the world . . . for money, it is true. But it was also to find my heart ravished by the discovery of love. . . . In your book, Mr Yate, you wrote of the anguish of joy, the pain of pleasure. . . .

YATE. If the love you found embraced the charity we spoke about, then I do not see your reason for the invocation which we also spoke about.

BUTLER. What I found was joy. I cannot deny that it was also suffering . . . . It was written that you too would meet your fate in those distant parts—and suffer the agony of love destroyed in public scandal.

YATE. Mr—

BUTLER. I am bold, perhaps not to be forgiven. But I do not apologize —nor for my endeavours to invoke your charity. It is a compliment I pay you. Who in these matters can truly understand unless his heart has known that rape? Can you appreciate that without the profoundest feelings of sympathy, coupled with humility, I could not have dared approach you?

YATE. Mr—

BUTLER. Although I am for quite some years returned from New Zealand, the love I found there still survives. Incredibly more—it is much increased. With the corollary that suffering has increased a thousandfold. Perhaps I might dare to say that the severity of your own suffering is not now beyond my experience. There, sir, you have the core of my approach to you—the reason why I beg for your charity. Mutual suffering may find a way to mutual relief.

YATE. Very well, Mr Butler. But I warn you—charity that falters in the face of sin is charity that has failed.

BUTLER. That word! One of those at the root of our misfortunes as I have mentioned. Do you recollect that the wise Frenchman has said that most of the occasions for our troubles in this world are grammatical? Sin! The word ties us to our century, our age, our island and our continent. Well! And what is sin?

YATE. From you, Mr Butler, that is a question which requires no answer.

BUTLER. But consider the Greeks of the days of our scholarship, Mr Yate—of whom it has been said that they were unable to distinguish the word from the thing. The word you say is sin. That word *can* be distinguished. It was the redemption of joy that I felt—a flood in my heart and throughout my being. Must I say sin?

YATE. Must I remind you of your texts? Adultery is the guilt of the man who looks upon a woman—

BUTLER. It was no woman—

YATE. That is neither here nor there. What you speak of was rooted in the lust of your loins. Its direction was its own sufficient warning —that no consecration could be granted you.

BUTLER. I am not to be held to account for its direction. What is of the constitution is no sin.

YATE. Not in its leaning—so long as leaning may be distinguished from the prompting of active desire.

BUTLER. You are too fine. If I were a consecrated clergyman the be-all and end-all of the Evangel I would preach would be the forgiveness of sins. But in any event, all was redeemed in charity—which I had then no need to invoke. Charity was already there. Do you suppose I conceived of my friend as an object for my pleasure regardless of every concern for his dignity and well-being? No, Mr Yate. I have mentioned since my return from New Zealand an increase—and there has been much increase of charity from which my love can never be wholly disentangled.

YATE. But you also mentioned a thousandfold increase in suffering.

BUTLER. There you have my reason for seeking your charity. . . .What is the worst suffering we may be obliged to endure?—that which may be compared with what your God must endure, Mr Yate.

YATE. I am not sure that what you say is not blasphemy.

BUTLER. It is written that God offers us love. If the offer is thrown back in his face—then it is beyond our understanding not to suppose that we cause God to suffer.

YATE. The love God offers is charity—which is not readily offended.

BUTLER. My analogy holds—neither is the charity which moves me. I have mentioned the common human love with which it is mingled. It is because I seek the balm of a charity from which common love has not been wholly purged that I have sought you out, Mr Yate.

Because of the tincture of mortality mingled with the charity you are already affording me, you may be assured it will not be thrown back in your face. . . .

YATE. Was the love you discovered in New Zealand for a native?—a Maori?

BUTLER. A European. He is about my own age—quick lively handsome confident carefree. All that besides much else—indeed, all that I am not. . . . Among the New Zealand settlers there were scandalous tongues to—

YATE. And your love is not thrown back in your face?—it is answered?

BUTLER. It was. It is not now.

YATE. And your charity?

BUTLER. That is . . . accepted. I have evidence in the most concrete sense. Money is . . . accepted.

YATE. Am I to understand that you are blackmailed?

BUTLER. Not in the legal sense. . . . You have already quoted the Apostle, Mr Yate—charity is not readily offended.

YATE. Your friend is not a worthy man?

BUTLER. I am not concerned with that word. What is relevant is his worth to me, which is beyond calculation. Perhaps I should say beyond words. . . .

YATE. This is strange matter—it revives in me what an old man might have wished to be done with. . . . Mr Butler, it surprises me to speak.

BUTLER. Speech that eases you, Mr Yate, may for me—no, I repeat myself.

YATE. You recall to me my College days, and a young man I first observed and then cared for. He became a great sorrow to me when I understood how greatly he was distressed by the promptings of what to him was his own natural self. It was only by the discipline of my prayers and fasting that I had imposed a truce upon my own longings. . . .You see, Mr Butler, you have won from me my trust. . . . But this young man—he had discovered, as no doubt many still do, that in towns of any size there are always those who will cater for our lusts. It would seem often in fear trembling and shame—at least that is what I inferred from my friend's behaviour. He was in company reluctant to meet any direct glance, and his own glances were the very spit of those described by Dante—you will remember he speaks of the looks which men exchange of an evening under a new moon, looks which call to mind an old tailor sharpening his vision at the eye of his needle. . . . His very walk became a silent gliding motion, curiously effacing. It was as though he had become already like the souls of the Inferno—the ghost of what he had formerly been. I cannot describe how much I felt his distress—on account of which I was prompted to offer him my charity along with my excuses for inquiring about his problem. And it was *his* excuse that he was engaged upon a search—a quest. He was obsessed by the belief that around one of the many street corners which he was impelled to turn—and turn and turn again, until it seemed that for him there was nothing upon earth except turning corners—I say he was obsessed by the illusory conviction that his search would end in the sublime happiness of his discovering another Platonic half. It was here I had the reason for his being unwilling to bother with me. There was so little time he could spare for anyone—when around the next corner was to be found the joy which he might miss if he was in any other way occupied—the joy which would be his when he achieved his completion. . . .

BUTLER. Yes?

YATE. I should tell you, Mr Butler, that he was a talented classical scholar. And one bright morning when the world seemed not an unpleasant place in which to be . . . he was taken from the river. Excuse and forgive me. . . . Very well, or rather perhaps, very ill. It was to myself the gravest warning, Mr Butler—and perhaps the more especially since it was not a great time afterwards that I found myself among the natives of the south seas, dedicated to the work of a Christian missionary. I was much too among the Europeans of Port Jackson—but my heart was fixed where the work was that I loved best, among the warm-hearted people of the Bay of Islands and tropical Tonga. . . . I will be frank—perhaps I am responding to what you called your invocation. Or perhaps, Mr Butler, it is more simply that your dark colouring of feature recalls vividly to me many a Polynesian for whom I conceived the most lively affection. . . .

BUTLER. I have read your book, Mr Yate.

YATE. Then you will know that I printed letters from a great number of my Maori friends—know too that if the language they wrote is to be credited my affection for them was tenderly reciprocated. . . . You would meet the native people in your part of New Zealand, Mr Butler?

BUTLER. In Canterbury they were scarce, almost not to be found—at least not by me.

YATE. You cannot conceive the readiness of their traits of affection . . . the tears of farewell, the smothering kisses . . . a New Zealander's love is all outside, in his eyes and his mouth. . . . It is not to be wondered at, at least not by you, Mr Butler . . . I was indiscreet. There are times for every one of us, it is something known to us all, when there is no answer to what we must endure in this world . . . there is no answer, no remedy—except the comfort, the protection we may find in a pair of enclosing arms. You will understand my special circumstances, the sleeping arrangements of those people are not as ours. . . . Indiscretion became my disgrace in a rage of scandal which you leave me in no doubt was echoed to you during your visit to those distant parts.

BUTLER. There were those who commended you. It was quoted to me that you were the victim of a conspiracy black as hell.

YATE. From you, now, in what we may agree to call this moment of truth, a moment which has so unexpectedly become mine in my old age, or should I more properly say yours-and-mine?—from you Mr Butler I will hold nothing back. You argued that the word sin ties us to our own times and country, to the continent of Europe and its civilization. You touched me—for it was part of my difficulty as a Christian missionary that I did not always discern a sense of sin where it seemed I might without fail expect to find it. It would sometimes surprise me that among these native friends I found nothing to remind me of the shame which had afflicted the young colleague of whom I spoke. And zealous Christian though I was, devoted to my work of conversion, the matter appeared important enough to require some investigation. As a worker in the mission field I was commissioned to bear the Gospel message, and when I discovered that many natives were possessed of qualities which seemed to distinguish them admirably from some Christians it had greatly distressed me to be familiar with—well, it was evident that I must make some inquiry into their own religious beliefs and practices. And to restrict myself to the matter in question, I discovered what struck me as immeasurably disturbing—for these people conceived of deities that inhabited the surrounding country, and resembled in their tastes the deities of ancient Greece. It may surprise you to learn, Mr Butler, that an affection for native Ganymedes was attributed to a native Zeus who was believed to be established upon the summit of a local Olympus. . . . Believe me, Mr Butler, there has been nothing in my life which has more sorely tempted me than these tentative explorations into native belief. It was perhaps for my soul's good that I became a target for scandal despite the unspeakable anguish I was obliged to endure. If it had not been in God's purpose to halt me, what licence might I not have been tempted into permitting myself?—as preparation for my own eternal destruction I do not doubt. . . .

BUTLER. I am grateful to you, Mr Yate. I understand, and I am moved. But for me any solution which depended upon Christian approval would not have satisfied. It would have entailed a lifetime's suffocation not to conceive of my freedom in a moral area where I might exercise my right to choose. Strong feelings may no doubt interfere with one's detachment in endeavouring to choose freely— but that may be remedied by a constant reference to the charity which I judge to be a constant need in all human relations. I am not aware that I am diminished in my stature as a man by my choice. Licence is not to me a temptation, nor am I convinced that a reason for what I suffer is to be found in the guilt which the tribal rules of the community I belong to demand that I feel. To you it may appear sacrilege, Mr Yate, but for me there are times of such happiness I can infer myself to be in a state of grace. . . . The contrary is also true—I confess that I suffer. But I suspect that suffering is the price exacted from any one of us who endeavours to establish harmonious relations with another human being. I resent my suffering, Mr Yate, because I am reluctant to believe that to suffer is to be enriched—my observations have often led me to an opposite conclusion. But today I am soothed—grateful that you have opened to me your heart. . . .

YATE. If I am not mistaken I hear the sound of my sister's teacups. . . . We must talk of other things, Mr Butler. May I recommend to you the thought that it is perhaps by God's grace that we have today reached across the gulf which separates us? I shall hope always that you may come to rely for your support upon the Christian faith. I am not your judge, Mr Butler—and I do agree with you in what you had to say about the forgiveness of sins.

Landfall, December 1966 (v.20, no.4), pp.344-57. William Yate was dismissed from his missionary duties in New Zealand following accusations of homosexuality. Sargeson returned to the topic in a review of a reprint of Yate's *An Account of New Zealand: and of the Formation and Progress of the Church Missionary Society's Mission in the Northern Island* (1835) in *Landfall,* September 1971 (v.25, no.3), pp.299-304.

23

AUSTRALIAN FICTION

My difficulties in writing a satisfactory note on this book are personal and special. Not long after I had learned to read I was preferring *Seven Little Australians* (Ethel Turner) to *Robin of the Round House* (Isabel Maude Peacock—Isabel Cluett to Auckland newspaper readers). I preferred Australian films (Snowy Baker in *The Man from Snowy River*) to anything from America except Charlie Chaplin. Later on I discovered the sentimental bloke, dad and Dave, and Bridgit McSweeney (by far my favourite in this genre was the last). I sang on my way to school 'Now the moon shines bright on Mrs Porter. . . .' and was eventually dismayed that T. S. Eliot had evidently not had my version 'reported' to him from Sydney. I thought *It's Never too Late to Mend* (Charles Reade), *Geoffry Hamlyn* (Henry Kingsley), and *Robbery Under Arms* the very best books I had ever read (now looking down a list of fifteen other Boldrewood books, it piques me that I never discovered *Babes in the Bush* and *War to the Knife*—the latter subtitled *Tangata Maori*; they are titles I would have been right out after if I had known they existed). And it all led eventually to Henry Lawson (his prose), about whose greatness I was never in doubt: it is true that I mistakenly supposed he was 'representing' an Australia which still existed, but I was right in my intuitive understanding that I was getting a literary line on what it meant to be alive and in the world anywhere at anytime. And perhaps it all in much later years came to a peak when I read the accounts of the

Australian explorers (among whom I would include Charles Darwin, who wrote in *The Voyage of the Beagle* his marvellous account of how those stupendous bluffs on the west side of the Blue Mountains may best be explained if we postulate origins for them at the bottom of the sea).

What did I find in New Zealand letters to compare with all these wonders? Why, except for our mountains even the terrain was unpropitious: our rivers were conventional, beginning in the mountains to end in the sea; Australian rivers crazily made off inland to end up ghosts in the desert. And desert? One could expect to find nothing human on the tops of mountains: 'desert' was a word that connoted romance as well as terror.

All of which is to say that this book will be valued by everyone susceptible to the spell of the Australian continent. It is perhaps aptly described by its editor as offering not always what is best from *Overland,* but what is most representative. There are far too many contributors to mention—writers of verse (which only rarely becomes poetry), stories, criticism, documentary, comment, obituary. The wonder is that such a handsome expensive volume can appear at all. Who reads?—we all know that reading in the Antipodes is something you do when nothing better offers, a substitute pastime for occasions when the weather is dirty enough to let you down.

A review of *Overland Muster: Selections from* Overland, *1954-1964,* in *Landfall,* June 1967 (v.21, no.2), pp.206-7.

CONVERSATION IN A TRAIN: or, What Happened to Michael's Boots

OLD MAN. I see that you have chosen a most appropriate book to read on your journey to the Coast.

YOUNG WOMAN. I am a student. I am to write a thesis on the New Zealand novel.

OLD MAN. Do I waste your time if I ask you to tell me something of what you intend to say? I warn you that I am a warm admirer of *Coal Flat*.

YOUNG WOMAN. I would prefer to call myself a compulsive admirer. My response is contradictory—I am held, but against my will. I think that for my own generation Mr Pearson is somewhat out of date. My thesis will explore the possibilities, and also the limitations of naturalism.

OLD MAN. I hope you will have a word to spare for the achievements.

YOUNG WOMAN. I have studied the theories and also the practice of the brothers Goncourt.

OLD MAN. Ah! Then you will know that the brothers encountered a difficulty. Committed as they were to the sensations of the moment they deprived themselves of all perspective. And although they endeavoured to detail at length the minutiae of daily living, they from time to time reminded themselves they were aesthetes, literary stylists. They owned up to the chances of a contradiction.

YOUNG WOMAN. Do you mind if I make a note of what you say?

OLD MAN. By no means. But can we return to achievements? May I assume that you have read the Zola novels, more especially *Germinal* which is surely a masterpiece among stories of coal-mining communities? In our own language you will not have overlooked the two Georges, Moore and Gissing. And I should also be sorry if you have missed Theodore Dreiser's *Sister Carrie*—not to mention many astonishing pages from his autobiography.

YOUNG WOMAN. I'll make another note. And would *you* be kind enough to note that I am a young woman? Clearly it is impossible for me to have read everything that is relevant.

OLD MAN. I have been told of a young man who boasted that he had secured his Honours without ever once looking into a book by his relevant poet. He read only the criticism the theory and the gossip.

YOUNG WOMAN. That is what we call academic vice.

OLD MAN. I think George Moore is probably our best demonstration of the Goncourt dilemma. When a naturalist is revealed in a man strongly inclined to be an aesthete, we may infer that in fiction-writing there is always a place for naturalism. Can you justly say that for your generation Mr Pearson is out of date?

YOUNG WOMAN. So you would argue that naturalism is what one must expect from the novel writer?

OLD MAN. I remember something from Santayana. Somewhere he says that everything in nature is lyric in its ideal essence, tragic in its fate, and comic in its existence. Lyric essence and tragic fate would be mainly over to the poet. Perhaps it is comic existence made manifest in the naturalist form that we mainly expect from the novelist.

YOUNG WOMAN. You said a moment ago, 'astonishing pages'. Would you say that we are astonished by *Coal Flat*?

OLD MAN. The astonishment is complex. The effort of energy and persistence which has sentence by sentence built so massive a work is by itself astonishing.

YOUNG WOMAN. Then you admire the author's prose?

OLD MAN. I don't say that. The prose is adequate to the purpose Mr Pearson has in hand. The Goncourts might have their aesthetic doubts, but I would expect Emile Zola to approve. It has been a part of Mr Pearson's purpose, and perhaps also his good fortune, to choose the right sequence of sentences to ensure that his story never slips out of focus. Provided always he has something to say, a writer who is master of focus ensures that he can be read with close attention. *Coal Flat* is eminently readable as you have admitted.

YOUNG WOMAN. But did you just now intend to suggest that the novel is a comedy?

OLD MAN. Perhaps we may come more readily to that question a little later. Will you in the meantime tell me what your thesis will say the novel is about?

YOUNG WOMAN. It is about people. And I would agree that it is impossible not to be concerned about what happens to them. But they are so specialized—regional. I can readily accept them as West Coast miners pub-keepers and so on, but they frequently irritate me with behaviour which does not seem to me true to human nature as I understand it. But I will be modest and add—from the standpoint of my limited years and experience.

OLD MAN. That is well put—but can I have an instance?

YOUNG WOMAN. There is Mrs Palmer, the pub-keeper's wife—the formidable materfamilias who dominates with a positive energy which terrifies because it is so immense and crude. But her absolute refusal to recognize that her children have grown up and must leave her to live their own lives renders her plainly insane. Surely it is wrong of a novelist to allow an insane person such a large slice of his story. And Mrs Palmer is not Mr Pearson's only insane character. There is the embittered recluse, old Mrs Seldom, and her equally insane daughter Nora Herlihy—not to mention Nora's son Peter, a boy not yet into his teens who is insane after a fashion made familiar to him by the book's older characters. I am compulsively obliged to read on as I have admitted—but with a constant distaste for the screaming outbursts of hatred and cruelty, the recurring emphasis on all that is sneering sullen scowling snarling sulking and sour. And all the words appear to have come readily to the author of *Coal Flat*.

OLD MAN. And do you assert that this Inferno is never leavened by the admission of any sweetness and light?

YOUNG WOMAN. That is what the author has intended in the figure of his young schoolteacher. Paul Rogers is the book's hero after the style of Nicholas Nickleby. That's to say, he is a kind of virtuous stick handy for dealing out blows to an assortment of demons and dragons. Paul, with a background of political radicalism, is approaching his mid-twenties, a returned soldier from the war. Yet despite his geographically wide experience he is presented to us as a naive idealist, well-intending but half-baked. He devotes himself to an endeavour to persuade the insane boy Peter Herlihy to behave rationally—and this could well be an admirable dedication, but the reader begins to doubt when it is revealed that Paul in his mid-twenties is virgin, apparently without sexual experience of any kind. And doubt develops into positive disquiet when he becomes engaged to a girl who is also in a state of sexual ignorance—because the young man shows no signs of being in any hurry. He is content to wait—while he fills in time by instructing his girl about the rights and wrongs of radical politics. . . . I expect I will sound wanton to anyone of your generation—but I must insist that Mr Pearson's schoolteacher does not in the least resemble the young man I am to meet in Greymouth. He too is a schoolteacher. We plan to cross a mountain—

OLD MAN. Forgive my interruption. I see you have closely read the book, and my own repeated readings were apparently necessary before I ceased to write off Paul Rogers as a relatively unimportant figure—although handy as a literary device. Let us say a kind of magnet with powerfully attracting and also repelling properties—to ensure that all the other figures will be kept in constant and at times violent motion.

YOUNG WOMAN. If you succeed in selling me Paul Rogers I think I might afterwards find myself in the market for the Southern Alps. In any case, my interest is vested—I would have to re-write my thesis.

OLD MAN. Pardon my vanity—with only the labour of an amanuensis you can re-write it now.

YOUNG WOMAN. I will pardon you—depending upon the value of what you supply me with.

OLD MAN. Let us forget talk of naturalism or any other label. Let us say instead that *Coal Flat* may be seen as detailed demonstration of what has happened to European civilization transported to this country. I think you are mistaken when you use the word regional—it is not far-fetched to see Mr Pearson's West Coast as readily standing for the whole of New Zealand. Note by the way that the background to the novel, coal, is a wasting asset—and so is a very great deal of our country's farming. But what I would emphasize is that if you will grant me that our civilization has slipped badly in Europe itself, then what Mr Pearson shows us is an Antipodean landslide.

YOUNG WOMAN. For my taste you are talking too big.

OLD MAN. I will be more particular. You were a little put out because Paul Rogers, instead of devoting himself to the primitive pursuit of love-making, prefers to instruct his girl in radical politics. Very well, in the *Paradiso* of Dante we find that the poet's girl Beatrice puts aside all question of any such primitive activity in favour of instructing her lover in theological questions raised by Aristotle and St Thomas Aquinas. Except that it is theology instead of politics, and the female instructs the male instead of the reverse, the situation is the same. But don't mistake me, there is shot through all the Divine Comedy a very powerful interest in what, for want of a better term, and despite the cinema and other vulgar connotations of our own day, we will call love. Dante's word is *amor,* I think the most constantly recurring word throughout the entire poem. I won't attempt to elucidate. As an educated young woman you will know that all elucidations are themselves elucidated in the concluding line, *l'amor che move il sole e l'altre stelle.*

YOUNG WOMAN. You continue to talk too big. The line you quote is all I know from the *Commedia* apart from, *lasciate ogni speranza, voi ch'entrate.*

OLD MAN. Forgive me, I am worried that the sour looks of our fellow-travellers have become a trifle sourer. Perhaps we should at least keep foreign languages out of our discussion. We must remember where we are. You will recall that in his essay called 'Fretful Sleepers' Mr Pearson has himself remarked upon the perils of revealing one's self an intellectual in a New Zealand public place.

YOUNG WOMAN. You were talking of *Coal Flat?*

OLD MAN. In the novel this same love that moves the cosmos makes its shy appearance in a manner which is dramatic and moving. I admit about the sulking and the snarling—and I agree that it can be tiresome at times. But keep always in mind the scene where the schoolteacher encounters Father Flaherty, who well knows what an impossible handful the insane boy Peter Herlihy can be, since he has previously been lodged and taught at the Convent. The priest maintains there is only one way to deal with such a problem, and that is to scare the boy. And when the teacher disagrees he is asked whether he knows any other way. He answers with one word. Love. And it is the priest's reply that he doesn't think the teacher would know what the word means.

YOUNG WOMAN. I think I understand. You are suggesting that the one word love, taken in its context, is intended to be loaded with a weight of meaning unsuspected by readers whose aim is simply to kill time with a story-book.

OLD MAN. It is not for me to know, or at any rate be certain about Mr Pearson's intentions. I can judge only from results. And are an author's intentions always relevant? Somewhere it has been remarked, I think by André Gide, that in every work of art there is always God's share. Nobody can say exactly what it is that sometimes gives to a naturalistic novel the lift which enables us to see it as though transformed and belonging to a different order of creation. Call it God or the Muse or creative magic or what you will—what does it matter? Anyhow, do you see now what I was driving at when I spoke of European civilization in the form of an Antipodean landslide?

YOUNG WOMAN. I understand you to mean that *Coal Flat* shows us our civilization in all its rags and tatters. That is to say, if we agree to take the Divine Comedy as a guide to inform us reliably about the nature of that civilization.

OLD MAN. Very good—you give me the confidence to say that we begin to see the novel only when we have forgotten about the naturalism. To take a simple point—you have referred to scenes of screaming human hatred, but do we notice that almost on the opening page of the novel we begin to hear the screaming of the river-dredge, and are seldom done with it until we have reached the last? To how many readers does it occur that the dredge is a kind of overall echo to the recurring cries of human rage and despair? What is the dredge screaming over anyhow? Over its frantic endeavours to provide the human haters with gold, a metal almost useless except for ornamental purposes—but a splendid additional excuse for the exercise of more and more yells of hatred. Or take another point—one which is not perhaps obvious or simple. You complained that the schoolteacher is a combined intellectual know-all and sexual ignoramus—but do you notice that he is brought nearly to disaster by his encounter with a boy in whom these properties are reversed? A boy who remains mentally undeveloped while his animal propensities are the terror of everybody unfortunate enough to have any dealings with him. Does it occur to you there is a sense in which it is true to say the schoolteacher and the boy are one and the same individual? The sexual drive which the schoolteacher has ignored or suppressed confronts him in the shape of that terrible boy. Does the significance of the names escape you? The teacher, Paul, the boy, Peter—two Christian apostles, the one an intellectual, worried and anxious over what goes on below the belt. And the other the natural man, rough bluff and hearty—and not a scrap worried or unhappy over being created basically animal. Will you not admit there is something in my claim for *Coal Flat* as a novel about this latterday Christian, that is to say Western civilization?

YOUNG WOMAN. You are plausible, but I think extravagant in stepping so far beyond the limits of the novel's naturalism. Here among my notes I have a quotation—which I think the most convincing evidence that Mr Pearson as a writer is literal-minded and intends himself to be taken as such. I have copied from an essay in which he tries to assess the place of the Maori as he figures in New Zealand fiction. The passage refers to a story entitled 'By the Lake' by Mr Dennis McEldowney, the scene being a Canterbury sheep-run. I quote: 'In this story a boy who enters an old burial-cave disappears and a new skull appears on the ledge; a shepherd had previously disappeared and they found only his boots. The man who returns to tell the news changes his mind when he gets back to the boy's nagging mother and decides to follow the boy instead. Now it is true that some of the old-time pakeha had a great respect for Maori beliefs, and it is true that breaking a *tapu* can or at least until recently could, so oppress a Maori with guilt that he becomes sick and dies. But *tapu* would not so affect these pakeha of Canterbury, to whom the Maoris are only a memory, as it is made out to do in this short story. And if *tapu* kills, the body is there waiting for *tangi* and burial; it does not just disappear, so that a new skull appears in a cave. Again, when the old shepherd was spirited away his boots were left behind, so what happens to Michael's?'

OLD MAN. May I repeat that intentions are not always relevant. In this instance an *un*intentional comic effect has been created. But let us face up to the paradox—without his literal-mindedness Mr Pearson would never have been enabled to create *Coal Flat*.

YOUNG WOMAN. Then you were not expecting to be taken seriously when you talked about forgetting the book's naturalism.

OLD MAN. I was never more serious. A moment ago I spoke loosely—I said that nobody knows what it is exactly that will sometimes give a novel the lift that takes it beyond what appears to be its own native category. We do however know that naturalistic detail, presented to us without any blurring comment—with on the contrary a literal-minded no-nonsense exactness and clarity, will at times prompt us to that intensity of feeling which is always a reliable sign that an important communication has reached us. How can it be explained that *Germinal*, although a much-detailed novel of a coal-mining community in northern France, is also a tremendous epic about the humanity-destroying workings of nineteenth-century *laissez-faire* capitalism? But for the moment never mind about Zola—or we might for a change say Daumier or Chardin or Goya. Instead I will give you one simple illustration from *Coal Flat*. A young miner's wife has the kitchen table laid for dinner and awaits her husband's return from work—and this, you will remember, is one of the scarce occasions when food is mentioned in the novel. I grant you that the lunch eaten by miners at work is often referred to, but we are never told what it consists of. Well, the potatoes and turnips are boiling, the mince is simmering, and the custard pudding is cooling—details which are all the more devastating for being plain and brief. It doesn't matter what Mr Pearson's intentions were, a triumph of the literal has been àchieved—one which has at least in part depended upon what the reader is able or willing to bring to his reading of the book. The miners, union-organized, are relatively-speaking affluent—so it is all the more dismaying that the civilized occasion of a dinner is founded on vegetables with the life boiled out of them, meat which has been poisoned with sulphur-dioxide, and a dessert which has almost certainly come from a coloured packet. I don't need to remind you that the novel is saturated with brewery-beer likely to have been chemically produced—and superfluous too to say that the dinner-occasion rapidly turns sour with the customary sneering and snarling.

YOUNG WOMAN. You are extreme.

OLD MAN. Blame it on *Coal Flat*—and since I am wound up pardon me if I continue. Our name-dropping has included the brothers Goncourt, Zola, Dante, several painters—why shouldn't we now say Balzac? What Mr Pearson's literal-mindedness has provided us with is the Human Comedy as he understands it from his experience of life as a New Zealander. I don't say he hasn't done so accidentally, but I do say it has all derived from his literal-minded, not to mention liberal-slanted concern for what happened to Michael's boots. Bootism—an admirable brand-name for the broad utilitarian philosophy associated with the Left Movement. But perhaps the word philosophy is too limiting. Bootism might more properly be called a religion—and who knows what mystique may have become attached to it during the long agony of the struggle with Hitler's Germany? Remember that before the war the Soviet Union aimed at providing about one hundred and fifty million peasants with boots. Perhaps in some frozen winter forest a peasant child defended his boots against a soldier who would have robbed him. Footwear had never been known in the child's family in a thousand years, and the boots were defended at the cost of a young life. Need I elaborate? What might the history of Europe have been if no mystical significance had ever been discerned in two pieces of wood laid crosswise? Who would be rash enough to deny that a pair of defended boots may not already enshrine the hopes of millions? Pieces of the true boot sold around the world *sub rosa*, down the Euphrates, and up the Yellow River—or the Waitaki. And the inevitable sectarians beginning already to appear. Uppers? Soles? Low Heels?

YOUNG WOMAN. You are joking.

OLD MAN. I know when to be serious. *Your* seriousness makes me suspect that you are a secret Bootist. Do you own a car?—will you deny that the status you derive from it may in part depend upon the style and size of its *boot*?

YOUNG WOMAN. I am sorry. I think you are mistaken in attributing so much suggestive power to Mr Pearson. I have found him unreliable. He has ludicrously misread Mr McEldowney's story—which undoubtedly concludes with the man's deciding, when he returns to the boy's nagging mother, *not* to follow the boy.

OLD MAN. Forgive me. Mr Pearson's inability to read is not in question. We are obliged at our peril not to neglect his ability to write. And are you quite certain about your own reading capacity?—given a fine summer's day for that Canterbury sheep-run expedition it wouldn't surprise me if the boy wasn't wearing his boots.

YOUNG WOMAN. You prod me into revealing that I am myself very much a New Zealander—I mean by replying with a snarl. You are too clever by half. But wait a minute, according to your arguments would we not expect Mr Pearson to be detached from his West Coast material? My researches have revealed the contrary—I have discovered him in a letter to the Broadcasting journal sourly defending West Coast behaviour.

OLD MAN. If the novelist as a West Coaster chooses to throw good love after bad that is entirely his own concern. But I don't intend to single out the West Coast for the insult—I mean what it stands for, our country in its entirety.

YOUNG WOMAN. I doubt whether you notice, but our train is about to enter the Otira tunnel—and upon emerging, if Mr Pearson is to be relied upon, we will be too much affected by our view of mountain and bush to continue our conversation.

OLD MAN. Before we are overcome by that emotional experience, may I remark that we might have begun an equally fruitful conversation if we had focused upon almost *any* figure in *Coal Flat*? It is odd that neither of us has mentioned Miss Dane, also a schoolteacher, and like Paul Rogers sexually ignorant although no longer young. And like Paul she credibly and convincingly attracts and repels. And then Don Palmer—the envied and admired easy-going young man for whom there is no aim in life except to take his pleasure without responsibility wherever he finds it. These figures oblige us to suspend our disbelief by stepping from the page in the full array and frequent horror of their full flesh and blood. But you have mentioned the bush, and perhaps of all the conversations we might be stimulated to, none would have been to me so congenial as an inquiry which would derive from the scene of mountain river and bush encountered towards the end of the novel. *Coal Flat* wryly shows us what human folly of the European brand has to date perpetrated in this country—but for balance we are provided with delights that add up to a kind of pastoral symphony. Most satisfyingly placed in the context of the story, that is what the author's account of the whitebaiting expedition amounts to. Subject the novel to all the rational analysis you can command, call it naturalistic literal-minded or what you will, you won't succeed in fully explaining that what we finally draw from it is an unusual and perhaps unexpected elation and illumination of spirit. But we should be grateful that the author's bush mountain and river pastoral is chiefly responsible.

Landfall, December 1967 (v.21, no.4), pp.352-61. Bill Pearson's novel *Coal Flat* (1963) is referred to through this dialogue, as is Pearson's essay 'Attitudes to the Maori in Some Pakeha Fiction' (1958). When he reprinted that essay in *Fretful Sleepers and Other Essays* (Auckland, Heinemann, 1974) Pearson acknowledged his revision of it in the light of Sargeson's observations.

]25[

CONVERSATION WITH FRANK SARGESON: an Interview with Michael Beveridge

I

BEVERIDGE: *Perhaps I can begin by raising the question of the function of the creative writer.*

SARGESON: You can't take this and limit it to the world we're living in now. One aspect of what you call creative writing is that unlike television and films it's got an enormous history behind it. I think this is a strength to a writer, that if he has a sense of history (and I have always been enormously interested in history), what he's doing is not just something limited to the present; it ties on to the past. I know a lot of people want to wipe us—the past—and I have a lot of sympathy for that viewpoint, but it's just not my own view.

You see yourself as continuing in this tradition?

Very much so. I think I can put it grandiosely and say that one's continuing civilization—other people would talk in terms of culture, but—well, put it this way: times when people didn't produce anything in the way of literature have become, historically speaking, the dark ages.

Do you object when it is suggested that your writing is moralistic or didactic?

I remember very clearly a speaker in the Reith lectures a few years ago resisting this idea that in modern times poetry shouldn't be didactic. He politely ridiculed the notion by pointing to poems of enormous merit and enormous interest which, taking an historical viewpoint, are didactic. If it's a question of moralizing I would say it all depends on quality. Tolstoy was a tremendous moralist. Some people are direct moralists—and Tolstoy was pretty direct—but some people are very indirect moralists. You could say that Flaubert was an enormous moralist; de Maupassant, a lesser person perhaps, but the moral quality of his stories is simply tremendous, isn't it?

What if we change the term to propaganda?

Propaganda? This seems to be bringing morality or moralism down on to a rather lower level. Propaganda seems to me to be something temporary as it were. The Church felt that what it called propaganda was a good thing and it was aiming at something very large. Propaganda to bring off a Communistic revolution, as it were, that's something pretty large too. I think the kind of literature has to be taken into account.

Professor Horsman in a Landfall *review of your* Collected Stories *said of the early stories that they were opinionated parables. In so much as you published these in the left-wing* Tomorrow, *did this make you feel you were allying yourself with a left-wing crusade?*

Beginning to write at that time—during the slump—affected me in two ways. It was no disgrace to be out of work. Although I had my qualifications as a lawyer there were lawyers on relief work as well as myself. These people, or many of them, no doubt would return to their law work when the slump was over. But for me the slump was also this opportunity. It put—I think I mentioned this in one of these so-called parables—a sort of comradeship into life which may have been in New Zealand life at one time, but which I think, to a certain extent, has been lost. The juxtaposition of a lot of people of various social grades had a good effect in that way. But also a great variety of people became very conscious of the injustices and hardships which were inflicted on people, and inflicted unjustly because it was through no fault of their own that they suffered.

Are you, in your early stories, advocating something like slump living, or the mentality that arose from the slump conditions?

I think, somewhere, I've recorded that my family came to New Zealand in the 1870s and that they were forced out of England because of poverty. Although my immediate parents felt that they had to some extent, anyhow, made good—although my father never got very rich, certainly not—I think I became conscious of Europeans living a long way from Europe. And it had come about through poverty. I think this gave me a leftist bias and seemed to tie up with what was going on in the thirties—that a new and juster world, a socialistic world if you like, would be created.

Can we shift territory to the question of how you write; of how you write a novel; how you experience the creative process? Does it come from a germ as with Henry James or do you envisage a novel as a whole before you begin?

Well, I should say, very much like Henry James. You're referring to the story of James with his fingers in his ears when he received the precious particle? I've never thought of myself as a realist or even a naturalist writer in the straight sense. I suppose one could use the term symbolic realism. I think Winston Rhodes may have used that or I may be fastening some expression on to him that he wouldn't think worthy. But yes—nearly all the fiction that I have written has come from just the vaguest thought. For instance, I could give you a quite good example in the play about Kendall *A Time for Sowing*. As far as I can remember now I got that out of one sentence in R. M. Burdon's essay on Kendall in which he referred to Kendall's drinking, and Mrs Kendall's reaction in throwing herself into the arms of their convict servant.

Are your novels conceived round an idea or characters or social setting or do they just start from this germ?

Well, that's enormously difficult to understand or explain, and I don't know that I really want to explain it for the reason that you can't get to the bottom of these things anyhow—not really—and if you're a working writer you have to be grateful for what I think André Gide calls somewhere 'God's share', something that's a gift, perhaps a kind of grace, that you can't explain. You hardly know where it comes from. It's a personal phenomenon that whatever I write, no matter how great the difficulties are, I'm never in doubt how long it's going to be. Before I begin I can calculate, almost to the page, how long it will be; and yet as I go along discovering it from day to day I just don't know for certain what it's going to be about—and yet I always know the dimensions of it. This is a mysterious thing that I've never been able to work out.

The process itself—is it pleasurable or painful for you?

It becomes your life. Of course the actual writing is suffering, although you become so absorbed in it—it's a matter of getting the right sentences in the right order, what each sentence has to convey in the way of visual image, sound for the ear; it has to carry thought. I recently talked of reading Dickens and discovering what a tremendous mandarin

Dickens is as a writer; he writes these highly organized sentences which are doing all sorts of things—carrying his humour for instance, his sentimentality—but anyhow they are very highly organized and they're written by a man who is a literary mandarin. And this is very hard to explain when Dickens was cashing in on the new literacy. It's quite a stringent criticism that one can't imagine present-day people confidently coping with literacy of the modern kind. Possibly it is the influence of journalism, with short snappy sentences and nothing much of weight in them, and yet these newly literate people in Dickens's time—one can only judge from his popularity—were willing to sit down and grapple with his sentences. And they meant something to them. For myself, I find I don't rewrite a lot. I have great difficulty in getting each page completed, but I can go about the rest of the day, after my writing, reasonably contented because I've done my work. I mean there is that satisfaction, surely. The difference between my work and that of people who work in modern jobs, factories and so forth, is that they're watching the clock and the clock goes very slowly. I'm not watching the clock. But when I do look at the clock I'm horrified to see how much time has gone by—my work makes time go very quickly. It doesn't drag. Now what I do is I write and I try to get this page of writing which may be the limit of the work of the day as right as possible, then next day I look at it and make obvious corrections that have never occurred to me—I work at it in longhand as much as I can, then I type it and add it to what's been typed before. Now it'll need a lot more corrections but you can see it differently—when it's typed and during the struggle to get a reasonable typing out of it. While you're typing it occurs to you how the thing is going to carry on. You may have a few notes down in the margin, how you hope it will carry on, but in this fixing up of the previous day's work you might see some of these notes are leading in the wrong direction. If you start going in the wrong direction—say for instance you have envisaged that a very important part in this book will be possible when a man says to a woman 'Will you do something?' and she says 'No', you see. Now the way you've worked it out in the actual writing is when you come to the point he says 'Will you do this' and she says 'Yes'. Well obviously the whole thing has gone wrong and you have to re-conceive it. Now that's not the sort of thing that very often occurs but I'm always conscious that it may occur, and this is why I'm always wary of going too far ahead in the wrong direction. Occasionally, admittedly, I do go in the wrong direction for a few pages and I have to scrap all that and tackle the problem all over again . . . but every page is a struggle. It presents problems, and they have to be solved.

Does it become obsessive? I mean, can you stop?

Ah well, I think Hemingway noted somewhere—he wrote a fair bit about the mechanics of writing—that you should never stop when you've written something to your satisfaction. You should always stop when you've got something in your mind. It's harder to break off if you can go on, but don't go on—put a few notes down if you like, because if you go on and write out everything that's been in your mind, then what are you going to work on next day? I read all this many many years ago and I tended to agree with it, and I think I tend to work that way.

Does criticism affect you? Have you learned from it?

Well, I think I've learned a lot in this matter from Janet Frame. It's hard to believe that writers can ignore criticism and not read reviews altogether, but Janet I've found can actually do this. For instance I have seen reviews or remarks passed about her work which I've thought might interest her and I've said, 'Look listen to this', and I've started to read it out and she won't let me do it. I'm quite sure that she doesn't read her critiques. I can't carry it to that length; but I would like to have some friendly person who would screen what is written about me and only show me a certain proportion of it. I say this because I think that if you are a working writer you have to protect yourself; criticism which appears to you destructive or completely non-understanding is not going to do you any good—or only as a reaction, you see. It's not going to positively encourage you.

And apparently constructive criticism?

Well that's difficult. One is I hope conscious of one's shortcomings. There are some shortcomings one can't overcome because they're just there and there's nothing much to be done. You can't remedy them: you can only compensate for them. Most writers are conscious they will never write a *War and Peace* for example. Each man, surely, if he is writing fiction can only do what is within his capacity and I should say be successful within his capacity—I don't mean successful in the material sense, but to produce what seems to be an entertaining and satisfying work of art, depends on knowing what you can do and what you can't do. Now if the critic or the reviewer is blaming you for something that you never attempted to do, never intended to do, and know that you can't do—well, this is naturally very irritating particularly if he shows no awareness of what you *were* attempting to do. I mean it's a cliché that it's a critic's duty to discover what the writer was intending to do and say how well he did it.

What do you see as some of your shortcomings? Have you ever come across something that has suggested, 'Here is something I can remedy'?

I think that what has gone down on paper and seemed satisfactory at the time, for better or worse, has to be let go. I don't think that anything that's been written can ever be remedied when it's got to the stage of reaching the public as it were. You can withdraw it. You can attempt to suppress it and as you know some writers do that sort of thing, or spend their old age, as James did, rewriting it . . . but I don't think you can do much in the way of altering it. What the writer could do, would be to make a note saying, 'My God, you know, I fell down on what I was really after there', but it means I must write another story and see if I can get it. The new story of course, seeing you have only manipulated the old, using real scenes, real people or people who have the appearance of reality as symbols, may present superficially an entirely different appearance.

Are you concerned about the position of writers in New Zealand—their influence; your influence?

This is a complicated thing because of the environment. I think we do need, somehow or another—I don't mind who pays them, whether it's the State or whether it's private patrons—a fair number of writers around in order to convince the community that writing is a legitimate activity. Nobody is supposed to be doing anything unless it's bringing them in a living. We're quite different from Australia in this respect. Because they had Lawson, because they had Adam Lindsay Gordon, they have the tradition of their ballads, and Lawson obviously created a great expectancy or tradition of short story writing. I don't know for certain, but I imagine that writers are tolerated in Australia in a way that they're not tolerated here. I should think Barry Crump to a very great extent has remedied this, but of course he's fortunate that he's also made it pay off—which makes it respectable anyhow.

Wouldn't you put Frank Sargeson in the same category? Walter Allen has said that you are a tradition maker. Were you very conscious of this?

A tradition maker? . . . I think the influence has not been on the public, only on other writers. I think Crump has carried the thing a stage further by carrying it over to the public. Though I think it would be impossible to go on writing in the New Zealand environment if you didn't feel that somewhere you had, say six people, who enjoyed what you wrote, were aware of what you wrote, aware of what you were attempting to do, aware of a certain kind of truth in it, aware of the artistic requirements. It's words on paper yet it's got to convey a reality, a reality of the spirit rather than a physical reality and so on.

That's claiming too little for you, isn't it, because you've got a good deal more than six readers and you exercised a strong influence on the way our literature has developed?

Well, I hope you don't mind me reminding you of something Rhodes has used: the anonymous girl student who, when I was talking in Dunedin, said that there were two tragedies in New Zealand literature —one was Katherine Mansfield and the other was Frank Sargeson. This is a tremendous thing—I think it's very very good indeed—salutory, all sorts of things could be said about it. There is this absurd talk about the great New Zealand novel. This is really nonsense because nobody would talk about the great English novel or look for it—and also this contradicts what I said just now that you should have writers around. There's no question of writing a great New Zealand novel; it's writing a good New Zealand novel, sentences well turned that can hold you and so forth. That's the essence of the whole thing. Writing is an ancient art and that somebody is practising it here, practising it tolerably well, should be a source of satisfaction and even pride to us.

Do you feel then, that there is some justification for the student naming Mansfield and Sargeson as 'tragedies'? Were you yourself affected by the 'Mansfield tragedy'? Were you writing under her shadow?

Oh, I wouldn't think so. I first saw her name, I suppose, somewhere round about 1920. But I remember when I was working as a government servant in Wellington and I was going on holiday I bought a volume—I'm not sure whether it was *The Garden Party* or the other one—and I read it in the train. I don't know that I was particularly struck by its literary quality or anything of that kind. I think that I was very much aware that this person was born in New Zealand and had left New Zealand. I was pretty ignorant about her then—very ignorant in fact. I was never conscious of writing in the shadow of Katherine Mansfield or reacting from her. But Mansfield imposed this feminine thing on New Zealand and it had a great influence overseas too. It was something that came and it appeared to be right that it should come because it meant something to a lot of people. Now this seemed to be so strongly a representation of New Zealand. The mistake that was made and is always made is that the writer's world is mistaken for a much wider world which it's related to. It mustn't be identified with this wide world; you must never confuse literature with life, as it were. But Mansfield, writing powerfully, imposed a pattern on our writing so that everybody was impressed and hosts of young women wrote Mansfield stories. Now, when I came along—and there's a very interesting little quote in Rhodes' book from Dennis McEldowney who said that when he first read Sargeson he thought that this was New Zealand and that no other story written about New Zealand that wasn't after this fashion would be valid or interesting, you see. Again, Dennis was a very young man and he made the same mistake of confusing art and literature. This was the sort of mistake that wouldn't have been made in an old culture. People would say that they know what life is and they know what literature is and they wouldn't get the two mixed up, but it's natural in New Zealand at this stage that the two should be confused; that the writer is measured not in terms of literature but in terms of something which would be an impure mixture of literature and life. When I came along a lot of people felt, I think (this sounds as though I'm flattering myself considerably but a lot of people have made this remark) that because of a certain amount of power in these early sketches they seemed to relate so much to New Zealand. And that's right, *relate*—it wasn't New Zealand itself; it related. But people felt, 'Ah, this is the way you write'. So therefore, instead of opening up something for New Zealand, both Mansfield and myself have tended to be constricting influences. I mean who wants all of New Zealand life to be seen in terms of Mansfield or in terms of Sargeson? Well of course fortunately now there are many writers. People who wish to, can see New Zealand in terms of Phillip Wilson or Ballantyne or Karl Stead. We're beginning to get the same area of choice as in an older culture, but of course this implies that what is needed is a very highly developed criticism and this is one thing where New Zealand falls down. You can find writers who've devoted their lives to writing—perhaps not quite so single-mindedly as I have myself—but I have yet to hear of a critic who you might infer has said to himself, 'I am going to be a literary critic and I'm not going to allow myself to be too much distracted by anything else. I know that I've got to live somehow or other, but my function is going to be that of literary critic and I'm not going to do any other job that is going to be too much distraction.' In newspaper reviewing you have a literary editor (I don't know whether he likes his work or not) who hands out books to a heterogeneous collection of people, school teachers, and so on. The pay is shocking; very often they don't get any pay at all, they just get the book. A lot of them are illiterate in the sense that they don't know what has been written in New Zealand; they don't know what has been written overseas; they're not particularly conversant with principles of literary criticism that began shall we say with Aristotle, and have come down through Horace right through Dryden; you know, the whole business down to the present day. I think that

these principles begun by Aristotle and so on, are still very very important and that people who are going to criticize literary work should have
this background.

*What about the academic critic here who presumably is conversant
with the principles of literary criticism? The state of criticism here generally?*

This is a very ambiguous thing or so it seems to me. For instance
you may have the phenomenon of a Catholic critic who will see everything from a Catholic point of view. He probably mellows a little in his
old age, but to over-simplify one could say that at times his attitude has
been no more and no less than, 'Look, is this book by a Catholic? Then
it's a good book; it will have a few bad features about it, maybe; that's
human. Things are imperfect anyhow. Is this book by a Protestant?
Well then it's a bad book; of course it will have some good points about
it because naturally Protestants partake.' No doubt you find this kind of
phenomenon in other modern cultures too.

*I suppose any critic and perhaps any writer too, is bound to be con-
strained by his prejudices to some extent.*

Yes, well true, but I can't help feeling that following on the nineteenth century there should have been more awareness that a work of art
is a self-contained thing and must be considered always, first and
foremost, as a self-contained work of art. It has its relation to life, but
you don't start off by bringing over from life a lot of principles that
you've collected and arbitrarily apply them. However, if the local writer
can see his environment with such intensity that it creates a reality of its
own, he'll now get away with it with the few discerning critics. If he is
successful in this way he will be recognized by a critic of the quality of
Eric McCormick. But the run of the mill critic will do this old business
of confusing literature with life instead of seeing the intensity of focus
which has created the work of art and created the self-contained world.
He'll say, 'But I've been down at Coromandel, or whatever, this Easter;
I know that place and it wasn't like that', and so on.

*Have there been any critics here who've shown this sort of discernment
with your work as it's been coming out?*

Well, one can never be sufficiently grateful. I mean, I would think
with writers starting work that the best luck that they can have is, early
in their career, to come to the notice of someone like Eric McCormick
—and for this person to say not very much, he doesn't have to go into
detail. He can say 'Look, I was so interested' and 'I've never felt this
before.' You see. He knows it's connected with New Zealand but that
it's not attempting a realism so that people can say 'This is New

Zealand'. He knows that it's sort of a reflection from New Zealand and it's the art that goes into it. Everybody is literate in the primary sense, in that they can write a letter, and then suppose writing is really nothing much at all. And yet you find many writers who speak—I mean professional writers—of the enormous difficulty of writing a satisfactory sentence, a sentence that they're really satisfied with. Writing is essentially just as difficult as composing music or painting pictures. Tolstoy has written well of all this.

You've managed to put forward some pretty penetrating criticism yourself—'Conversation in a Train' for instance and the review of A. P. Gaskell's stories.

I like to think—you see this is one of my escapes from puritanism —that if you're a professional writer you can write anything if you're asked to. To be a writer, to me anyhow, unless you're a primitive or virtually a primitive like Barry Crump, you're tremendously well read. I suppose a lot of my writing is a form of devilment, a sort of demonstration that you can have people who are writers in New Zealand who know how to shape their sentences and who know how to do what is required of them. I have no objections to journalism *per se* but I do recognize the strange contradiction that you can write something hot— hot news as it were—and by good luck it can also be something permanent, something universal, that's fulfilling Goethe's dictum that you think about the particular first and if you do your stuff as it can be done then the universal will be there in it without your ever giving one thought to the universal. On the other hand it may be something that might amuse somebody and is quite valuable for the moment. Well, O.K. I'm willing to do that, but I'm not particularly willing to do it if I'm deeply engaged in what I would call trying to create a serious work of literary art. In that event I have a notice on my door warning people off and I just don't want to be disturbed—not during working hours anyhow. I think association with Fairburn had something to do with it. Fairburn was, at his best, such a marvellous breath of fresh air. It was a great privilege to know him when one first did know him and his fertility . . . the epigrams used to stream from him at the drop of a hat. You could have him laughing tremendously at his own jokes which you repeated to him and which he'd invented or reinvented a few weeks before and had now completely forgotten. His laughter seemed so genuine. To be with a person like that was to realize that if it was connected with a capacity to write sentences on paper then you needed all this versatility.

You see yourself, then, as very much a full-time writer?

One would hesitate to go to a part-time doctor wouldn't one? You might go to a part-time physician and not come to any harm, but imagine going to a part-time surgeon. Is it so very different for a writer? I mean he is not coming out of the blue; he is part of the chain; he takes his place in literary tradition. You can have literary primitives but they're very rare. I suppose in some of my early fables, for instance 'Cats by the Tail', 'A Piece of Yellow Soap', there was a more than faintly conscious effort to be a primitive (which is a contradiction in terms anyway). In a little sketch called 'Toothache', for instance, I'm using almost all one-syllable words and I've pared the thing down to just this horror of human life, of our isolation, our solitude, grief and pain that we don't understand and I've tried to put it into just a few lines. Of course it's obviously a bit akin to poetry. I think I'm pretty firm on the six people, as it were—I'd written quite a lot before I began to be published in *Tomorrow,* but I can remember the excitement that I experienced at the first of those sketches that I wrote in this new way, 'Conversation with my Uncle'. I remember the excitement I felt when I looked at it when it was finished feeling that I'd discovered a new way of writing and this new way consisted in writing sentences which suggested more than they said, as it were.

That Summer *was a summary of achievement in this particular genre but also a gesture of farewell—do you think it was a gesture of farewell to a more difficult craft, to craftsmanship?*

I think it probably occurred to me that I couldn't go on writing in this way indefinitely, but I had a lot of notes of possible stories to write. Somebody said, I think it was Robert Chapman, that *That Summer* is constructed in the way of a lot of clothes on a clothesline. I think the reason for that is that I looked at what notes I had and found that they all could be run together, as it were, rounding off a single theme and this was connected up with my obvious wish or desire to write something longer, to write a novel. I think I thought I was writing a novel. I wrote it in the first person and I think at one stage when I was writing I realized that I couldn't carry on this technique for too long. The theme is just the older man and the younger man and the idea 'mateship'.

I would have thought the change to a different style must have been very conscious, deliberate; I mean you were leaving behind something of which you were a master. You were saying you had gone as far as you could.

I can recall certain conversations with Fairburn—for instance I would go for a walk with Fairburn on the beach and he would quote lines of verse at me and I would say 'Who wrote that Rex?' and he had obviously written it himself. 'But where has it been published?' and he'd say, 'Oh well it's not worth publishing.' He'd done so much; he could do this sort of thing and he didn't see any point in doing it any more. I don't know whether I mentioned it to him but I was feeling that I was in much the same sort of situation with the stories I was writing. I think I was always pretty conscious that such a high proportion were written in the first person, and this implied I would go on assuming an infinite variety of masks, as it were, and I thought that seeing there is a relation between all these stories there must be a limit somewhere.

Do you feel to some extent the masks have now been dropped?

No, not at all. I think that when you are doing longer work you have the mask—I mean, what could be more of a mask, surely, than that of Newhouse in *Memoirs of a Peon*? Let's put it this way: in *That Summer* you have a first person narrative but you have this first person speaking in a very limited fashion. Now this is obviously presenting enormous problems, this represents a great constriction. From this point of view Copland in his *Landfall* essay is quite right—there is a constricting factor in using the first person, more particularly when I have assumed the mask of a person who is not literate. Perhaps I flatter myself a little but I think at this stage I managed to solve these problems in a way which is not too disgraceful to myself. But by the time I wrote *Memoirs of a Peon* I realized that if I could assume the mask of a more literate person it opened up a good deal more.

What about I Saw in My Dream *then; the question of a mask there?*

As everybody knows, I suppose, it wasn't originally conceived as a novel. There was *When the Wind Blows*. I remember Denis Glover was one who, when he first saw the manuscript, perhaps, up to a point, misled me by being so enthusiastic. He said, 'It's crystal clear', and so on—I can't remember exactly—he was just back from the war, and he was keen to do it and so on. Later on I think Glover changed his views, very much about this—perhaps when he saw the second part. Of course I dedicated the work to Glover, printer and poet—he'd been another one who had encouraged me in my early work. I feel probably a lot of writers, at least once in their lifetime, feel that they can get round to a book and use a mask which is fairly close to, but not exactly the same as, the author behind the work. You've got to remember, though, that we all wear masks in real life because real life would be intolerable if we didn't. As a matter of fact this is a remark which could be made about the hippie generation. One of the perhaps disconcerting aspects of the hippie and suchlike modern movements is that they sometimes appear to be people who want to live without masks. This is a fallacy obviously because nobody can; it's the essence of being human that you are wearing a mask.

You really don't feel that you can live maskless?

Of course you know Wilde's dialogue with those marvellously perceptive things that he throws off about writers such as de Maupassant who're simply trying to strip life of the few poor rags which cover it. There is an enormous truth in this. If you get a maskless civilization you have no civilization at all I would think. Again, it depends on the quality of the mask.

So, in the case of I Saw in My Dream *you still object very strongly to being identified with Henry/Dave?*

I think so, because I remember when writing that, over long stretches I didn't think of myself; I thought of somebody I knew very well when I was a boy who was an even more extreme example of what I seemed to be myself.

What about the shift from short short form to long form? What have you found to be the benefits?

I think it's the same for the writer as it is for the reader. As you know in this age short stories don't sell very well; they're used in magazines but they don't sell well in collections and this is because the reader has to make a fresh effort each time. The story might be quite short but nevertheless he's got to key his mind up and grapple with these people the author's talking about; what's the situation, what's going to happen and so on and so on. That doesn't happen in the novel. You know the famous dictum of Flaubert? *'Il faut intéresser'*. I fully subscribe to that—that you're there to hook the reader. Now, I'm not there to hook *any* reader; I'm there to hook the reader of goodwill, and in my later work a literate reader, a reader who's able to appreciate sentences—what they're up to, what they're doing, how they're written, and so on—but behind it all there must be this business of hooking.

Do you feel the same sense of impatience with the story as does Forster? He says, I think, 'Novels have stories. Oh, dear me, yes.'

No I don't. Some people have compared my writing with music of the sonata form. You announce a theme then you drop it, then you take it up again and you've slightly altered it—there's been a slight variation, perhaps you have changed key, then you amplify and so on. Well this, to me, is writing; you do it in a short story in a much reduced form and you do it in a novel. This has its perils obviously, because if you drop something in that's going to be very important you've got to have the technique to ensure that the reader won't overlook it. A lot of readers do overlook it, and then when it's amplified they've either forgotten it or haven't seen the connection. For instance, in *Memoirs of a Peon* some critics have said that part of the humour, part of the success of the book in a curiously inverted way, depends on the gap between the extraordinary language applied to New Zealand situations and the situations themselves, but I thought I'd made it crystal clear in the opening parts of the book when Michael is living with his grandmother who had such an influence on him and created his literary taste or brought out his literary taste. This aspect is focused in the episode when he's on the street with his grandmother and the children are playing in the gutter pelting each other with mud. The boy stares fascinated, doesn't say anything until they've passed, then says to his grandmother, 'They seem to be three merry young ruffians, don't they, granny?' This is setting the tone for the way he is writing the book; this was his literary approach to life and his appreciation of the comedy that could be got out of words—not the transparency of words but the enriching complicated thing where you take life and you work it up and it's so enriched with words. Still, I say there's a *relation* with life; there's no actual rendering of life on the pages—you just can't do that.

Did you find your undoubted mastery of the concise almost poetic technique of the short story was any hindrance in writing novels? You must have had to apply such compression earlier on.

Well yes—that's a point that Horsman made in his article—the pressure that the material had been subjected to. It is gratifying I think to have a critic say something like that but I don't think one's conscious of it, you know. One's conscious of a struggle but one takes this for granted, that my manuscripts are overwritten and they're corrected and the typescript is corrected and so forth, and it goes through your mind that it's so difficult; I can't do it, you see, but after a certain amount of experience you know that you can and will do it, for better or for worse. You've got to remember I've never read my work since it was done. In a sense I don't know what's in it. . . .

The impression I as a reader get is there is a terrific effort to put it all . . . .

You feel that in the writing do you? You, as a literary person, are conscious of it? I mean, surely it doesn't stick out—it doesn't show.

Oh, no. But I think that once you go under the surface it seems to me that a discerning person would realize the amount of compression and effort that goes into the stories, that lies behind their apparent simplicity.

Certain critics had informed me that I couldn't write a novel. I think to stick to longer things and try to write longer things was a determination, to say, 'Why are you writing about me now, why don't you let me have my career and see what happens first?' I think that even bad criticism, or perhaps I shouldn't use the word 'even', bad criticism can be an enormous stimulant. I think I have been stimulated and irritated into writing novels—I mean that's part of the story, I think. And as for the technique—I admit short stories might be difficult, but you know that the struggle and the labour will be over soon. With longer things you see in the far distance, perhaps years hence, you'll get to the end of the damn thing, but the actual day-to-day work I agree is not so difficult because you simply carry on the thing from day to day, and there *must* be more looseness because you couldn't expect to keep a reader if you made the same demand on his concentration over 400 pages.

That is to say perhaps Virginia Woolf wouldn't keep her readers' interest?

Well there you pose me quite a problem because I happen to know that now Virginia Woolf is dead (and in her lifetime she was never much of a seller) she sells about 80,000 copies a year, which is very good.

I think in 'Up Onto the Roof' you said that you had to create a new language and that the language of those who had written in New Zealand before you seemed irrelevant. Wasn't it much more than this—more than the language? I mean did you find New Zealand anywhere before?

Well, yes I did, but I didn't find it in New Zealand literature. I found it in say Sherwood Anderson for instance. At the same time when I first read Katherine Mansfield I was being much more moved by something I read in the *London Mercury*. It was a curious kind of a story by Sherwood Anderson; it was something called 'Small Town Notes'. It was just some observations about a very ordinary person living in a very ordinary little American town and the doubts he had about this and that, how he went to bed feeling very troubled, and how he was interested in a certain girl but he was too shy to speak to her and so on. And it was all a way of writing that to my mind had never been done before. Perhaps I didn't understand at that moment that Anderson was a real successor to the Mark Twain of *Huckleberry Finn*, that he was carrying on something. I got so excited over this because it related to my experience of New Zealand.

With the stylistic changes which have appeared in your work lately do you feel that it has been something of a volte face, *that you've turned from the Huck Finn side to the Tom Sawyer side?*

I don't know. I feel that if you're a professional writer you have to go on writing. Now that can be a terrible statement to make, but surely, if I'm doing the Huck Finn side another side exists in New Zealand which I'm not so dumb as not to be aware of and I can look at this too. Surely.

You once said that in the end it would be seen that your work 'all hangs together'. Still so?

If you write over a certain period there must be a relationship—a thread going through it. Besides the threads, the obsessions and all the rest of it which is grist to the mill, all the material has to be focused through one pair of eyes, one personality, as it were. Of course I would think that it all hangs together. I don't see any contradiction. I'm thinking of the railway man who tells Jeremy his wife is missing in *Joy of the Worm*. I just do it in flat language and some people might say, 'Well there is Sargeson—he's turned on this character who he would have dealt sympathetically with before. Now he just introduces him as a flat character of no account and is possibly concealing a sneer for his simplicity and for the language that he uses.' O.K. But couldn't it be seen as a rendering of how New Zealanders who wouldn't be particularly interested in reading my books would see this character? Because I present a character in a story and perhaps get the readers' sympathy and approval and so on it doesn't mean there wouldn't be an enormous number of people who wouldn't read the story and who would see the material or similar material, raw material for a story like this, quite differently. Well, can't I present that?

I didn't mean to imply that there was any discrepancy. But as the process goes on have you been conscious—as you expand in sheer length—of having less didactic intentions, dealing in more straightforward humour, more outright hilarity? Do you think it has been a sort of mellowing?

Well, I suppose one must mellow with age. I think I have a comic sense and I think many readers have overlooked the fact that I have this comic sense. I have my own particular sense of comedy and sense of what makes comedy. I find it hard to see these things as a reader would see them; I am asserting that there is a thread of cohesion but it is mainly a *feeling* that there's this cohesion. I couldn't work it out as a critic might when approaching my work.

Reaching a wider audience, entertaining, has been at the back of your mind lately. Is this part, or even a small part, of an explanation of a shift in style?

I don't think I can be seeking a bigger audience with a more 'literary' style because this implies a literacy which isn't very general in New Zealand. I can't possibly be seeking to widen my audience in New Zealand, can I?

I don't know. You mentioned the popularity of a 'mandarin' writer like Dickens.

Yes, but Dickens wasn't competing with television. You've only got to walk down the street and see the blue lights flickering every night; these people aren't going to be reading books. They're crouched over their television sets. For Dickens there was *good* competition, Thackeray, the Brontës, George Eliot, a host of people, but no radio, films, television.

Critics have noted in your work a preoccupation with seediness, horror, death, violence, squalor. Do you exaggerate these aspects or are they as you see them?

Do you mind if I say one notes all these things in Dickens? One can take the God's eye view, and the critic might want one to take the God's eye view, but obviously one isn't a God and one hasn't got a God's eye, has one? All one's imperfections, one's slants, one's impurities must get into the thing. I'd agree about that as a broad general principle—but, do you know, I think it's almost just a mechanical question. To make my contribution to New Zealand literature as I can see it—I suppose after I'd put my hand to the plough, after I'd ploughed so far, there was, probably because of my innate puritanism, the discipline of my puritanism, no turning back. Now this meant that I had to be a full-time writer. I just didn't have the money (you've got to remember that until 1966 when my widowed aunt who had no children died, she was 93, and whoever benefited under her will had to wait a long long while), I had to live officially on only £4 a week. I don't say that was all the money I had because I've been fortunate in having friends who've been enormously kind. We won't go into the question of whether they could afford to be kind or not—possibly I don't know the answer to that question—but whatever help was afforded me wasn't going to lift me into the grade of society in which you just didn't have to worry. This meant that my contacts were mainly with people isolated, not necessarily by money—although if you have a very small income you're isolated, take that for granted (I think one of the things that attracted me to the clergyman in *Joy of the Worm* is his isolation). People are isolated for various reasons; it might be because of their quirks of temperament, it might be because they choose to be poor. Naturally there's a lot of sordidness. There's going to be unwashed clothes, unwashed bodies too, where there should be washed clothes and washed bodies and things of that kind. Is this what you mean by a grubby seedy world? There's also, through it all, the spectre of old age, the end and dissolution of everything; the decay and the humiliations of age. In other words I've simply made use of the material that seems to have been there.

And yet in your work this thing permeates society. It's not restricted to a class or to isolated people. There's a spiritual sordidness, too, isn't there? It doesn't just relate to the down and out but also to men like 'my uncle' who's spiritually certainly unwashed, certainly grubby.

Oh, the uncle in 'Conversation with my Uncle'. Ah, well, that particular uncle was chairman of a transport board, he—it comes out in the story—stood for Parliament, he was on borough councils and things like that. If you mean that, I would say that New Zealand society is sort of kidding itself; that it does present a general spectacle of spiritual impoverishment and this might be one of the most devastating aspects of New Zealand society. Just the same as in a later story 'An International Occasion' I have xenophobia, the dislike of non-New Zealand ways brought out. Twice in my lifetime, during the two world wars, I've seen the New Zealand thing, the isolation, break down. The soldiers have been absolutely appalled at the narrowness of the scene they've returned to, but they soon get over this and the Kiwi thing comes up again. Of course if a writer is depending on an audience for the sort of sophisticated and civilized entertainment that I'm trying to write with a certain level of literacy your audience must of necessity be very small.

At times, you must have felt very lonely?

Well yes, I think that comes out. The isolation of various people and types of people in my work is all connected with the isolation that I've felt myself. I feel the two things: that this is a New Zealand thing and it's particularly so in my case because of the unusualness of my occupation. I think I said somewhere that after the slump, living in a suburb in which I lived only because my father owned a section and a bach on it where I was able for a long time to live very cheaply, I think, for a lot of people in my environment, I was a figure of fun. That hasn't greatly worried me—I'd discovered this about Montaigne. His career as a writer was carried out near Bordeaux. He had been at court and all the rest of it, but he'd more or less given that up. He was the mayor of Bordeaux at one time. But naturally, as a local person who wrote, a local writer as it were, they didn't think much of him—as is demonstrated by the fact that he said: 'If I write anything and I want it printed in Bordeaux,* I have to pay for it to be printed, but if I have it published

---

*Actually Guienne.—M.B.

in Paris, they pay me.' We are provincial and if you're provincial certain things happen. You're working in a certain kind of environment. 'He's one of the local boys. Is he any good? The chances are that he's not any good at all.' This is obviously connected with New Zealand writers sending their manuscripts to New York, or London because they want to find that they can be accepted by somebody who doesn't know them, doesn't know anything about them, and is not going to make the confusion of life and literature.

James K. Baxter remarks in his essay in The Puritan and the Waif *that your stories show a crude and sneering insistence on sexual abnormality.*

I remember Cresswell used to say very solemnly to me that New Zealanders are very sexually aberrated. I don't think I've over-emphasized this. But . . . I don't know about the word sneering. Possibly when I was young—in a story for instance called 'I've Lost my Pal'—I think there may be a suggestion of sneering because I was young, and I found difficulty in taking what would appear to me then as the hypocrisy of a Sunday-school teacher having double standards. Obviously I'd approach such a situation differently now but I don't see that in that particular story, in the chief protagonists, that there is any sneering at all. What were the other words that Baxter used?

Crude insistence.

I think if you isolate a character and if you are alive to the fantastic loneliness and isolation of many many people in this sort of society I think you find that deviations, or what people would call deviations, are much more widespread than the average person—if there is any such person as the average person—would suppose. One is inclined to get very balled up in this question of sexual variety. I don't think Anglo-Saxon people can really understand that what seems to worry them so much is not even a question or an issue for numerous peoples who live outside the Anglo-Saxon communities. Mr Kirk was reported to have got very hot and bothered when it was suggested that on statistics they could count on there being four homosexual members of Parliament—the *Evening Post* put its foot in it because it headlined a column 'Four Homosexuals in Parliament' and this led to a real fuss. In France, Italy and Spain or Asiatic countries it's just unthinkable that there should be any question of enquiring into this sort of thing anyhow. It would all be just completely taken for granted. Later Mr Kirk was reported to have said that if the Labour Party took up the question it would deal with it from a medical not a criminal point of view. This seems to me the last word in the ludicrous. As a last word on this I would say, 'Men have tits. Why?' Doesn't it occur to people that we must naturally be bi-sexual. Some have held that the male is concerned with culture and was differentiated out at a late stage in human development and that if you want to look at the type figure of the human race you look to the female. I think that's probably a sound idea. No doubt you do get the absolute pure heterosexual. At the other end you get— well we've all seen pure homosexuals. But all the rest of us are somewhere in between.

In your work men seem to have more redemptive capacities and qualities than women. You don't have women, do you, with the qualities of Bill and Terry in That Summer? *These bonds you show between men like Bill and Terry don't seem to exist between women, or heterosexually. In some ways the women seem to get a rough deal. For instance, Queenie's and Maisie's horrible deaths in* Joy of the Worm.

Queenie's death? There's an intention of ironic contrast. She envies Maisie the children, and she refers in her letter to the dolly that she's had. She is deprived of her human dolly but she became someone else's macabre doll. I suppose this is absolutely horrible is it? It's an indication of my well-known cynicism or deplorable qualities or something or other. Are you saying that I've never written a piece of fiction about a standard heterosexual situation?

No, obviously not, but . . .

In conversation I find myself saying, 'How can you expect a marriage to last, when people are jammed together in these little houses?' In aristocratic society, where nobody counted except the upper class, husbands and wives didn't have to see each other much.

Do you think the woman is the instigator of the difficulties? Apart from the social aspect, apart from the cramming together? Wives often seem to be millstones in stories such as 'The Hole that Jack Dug' or 'Big Ben'.

There is this idea that the woman is the type figure of humanity, the great immoveable mass, as it were, round which the male has to move in orbit. I think the Molly Bloom and Bloom relationship is a fair enough depiction of this relationship.

In the three later novels you laugh at a lot of things, poke fun at a lot of things. Are you one of them?

What do you mean laugh at things? If I create comic situations is that 'laughing at'?

Perhaps mocking your own erudition for instance—in the style of Newhouse in Memoirs of a Peon. *Is there any intention there of having a dig at yourself?*

I don't think so, although I am quite capable of ridiculing myself, telling stories against myself. I think it's related to having a comic sense of life. I think I have a combination of a tragic sense of life and a comic sense of life, and maybe these are very closely related.

In Joy of the Worm *when old Bohun is having his naked dip and standing on his head, this isn't Frank Sargeson having a dip is it, and also Frank Sargeson up on the hill with the binoculars?*

Well, I don't think I can honestly go along with that. Is this because I'm an elderly novelist? I might be an exhibitionist, but I'm not an exhibitionist of that kind. My exhibitionism resides in exhibiting the Rev. Bohun. The idea fascinates me that he has set this family in motion. He is a very civilized person. He doesn't stand on his head for prurient reasons at all. He's an egotist, of course. How many of us are not? He does it out of sheer vitality. There is a certain limitation of imagination in that he obviously hasn't considered the fantastic spectacle he would make if he succeeds in standing on his head. It's commented on later of course.

An English reviewer of Joy of the Worm *suggested that you are intending to show the old man up for the monster he was, but I was reminded most strongly of that sentence in 'Up Onto the Roof and Down Again' where you talk about the old man who used to tog himself up with cane, top hat, and so on and go off in search of erotic adventure. You noted then the immense vitality and exuberance of human life.*

That is perfectly true. This book is, in a sense, the celebration of Bohun vitality. Of course the Bohuns are impure but so what?

Impure, but deserving of forgiveness? This is something that recurs through your work—the idea of forgiveness. Jeremy Bohun says that the best we probably can do is promptly forgive the lot, sin, sinner, everything. In 'Imaginary Conversation' in Landfall *you picture Butler in the frame of mind where forgiveness is all that matters. Is this close to your own attitude?*

Well, of course, that's an idea that's very strongly in some literary figure I'm trying to think of—it may be Blake, but I'm not quite sure. I've heard of Christ, too.

And yet, there's another side to the question because, although perhaps 'forgiving sin, sinner' is close to your view, you seem unable to forgive the sin of 'puritanism'—the side of puritanism that says acquisitiveness is a virtue.

In this society in which this puritanism is very strong there are certain ways in which it rings a bell for everybody. Virtually everybody thinks that it would be a very good thing to make good, to materially make good, and the material affluence or prosperity in a country like

New Zealand is a sort of double thing—it is a puritanical thing in itself and it is also a reflex from the other puritan manifestations. I mean, if you have to be a sexual puritan—and this means that you are constricted as far as your sexual energies are concerned—then put it all into that department of life where you approve of the puritanism and the whole set-up will approve of you and so on. You have to be a hundred per cent pure in your morals and you have to be a hundred per cent in your devotion to business too. And I would think this is at the root of a lot of the mental hospital set-up in a country like New Zealand, that there are a lot of people who cannot work out a reconciliation of this contradiction, because you can only be a hundred per cent in your business if you are going against your conscience. Surely this is so because, as there is only so much wealth or income to go round, the whole pressure of business is to get more than your share.

Would you call yourself then a thorough-going puritan?

Well, I must be honest enough to say I recognize this discipline is very valuable to me, but I have obviously reacted against the puritanism of open slather for material belongings and all the rest of it. But, on the other hand, I can see that this leads me into difficulties too. For instance I might look at some working class friend and say 'Oh well he is unjustly treated because he takes *less* than his share.' But I am thinking of a working man of the more old-fashioned kind. Now a really civilized non-puritanical person would say, 'Look, this man has his own soul, his own destiny to cope with and work out. You can't remedy the injustices of this world.' Now that is possibly the civilized way. You have older civilizations that worked that way; you've got people like Montaigne. But now you have this drive for the view that every human being has his own dignity and his own rights and that he should share and so on; in extreme form you have the socialist idea that we should all be, economically anyhow, equal. Now is this too a form of puritanism? I think probably it is, and that is a thing that is allied to this background of coming to New Zealand in the seventies last century and being forced out of England by poverty. Admittedly it would be a great problem for me if I were rich myself because I'd feel that I had no right to be rich—something that Montaigne, for instance, would not feel. I venerate a man like Montaigne, and he was the product of privilege, social injustice and so on. Now I'm caught in a cleft stick. I will admit that. If I were rich I think I would want to give an enormous amount of these riches away, distribute them where they were called for. This might be sentimentality or this might be my own personal adhesion to something that is in the air, and yet the contradiction of all this is that you never had so many people who were so rich in this society—oil kings and all the rest of it—and some of them are contributing to and patronizing art, contributing to this culture which is a continuity from the past. In other words you are asking me something which I'm not really called upon to answer at all, because all I can do is to be aware of this terribly complicated and difficult situation, and I can only make marginal comments in the form that seems to suit me best—that is, by creating fictions.

II

In the 'Writing a Novel' broadcast you said you were attempting to conceive of the New Zealander, that you were still in the process of 'defining the background'. Does this still apply to your last three novels?

Two are set back, one is set a little way back. You can't have anything quite contemporary because of the delay in publishing. My next unpublished work is brought up to date again, and I have had the idea that if I go on writing novels I am going back and forwards all the time. Some historians do say—although historians generally are not really in favour of people who write fictions—that fiction can fill out the picture of New Zealand, that someone with imagination has a place in history as much as someone who takes part in a county council meeting.

Are you thinking about Chapman writing about your work?

As a matter of fact I was thinking about Chapman. I remember when I was depressed about not being able to get *Memoirs of a Peon* published, that Chapman read it for a publisher and sent in a favourable report. The publisher still didn't take it on and I remember Chapman saying 'We should have it' meaning the public, and he, as a historian, should have it—which was quite pleasant. I've got an historical sense but I can't be much interested in historical documentation. I get bored by it. But whether I'm still attempting to conceive of the New Zealander. . . . Perhaps I think there is no such thing as a New Zealander but that if you have a lot of New Zealanders some composite thing comes out of it and each figure in this composite portrait makes his contribution. I think of myself as very much a New Zealander but in a double sense. I am basically quite representative of New Zealanders but I have my oddities which somewhat set me apart. But I think New Zealanders are much more isolated than they imagine anyhow—each as an individual is.

You could say then that Michael Newhouse, Dick Lennie in The Hangover *and the Bohuns are types in a sense—that they are isolated?*

I hadn't quite thought of it in that way but I think that would be right.

So you are still defining the background?

Yes. . . . People and background, they go together, even though they can at times be antagonistic. Readers who have never been in New Zealand sometimes say they get a strong sense of it from my books.

Among Maoris perhaps there isn't the sense of solitude evident in your New Zealanders and yet Forster by the time the Collected Stories *came out was able to say on the basis of the stories that you knew 'heaps about the Maoris'.*

Which I don't of course. He was mistaken.

How do you think he deduced this, and why hadn't you, up to that point, used the Maoris as the antithesis of the solitary. Why hadn't you used them to show what was missing? Was it because they had been sentimentalized earlier?

I don't know. . . . I think I mentioned earlier that New Zealand authors haven't generally been very successful in handling the Maoris. That has been the view of Eric McCormick. Perhaps Noel Hilliard has altered matters, perhaps too O. E. Middleton—as Rod Finlayson did further back. Without ever having formulated this to myself I think I was wary that a problem was involved; but there is another thing. You know the Te Aute type of Maori—the upper class, the superior Maori. Well, when my new novel is published, *A Game of Hide and Seek,* if it is ever published, I think I'll get a fair amount of criticism the gist of which will be that the Samoan I've used is the Maori equivalent of Bill in *That Summer,* not the Maori equivalent of the Rev. Bohun or of Michael Newhouse. In using Maoris I would tend to steer clear of the Te Aute type of Maori. This is a very difficult problem because there are so many people who are quite doctrinaire about this. They would be searching everything written for any derogatory view of the Maoris. Now I think this is fundamentally phony because the Maoris are just as individualized: they have this sense of community and they're not isolated, but if you sort them out as individuals they're just as individualized as we are. I have my Samoan speaking, 'You, boy, eh—you come to the pub'—I sometimes have him speaking in this kind of way. Now I can imagine a lot of these Maori supporters will be absolutely disgusted and say, 'Oh but this is Old Hat' and so on because they will be thinking in terms of Maoris going to university. This touches on much that I've said in talking with you. What I think is that, 'Oh well, bugger all this. To hell with it, in fact. I'm doing a work of art, you see. I'm not falsifying.' Look, let's put it in an extreme form. You know the resistance to, and contempt that has been poured on, the Hori stories. But Hori stories are still going on all of the time. It's only that what is the basis of the Hori story is badly used or is a fatigued artistic form, not that it doesn't exist. I have a nephew who is a school teacher and he's been teaching way up on those mountains towards the East Cape—on the Divide there. My God! He comes up here and tells me stories about . . . . it's a Maori community. All right. This is all material for art isn't it? But you're running a greak risk, I admit that too, because this is the time when the whole question of brown skinned people and apartheid is prominent. We're living in the day of the documentary, and social anthropology, and all the rest of it, and therefore the Maori insomuch as he is the basis of the Hori stories, is supposed to be forgotten about. We are meant to pretend that he doesn't exist. This Samoan boy drives a bulldozer. He's here to make money. He's got to get on in the world. While he's here he has to get on in the Pakeha world. Back home he has a mother with a swollen leg. He has a father who is blind. It is a pitiful personal situation and he is operating in the Pakeha world. This is something that moves me, touches me, whereas if he were of a well-to-do Samoan family, here to become an engineer, or something of the kind, well this wouldn't interest me because this wouldn't be the basic stuff of what I conceive I'm dealing in—that which is permanent in human nature. Because he would probably go to America and he would get a degree at Indiana University, and then he would go and teach anthropology in a Japanese university, you see; and this would seem to me to be so artificial, so temporary, so much part of the contemporary world, and with these permanent elements which I'm after much obscured.

This fumbling happiness and comradeship and sense of community —and Professor Rhodes talks about your return to natural man. . . .

Yes I suppose he's thinking of this hunger for the dropping of all the trappings. . . .

Didn't the Maoris appear to you as an admirable contrast?

Yes, yes they would, if they were left alone. They're like the people at the opening of *Joy of the Worm*—primitive people, uncontaminated by western phoniness—but there's nobody anymore like that. I suppose a lot of my work is concerned with trying to heighten or bring out these old elements of natural man, as it were. In whatever society there is natural goodness besides natural wickedness, and natural joy besides natural gloom. I remember I was sitting with Dennis McEldowney near the civic square in town and he was waiting for a bus and we were saying goodbye and up came—it was high summer—up came a water cart and it had to water the plants that were in tubs around the civic square. Two people on it, the man in charge and a boy of about sixteen who was beginning his working-life apparently. He'd been able to leave school and this was his job, you see. There was this enormous hose to be taken off, and they watered the plants and they drove off and they were talking and jesting together. We couldn't hear what they said, and I said: 'Isn't it marvellous Dennis—especially in summer' and we agreed how wonderful it would be for this boy to go around on the water cart. I think I said, 'Think how awful it would be if someone got hold of him and said, "Now look there's no future in this. You should be enrolling for a course of adult education." ' We began our own jesting and laughing about it. But it was awful to think of this knockabout boy enjoying himself thoroughly every hour of the day in his job who was to be put to read about the problems of social adjustment and race relations and God knows what. I think I'm endeavouring to depict this sort of thing, that still exists just the same, in the new book. I'm depicting a person who does exist and it seems to me that, because of the modern context and so forth, a lot of people are wilfully denying that these people are still there. And they're very much there. I know you have Maori anthropologists and all the rest of it at the university, Maori linguists with terrific Oxford degrees. Well, that's all right with me, but it doesn't particularly interest me. Although I might get round to being interested eventually. I suppose that before I wrote *Joy of the Worm* I didn't conceive that I'd ever be all that much interested in depicting an old Methodist clergyman.

You're interested in the Beat and Hippie generation. Why? Do you see something, particularly in the latter, that reminds you of slum living—the idea of all barriers being down, all conventions, all inhibitions? Natural man if you like.

To see young people with all their energy and vitality confronted with these social facts of life interests and touches me. I think the whole of my work as a novelist is to demonstrate human nature seen through a particular lens or a particular personality. Sometimes the lens I use is one of my own, but often for a host of reasons which could occur to anyone, I prefer to borrow a convenient lens from one of my own characters.

Reviewers of The Hangover *seemed to be uncertain about what you were trying to do. I feel the difficulties arise from your being a symbolic realist rather than just a realist.*

When writing *The Hangover* I think I had at the back of my mind an actual happening—two boys from a very narrowly religious family, a little sister shot, and an apparent intention to shoot parents. To cap the whole horror of this thing, I think I'm right in remembering that the father, still holding to his beliefs—a very narrow form of protestantism—was reported as saying he was going home to begin replacing his family. Who had learned what? The public? The father? The public had been thrilled to have their hair stand on end, provided with what they wanted by the popular press. But the author who writes a serious novel, if he uses such material, is going to be dismissed as morbid. I think you must expect a very ambiguous reception to a thing like *The Hangover* because it's cutting so close to the bone. But I couldn't write up a story of this kind as Truman Capote did with *In Cold Blood*. Capote hasn't added one fraction of understanding to the dreadful affair he deals in. He has simply done a very superior *Truth* story. I deplore this book.

As far as the whole method of symbolic realism is concerned do you not feel bound by the strictures of a realist novelist, a conventional novelist? The nervous onion skins, the plastic raincoats, do they function as really earned symbolism? They're obviously symbolic, and it was obvious enough what they symbolized, but what precisely were they objective correlatives of? Was this clear?

I have Lennie do the analysis of the thing. I'm not prepared to make many stabs at what's going on in Alan's mind because I don't think anyone can do that, not convincingly, but you have to select just a few things you see. Remember, this is still fiction; it is not documentary, not a psychiatrist's report. This is a work of art and I had already indicated at the beginning, with Solly and the plum tree coming out of his heart, as it were, and Alan—this had occurred to him too, had come up naturally. Then there is the beautiful little bit of the garden of Eden—and then the horror that follows. . . . I think what people think of as reality is useful, but you have to know how to handle it. Doesn't Maurice Duggan say in one of his clever short pieces, 'Don't let yourself be imposed upon by reality'?

And you'd feel this?

Yes I think so. I think that's a very clever saying of Duggan's. Reality, we can't handle it, we must interpose a style. Look at the *New Statesman* review of *Joy of the Worm* where the reviewer says, 'Well, this is the author, and all his people, interposing a style.' This would apply to America with its violence and crime: no one can take this. You must interpose something to take the edge off it. Lewis Mumford has said that the great failure of America is the failure to achieve form.

Nobody knows where they are. With simple people, when something comes up like a bereavement or a calamity, they know what to do: they send the banal bloody card, you see, and never think. I'm trying in a situation to extract some truth, something from my heart, you see—puritanism again. You need the form. Just the same, I can't do it in real life, but I do it on paper. If I'm going to convey something that's truthful that will focus people's attention, something terrible—and terror is a legitimate subject for art—I've got to do it according to certain literary forms and conventions, and this, once and for all, rules out, for me, the straight realist novel completely. There's no such thing. But I suppose no matter how you're not going to be imposed upon by reality, you have to pick out some dreadful facts of reality and you have to start from there. I mean death—you can't get round it so you have to do something about it. I suppose it's sort of rubbing it in, in an entertaining, artistic way.

So reality functions as a take-off platform?

A springboard. And then the thing becomes self-contained, *sui generis*. It has an identity of its own. You've got to remember that the realism or the reality you allegedly talk about, in a few years, will have disappeared completely and all that will remain is the transmuted thing. Isn't that the characteristic of a work of art? Look at Catullus—all that crap and dirt, obscenity and so forth that was part of Roman life and see how he's distilled it, at his best. It might be something as commonplace as the sea breaking on the beach, and there he's got it once and for all and for ever—*litus ut longe resonante Eoa/tunditur unda.*

You use realism but what matters is that a work of art is more than the sum of its parts. Is this it?

Yes, agreed. If you're writing a *Hangover* you first of all select those things that are going to hit you in the face from reality—you needn't select those if you're Jane Austen; you deliberately avoid them. It's a matter of ingredients on which your imagination can best act as a catalytic agent. There's all sorts of things going on and finally out of it you get a new unity which refers to the original material but is not the original material.

Some years ago you said that you thought that the naturalistic novel was the most likely kind to appear in New Zealand. Do you think this is still so or have we passed it?

This might have been in connection with my interest in publications such as *New Directions* during the war years. It was a very odd thing, the differences between *New Writing* in England and *New Directions* in America. *New Writing* proceeded more or less along naturalistic lines but in America they were all modernistic. It was a sort of hangover in America from the Paris period of *transition* where people like Gertrude Stein appeared. I think as a country becomes more sophisticated, as what culture it has becomes more sophisticated and civilized, that you tend to get away from naturalism—although that's contradicted by Zola. But although Zola wrote some very good novels on naturalistic lines perhaps they weren't as naturalistic as he and people at the time supposed. Think of *Germinal* for example, which is epic. One thinks of Homer. But yes, I would think there's always a place for good naturalism. Think of how good Céline is at his best, and how his naturalism transcends itself. How Dreiser's does too—and how Farrell's mainly doesn't.

This seems very much contradicted by the fact that in the English New Writing *you were getting naturalism after Forster and Woolf.*

That's sort of pressing it a bit far because I imagine some people would tend to call Forster a kind of naturalist. You are only attaching these labels to people.

But you've certainly got to say that symbolism is what matters to Forster up to Passage to India, *which is in a class of its own.*

Well, you mustn't limit naturalism to what Zola would call naturalism. I mean there must be a basis in naturalism surely. One must remember a lot of people might read something and enjoy it without being very strongly aware of the symbolic levels. For instance, take another Forster, *Where Angels Fear to Tread,* which I think is a very delightful Forster. That scene on the railway platform which it opens with—in a sense nothing could be more everyday, if you like, more naturalistic. I know all the symbolism that carries over beyond the real facts, but didn't I make the point in 'Conversation in a Train' that if naturalism is intense enough, if it is rendered with sufficient intensity then out of it arises overtones—it gets a lift, transcends its own limits? But to answer your question I don't think that the naturalistic novel is any more the most likely kind to appear in New Zealand. I think there is a sophistication taking place which is becoming more complicated all the time. One has only to think of Janet Frame. There is a recent novel by Joy Cowley called *Nest in a Falling Tree,* which is about a woman more or less unattached and her affair with a teenage boy. This obviously has a naturalistic basis, but it should be plain to everyone, I think, that you are to see it as a great deal more than that. And you get non-naturalistic novels which vary from each other as much as Michael Joseph's *Hole in the Zero* does from Sylvia Ashton-Warner's *Spinster.*

Why have you published so much here, particularly in Landfall, *when you could perhaps have published overseas?*

One needs so much help if one has lived as I have done and if you have an editor as I had in Charles Brasch who encouraged you and who felt that you knew what you were up to and that you were producing something of some value, a question of loyalty comes in. That is it. John Lehmann published two books and he published my material in *New Writing*. And I have to confess that when he began *London Magazine* I was naturally interested. I sent him 'The Undertaker's Story' and he didn't want that and I sent him 'The Colonel's Daughter' and he didn't want that, and I think he wrote in one of his little rejection notes that, ah well, I didn't achieve the same tension that he was looking for. I felt this was a little bit slick, but times had moved on and what he would think of as proletarian literature was no longer a fashionable thing in England. He wanted to move on to something else and although I had moved on too my direction was not the one he had hoped for.

Has there been anything in your mind about promoting or helping to promote New Zealand literature—has that influenced you at all?

Well, I think that is answered by the fact that I did put quite a bit of time and attention into editing and bringing out *Speaking for Ourselves.* *

Have you read Holcroft's Reluctant Editor?

No, I haven't.

I'll probably spoil it for you by saying that in that book Holcroft treats with a fair amount of acerbity his relationship with you.

Does he?

And perhaps more surprisingly, yours with Fairburn suggesting that you and Fairburn fell out. . . .

That's true.

. . . because you were not masculine enough for Fairburn. He . . .

That's crap.

. . . actually says: 'Rex Fairburn could not be numbered among the admirers of Frank Sargeson. In spite of the female sensitivity which all writers must have, he was a masculine man, and I think he found Sargeson

---

*Published 1945 by The Caxton Press, and printed by R. W. Lowry, with stories by Audrey King, Roderick Finlayson, Lyndahl Chapple Gee, A. P. Gaskell, E. M. Lyders, G. R. Gilbert, D. W. Ballantyne, Helen Shaw, John Reece Cole, Max Harris, Greville Texidor, E. P. Dawson, Maurice Duggan, D. M. Anderson, and Frank Sargeson.

incompatible. I am not suggesting effeminancy in Sargeson: . . . but I think he could be temperamental in ways which Fairburn might have found disconcerting.'

I knew Fairburn for twenty-two years, and it was only in the last five or six years that we ceased to be good friends. I first saw Fairburn in my very early twenties when I did not know who he was—an immensely tall slender young man with a crop of curls—the 'pale youth' of his poem perhaps, but I remember patches of high colour on his cheeks. He was taking long slow strides down Queen Street, and appeared quite absorbed in the contemplation of a bunch of flowers held out in front of him—I forget what they were, but I would think not gladioli because much later he told me of his dislike for their vulgarity. Anyhow, I felt the gods must be at large in Queen Street. But what was Holcroft's acerbity about? He assesses me as a writer does he?

Yes he does that.

And points out my limitations I would take it?

Yes. Though confessing that he thinks it's a limitation on his part too—not being able to appreciate you as much as he sees other people can. For instance he says that when he read The Puritan and the Waif *he was most surprised by what he found there, by what people had got from you, and thought this was perhaps his limitation.*

I think that when I began writing Holcroft had made his shot overseas, as it were, and then he came back to New Zealand. When he first saw my stuff I think he was interested, but you know, it can be the same thing in the universities: a professor might like a brilliant pupil so long as he remains a pupil but he doesn't like him as a competitor. Isn't it one of La Rochefoucauld's maxims that we like imitators but we don't like competitors? I think that Holcroft when he returned to New Zealand and before he committed himself to a life of editorship, which presumably he had to do because he was married and was producing a family and all the rest of it—I think he conceived of himself in the role of *the* New Zealand writer. I must say that I never at any stage conceived of myself as quite like that—I think I was surprised as anyone when I began to draw attention—and oddly enough, from Holcroft's predecessor on the *Listener,* Oliver Duff, who was immensely kind to me, generous with his appreciation, printing my sketches and stories, sending me books to write notes on, and I think paying me fees which I believe were rather in advance of what most contributors received. And here too I should not forget to mention that in one of my times of greatest stress and difficulty I was done a kindness by John A. Lee. I think Holcroft's whole attitude to me would probably be coloured by his imagining that I had collected certain advantages which he'd have liked to have had himself. He probably knew I received a small pension, and perhaps conceived of my being set absolutely free. I know at one stage I was greatly surprised that after he had written a very enthusiastic critique, I think in the *Southland Times,* on *A Man and his Wife* he changed his tune. He seemed, very obtusely to me, to change his tune with *When the Wind Blows.* He didn't seem to see the point of the book—which is that once the boy understands that his father is involved in all the human frailties, the way is open for the healing of his traumatic condition. It's much the same as the birth of charity at the end of 'Old Man's Story'. He can now think 'Poor father. Poor mother' and so on. He can now include his father and his mother in his own self-pity, you see. But tell me, do you feel that in this thing of Holcroft's that he is really trying to derate me? Later on we had our quarrel when I tried to get the *Listener* fees raised, and when he said I had to sign my name to contributions and I refused because it was clear he didn't insist about this to all his contributors—well, later on it all boiled into a fearful row, because he forgot about this insistence, saying in an editorial or in a note to a letter that it was up to the author to decide about signing his name. But it hadn't been up to me to decide. . . .

He mentions this. He goes into the whole thing. . . .

The whole thing? Does he? This goes on over pages?

Yes.

I haven't read it but I have no intention of reading it, I'm sorry—I mean not while I'm writing. I can't be bothered. I've got my writing to do. You see I felt strongly at one stage—I was never offered another book, times changed and the fees *did* go up but I never got the pay-off. But it's extremely interesting about *The Puritan and the Waif.* It was sent to the *Listener,* but it was never reviewed. No, never, and I remember this clearly because I expected it would be, and Helen Shaw was very surprised too.

There was, seemingly, a fallow period between I For One *and* Memoirs of a Peon.

I admit that in that part of the fifties I went through a tough period. You've got to remember that the great changes of this century came in the fifties and it was all awfully difficult to take in. I'd sort of missed the war, I'd had surgical tuberculosis. Glover in his blatant way used to say, 'Remember you'll be pre-war—you'll be completely out of it now—forget that you ever put pen to paper.' I was groping round for a while. I had come from my bach down the garden into this little house. I admit to going through this groping period, you see, but then I met

Richard Campion, and I started to write my plays but got nowhere with them. I started to write *The Peon* in 1957 after I had helped John Graham, as many others did too, with his tomato growing. I was not going to mope after writing the first play so I sat down and I wrote the second one. It still was no good—I mean trying to get a production, and then I did have a short time of great despair and that was when I went tomato growing. But when it collapsed I was conscious of an amount of accumulated energy. I looked over notes I had here and there and saw immense masses of material which I'd never used . . . and I thought, 'Ahh! I'll make one last endeavour.' I remember that James Courage—he had written an inscription in one of his books, 'To Frank Sargeson who writes the books that I would like to write'—asked what I was doing and I said, 'Oh well it will take me a long time, I work so slowly, but I'm writing a picaresque novel.' And he replied, 'Oh yes. This is good. Frank Sargeson ought to write the *Felix Krull* of New Zealand.' I felt that *The Peon* was to be my final thing, that I was writing the last thing I would ever write, so I would put everything into it. This was when I was friendly with a man a good deal older than myself, Bake—the plays are dedicated to him—William Levener Chadwick Bakewell. He has daughters who greatly admire *The Peon* by the way, because they recognize Daddy and don't think it's a bit unfair or unkind. Not really. They just regret that I didn't find room for some of Daddy's fruitier stories and I say, 'Oh well, they just didn't fit. A work of art is a work of art.' Of course all this must make it sound as if I really copied from life but I'm leading you up the garden path. With *The Peon* I felt I was writing my literary last will and testament. I started in May 1957 and I wrote through '57, '58, '59, and I finished it at the end of '59 at a time of great difficulty and great poverty. And then I put it aside. I thought it was no good. I had this immense mass of manuscript and I had typescript drafts of most of it and I put it away for six months and then I started to think twice and I thought it might be all right, see, and I typed and typed and typed on an old typewriter and so I finally got it done and when I'd got it all corrected and I'd done three copies on this poor miserable typewriter and I started to send it away—well, I collapsed again because no one was interested. Some wouldn't read it. Somebody said it was unreadable, and so forth. I tried endless English publishers and I really went into another period of despair. But I was hooked out of this by meeting Chris Cathcart who then took an interest in the plays. Mr Cathcart was a government meat inspector but he was also a very good play producer and a very good actor. He came from Scotland with it's tradition of Scottish folk theatre and one of his first questions was 'But where is your own theatre?' meaning where are your own plays? He was shocked and surprised. It was marvellous to meet Mr Cathcart. And, of course, while Chris and I worked together I was able to show why there was this dearth of New Zealand plays. We have the theatre controlled mainly by people who *'know'*—these are the intermediaries. If the playwright is to be eliminated you can say that it is not so much the exigencies of the time as the behaviour of the people who have the most say in the theatre. If you write a play the first person you run up against is somebody who is a theatrical entrepreneur or producer and you find that you know nothing whatsoever about writing plays—you can take this for granted. This is why New Zealand theatre in an international sense might have some performances that wouldn't disgrace some provincial city in England or a London suburb—but a handful of playwrights who really are a bunch of poor relations. But *The Peon* was put away from 1960 until near the end of 1963. Then some New Zealand boys, Kevin Ireland who used to be Kevin Jowsey, the man who works in the Turnbull Library, Ray Grover, and a New Zealand doctor, Neil Perrett, were at a London party and they met Martin Green who is the man I deal with at MacGibbon and Kee and he wanted to know if there were any New Zealand writers and they said, 'Well, Frank Sargeson', and that's how all that came about and that was the end of 1963. By 1964 we had produced my two plays: we'd produced a play by John Graham, *Lest We Resemble*; we'd produced D'Arcy Cresswell's *The Forest* and this took up all my time, you see, from the time I finished *The Peon.* This work was done with the three of us collaborating— myself, Chris Cathcart and Colin McCahon. Putting on a play is an enormous undertaking and I had to hold the whole thing together and organize and do the donkey work, you see, and I can still feel the marvellous feeling of release I got when it was decided, 'Look, we can't get money; the people in Wellington that should subsidize us, won't; nobody is interested'; and it all collapsed and with this marvellous feeling of release I started writing again. I wrote 'Just Trespassing, Thanks', I wrote 'City and Suburban', and I wrote 'Beau'. I saw that I could still do things and that really set me going again. That and the release from the plays, and the interest Martin Green took in *Memoirs of a Peon.* He was much taken by the abundance of comic episode and that was exactly what I was trying for. Rhodes says that I don't tie up all the threads, but I don't think in a picaresque novel you have necessarily to tie up every thread. Dickens in his novels does it in a mechanical way anyhow, devoting pages to characters who have been dropped ages ago and explaining what has happened to them meantime, a kind of formal tidying up. I would always prefer myself to tie up more meaningfully.

Did you have much difficulty getting your early work published?

The first thing I ever had published was an article in the *N.Z. Herald* called 'A New Tramp Abroad' or some such title.

I mean other than in Tomorrow. *Were you trying for magazines that rejected you?*

I can't remember details, but I did get a lot of rejection slips.

Within this country?

Not for stories. No, all my stories I think went to *Tomorrow* which of course could not afford to pay. I nearly had a story, 'Henry's Birthday', published by the *London Mercury*. I sent some verse but the editor John Squire thought that was no good but he nearly published the story. And Jonathan Cape said he nearly published my novel *Southern Rebels*—as I called it then. Later it became *Blind Alleys,* and was also changed into a play. Then my boarding-house play *Secret Places*—A. D. Peters, who is a very well known London theatrical agent, was very hopeful of getting that put on in London. This was way back at the end of the twenties or thirties.

No question of these being revamped . . .?

None whatsoever. I've read passages of *Blind Alleys* to Janet and I knew from the way she looked, the way she laughed. . . . At the time that it was written I thought it was written very nicely, very Galsworthy you might say. Perhaps that was why Edward Garnett at Cape's admired it.

I think in 'Up Onto the Roof' you said that after you had first started to publish you realized that there were people doing parallel things to you and that you were far too long unconscious or unaware of what they were doing. Who did you make contact with early on?

Rod Finlayson. Rod Finlayson had got to know D'Arcy Cresswell and D'Arcy had introduced us, and he was at a beginning stage too. He wrote a looser story than I did, and he was in some senses further ahead than I was. I don't think he was perplexed nearly so much by problems as they presented themselves to me.

Was this sort of contact very fruitful?

With Rod? Oh, over a period, yes, very.

Was there a North Shore artistic community?

Robin Hyde lived at Castor Bay and I saw a lot of her. She could be very difficult, she was very unstable, but I greatly liked Robin Hyde. This 'community' was often talked about. When David Ballantyne came along I remember he spoke of North Shore intellectuals. I suppose with Robin Hyde and Cresswell at Castor Bay, and myself in Takapuna, and later on Fairburn in Devonport, the label was to be expected. I should mention too there was at Northcote, Jess Whitworth, who had formerly been married to Oliver Duff of the *Listener*. A ready journalist, she also wrote *Otago Interval*. But for me the Auckland writer I found most congenial was an occasional visitor to the North Shore, Jane Mander. I met her at Cresswell's bach, and I'm afraid that afternoon he may have somewhat regretted he invited me because it turned out that I was pretty familiar with the work of American writers who had been Jane's friends during the 1914-18 war and afterwards when she had lived in New York. I'm afraid that Cresswell felt a little out of it despite his brief inquiries about the work we were discussing—afterwards followed by his doubts about its value. I received many kindnesses from Jane Mander, and so did Rex Fairburn. She would send us expensive tickets to the visiting ballet companies, I mean from overseas. She used to invite us to evening meals in town which she generously paid for, and did not complain if we perhaps stayed too long in the pub and turned up late—perhaps with one or two odds and ends tagging along. I used to make long journeys to the Mander home at Meadowbank, where I was paid for working in the garden, and where one day I was introduced to Jane's father, frail and bedridden after his life as saw-miller of the kauri forest of the North—and later a member of the Legislative Council. I remember he told me that to get on in life I should get out of New Zealand, there weren't the opportunities there had been for young men in his day. I found all this fascinating for a beginning writer, particularly as I was reading Jane's books—in which her father's activities so largely and so vividly figured. Jane Mander, together with William Satchell, remain with me the only New Zealand novelists whose books I have consistently hunted down until I have read the lot. I have an inscribed first edition copy of *The Story of a New Zealand River*. I think the book first appeared in New York in 1920. Also I have *Allen Adair*, bought in a secondhand shop for two shillings, very probably the finest thing she wrote, and now a very rare book. I love to remember her story about a publisher, a very old man, who was to publish one of her books—who tried to seduce her in a taxicab.

Did the group actually meet and exchange ideas?

Ah! Cresswell gives a portrait of us all sitting lovingly around the fire listening to his reading aloud *The Forest*. As a matter of fact I was never there. He was mistaken. He used to come down and read me parts of *The Forest* in my hut. I remember I had an elderly friend, the friend I used as the basis of my story 'Beau'. He came in one day. He was so poor he used to come to read the newspaper and he rustled the newspaper and Cresswell very obviously paused, in a superior way, and said if he had finished crackling the newspaper, and then he read on . . . ha. . . . I suppose in the thirties there was a sort of grouping as it were. *Tomorrow* was an outlet. There isn't an outlet now, in the sense that there was with *Tomorrow*. You've got to remember that *Tomorrow* used to be a *weekly* to begin with then it became a fortnightly then a monthly. But we did have something that we haven't got now, apart perhaps from *Monthly Review*. Publication takes so long. *Arena*, you never know when it will come out, *Mate* is the same, *Landfall* only every three months—whereas with *Tomorrow* you *always* had a date line. I wrote for years for *Tomorrow*. I wrote as 'A Radical Man About Town'; I wrote all sorts of comments and so on. It was almost like Wordsworth you know, 'Bliss was it in that dawn . . . /but to be young was very heaven!'

There was a great deal of excitement?

Oh, infinitely yes, yes. There was a great fuss when Glover brought out 'The Arraignment of Paris' and it was rumoured that Marris, the editor who was Glover's target, was threatening him with libel. I think we wrote Marris indignant letters and things of that kind. And then things happening like all the fuss over *Children of the Poor* you know. It was really nonsense, people not understanding, and Lee getting blamed for denigrating his mother, as it were, when this is just contrary to the truth. And Jane Mander coming back from England—and once again let me say what a marvellous person Jane was! It was the greatest privilege to know her. It was so much more relaxed then. Somewhere I say there was a comradeship in life which you don't find now. There was not the pressure of time. . . . They're very happy days to remember. I didn't quite come in on the founding of *Tomorrow* but I remember I sent little scraps of verse. We used to get excited when *Tomorrow* was quoted in Parliament by somebody.

Tomorrow *was a sort of cheerful crusade?*

Yes. Well, Kennaway Henderson, the editor—he was not a very good cartoonist perhaps; he was a painter, a visual artist—and we all felt sympathetic to him. I don't know whether it's different now, or whether I have a lot of sympathy from younger people, but it seemed marvellous that he was older, that he was radical when he was old.

What about the people you've helped? Crump perhaps, and Janet Frame?

Oh. I can't claim to have helped Crump. My intentions were all right but they never came to anything. Janet wrote *Owls Do Cry* here. I knew about her and her sister turned up with her in a car one day and said this is Janet Frame, and *The Lagoon* had been published by then, although before Glover managed to get it out something had been published in *Landfall.* You could see this girl had this marvellous intelligence. She was very shy, retiring, and I showed her the army hut and I said, 'You know it's summertime. You come and write here,' and later I said, 'Well why not come and live in the hut?' and she did and she stayed about eighteen months. She has become perhaps the most wonderful of all our writers, and she remains my very good friend. I helped Ted Middleton by circulating a petition. This was when Middleton's eyesight was becoming a trouble. I concocted a petition which went all over New Zealand begging the Literary Fund to help him because he wouldn't be able to see. They did help, although I remember some people objected, saying I was mixing up personal and literary grounds.

What do you think has been the best New Zealand novel in the last ten years, and why?

Best New Zealand novel in the last ten years. . . .

Excluding yours.

Ha. Look I don't know—I don't like to deal in this. The great New Zealand novel—it's the same as saying the best. . . . I think it does authors good to hear opinions. Often you can publish something and you might feel that nobody has read it. You don't hear any comment. This is all right. You have to take it whatever happens, but it's nice to hear—not fulsome stuff, not analysis. For instance if I was writing to Maurice Gee I would say it is nice to read somebody who knows how to write a sentence, you see, and I enjoyed reading such and such and so forth. Somebody wrote to me a little while ago and said *Joy of the Worm* was the best New Zealand novel, and I just can't take this at all. There's no best; only good novels. If you have a very good dinner there's nothing to say about it—it is only when the dinner is sort of. . . . I can say plenty about certain writers' books because they so open themselves to comment. There's nothing particular I want to say about Janet's novels because it's just Janet and I'm fond of Janet and I know I so much enjoy her company and I know what a marvellously intelligent sensitive person she is. There's nothing else. There's just this talent she has—in her case probably genius.

How much have you seen the literary public and climate and response in New Zealand change in your thirty or forty years?

There has been these great changes. There was this business which has been knocked back a bit now, about Commonwealth literature. I think to a certain extent the Twayne series is a sort of hangover. It's a little bit out of date already. I think this sort of burst of interest in Commonwealth literature has received a little bit of a setback. It's tied up I think with a general recession, the effect of television, and so on. I remember I wrote to my publisher in London, 'I see that this Commonwealth literature is going to be the coming thing', and then I think I put in brackets 'it looks as if a lot of readers are going to be in for a lot of very dull reading'—I won't say that I include myself on that.

What's to come?

Well, just going on writing I suppose. I'm still interested in people and presumably I'm still interested in this reflection of people on paper.

You've got A Game of Hide and Seek?

Publishers are such extraordinary people. One must just wait and see.

You haven't got anything else specific under way now?

Well I've written the story—'An International Occasion'—and I'm working on another thing about which for once I may be mistaken, I mean as to its length. It is about a good person, rather unusual in that respect, a thoroughly good person without any qualifications whatsoever. And of course you can't sustain a story about a good person for very long. So I have to wait until I remember some material about a wicked person.

I can't agree. What about Fanny Price?

Fanny Price?

In Mansfield Park.

Oh, *Mansfield Park*. I was thinking of Fanny Hill. What a terrible mix-up! Well, yes—Fanny Price . . . it's surely a mark of Austen's genius. I think she brings the novel off, although it's not a very well-proportioned novel. But I don't mind. Fanny Price can be half-witted and Edmund can be even worse, but it's still a great novel. That's Miss Austen's genius which it's folly to analyse too much perhaps.

Landfall, March 1970 (v.24, no.1), pp.4-27; and June 1970 (v.24, no.2), pp.142-60.

TWO NOVELS BY RONALD HUGH MORRIESON: an Appreciation

I

'Herbert had told me on the quiet that he reckoned Uncle Athol had got his teeth from Mr Dabney, the undertaker.'

I recommended *The Scarecrow* to a friend who afterwards commented that he found so much life in the novel it had clearly required no author, having in some miraculous way written itself. I daresay there is a naivety somewhere concealed in this statement; but I have no complaints if it can be taken to mean that 'life' is so very much there in the novel, only because Mr Morrieson's powerfully inventive imagination has worked along hand in glove with his superb gift for story-telling.

In the opening two chapters we are introduced into a world of pubescent childhood: the narrative is first-person, and without any difficulty we accept that all appears as it would to a boy about to enter his teens. Nothing much different from a good deal of New Zealand fiction, you may say. But besides the density, the resonant suggestion of the sentences, there is Mr Morrieson's story-telling skill to reckon with. And within a few pages sufficient hints have been dropped to ensure that this is *not* one of those novels which, once picked up, are (more or less in the immortal words of Ivy Compton-Burnett) impossible *not* to put down again. We meet for example Sam Finn, the local half-wit, and are told by the narrator that he alone knows 'the secret of his disappearance, even the secret of his grave'. But then immediately after that we are told that Sam Finn, along with 'the equally ill-fated Mabel Collinson', tied up with the story though they may be, 'will have to wait their cue'.

Now read on.

And Mr Morrison soon proves himself a perfect showman in the timing of his cues. In chapter three for example, a cunning sleight of hand takes place whereby the boy narrator seems temporarily to become silent (now you hear him, now you don't), to be replaced by (I won't say Mr Morrieson in person), but somebody we may perhaps identify as the boy grown a good many years older, with the author discreetly some distance off in his role as prompt: the prose style temporarily changes too—and all has been designed to introduce middle-aged melodramatic-tragic Hubert Salter, himself too a sleight of hand man, but out of work, whose macabre 'thing' is young girls (but for the perfect satisfaction of the love he makes to them they must die first).

Now read on!

And so with our eyes adhering to the lines of print we turn the pages —but not too rapidly, or we will sometimes miss what Mr Morrieson's prose sometimes conceals. The boy narrator returns, or rather he comes and goes, and the prose style changes accordingly. Will Prudence, the narrator's sister, be killed and raped by the necrophile? And the macabre peak is scaled when it becomes clear to the reader that unknown to anybody in the town (except the luckless and rapidly despatched Sam Finn), the corpse ravisher is secretly at large in the rambling and decayed old premises of a drunken undertaker. As for the comic-macabre, that is crowningly arrived at when two funerals and two corpses become irremediably scrambled owing to the intoxicated condition of the undertaker and his right-hand man. But shot through the novel there is also another kind of comedy, scenes from small town poor-family life—the sort of thing which has come to us in New Zealand partly from Dickens, from Australia, and as much perhaps too from Mark Twain. There is for example Uncle, who helps to paint the house and nearly burns it down with his blow-lamp: and there is Ma, who sometimes reveals herself as another incarnation of Mrs Malaprop:

> On the Thursday Ma said, 'I passed Mrs Quinn in the main street this afternoon and she cut me dead. Just sailed past me like a gallon on the main street.'

'Galleon,' I said.

'Galleying she certainly was', declared Ma. 'With her nose stuck up in the air like an empty cannon in the park. I can hardly bring myself to credit she did not see me, or overhear me speaking to her very politely, and it is plain to me, as a consequence of being humiliated like this on the main street, that she considers herself a cut above the likes of us. And who would she have been, I ask yuh, before she trapped into matrimony this Quin with all his money, but plain Lizzie Haywood, whose father as near as dammit went to jail for stealing a horse? Next time I come across that stuck-up piece of goods I'll let her know in no uncertain manner that, much as she would like to forget her humble early oranges, other memories around Klynham are not so short, even if they are wedded to toilers and junk collectors.'

II

In *Came a Hot Friday,* there is much to remind readers of *The Scarecrow*: but among a number of differences, there is the important one that whereas the inter-related (and therefore much complicated) worlds of children and adults are crucially important in the first-published novel, there is no such complication in the second (although there is in fact one minor exception which I need not mention here).

I think it is probably the presence and importance of the children in *The Scarecrow* (they see their 'horror' films at the town cinema, and it is the children, in particular the narrator, who first become aware that a kind of complementary 'real life horror' is very much alive in the community), that induces us to see the novel as a kind of modern 'Gothic' affair. But it seems to me that *Came a Hot Friday* is best appreciated if we see it all happening within a framework which derives from a clear simple and perhaps 'Classical' idea.

The novel begins with a fire, the work of a young man who burns down a decayed town building. He has been bribed into setting the place on fire by the owner of the property, whose aim it is to collect the fire-insurance; and although the owner knows that an upstairs room is occupied by an old man, he conceals this knowledge from the young arsonist he employs. At the end of the book there is another burning, the building destroyed on this occasion being a woolshed used as a resort for drinking, and crown and anchor; and for this fire, in which the fraudulent collector of insurance is himself destroyed, the duped young man is partly responsible.

Unlike *The Scarecrow* however, it is not the framework or scheme of the story which is important: in that novel the melodrama is shot right through the story, and should not be mistaken for a flaw when it is in fact a device. In the second novel the melodrama is largely confined to the beginning and the end, it is comparatively speaking unimportant, and what matters in between is a series of extraordinarily exciting scenes of demoniac energy. Everybody is drinking betting cheating whoring; or if not, hoping to. And all these activities depend on powerful cars which cover country roads at suicidal speed. There are bashings too. And at the centre of it all is Wesley Pennington, perhaps Mr Morrieson's most notable achievement in character-creation:

> 'They reckon there's a life hereafter . . . But, berrrother, it'll have to be good to beat this one.'

Wes is young, an accomplished con-man with charming manners and never-failing comeback. But besides being the most outstanding among the demons of energy he is notably intelligent, a young man who appears to have consciously decided that within the framework of the only environment in his experience, the only sensible thing to do is to accept cheerfully the plain fact of his own damnation. And all is brilliantly explicated by Mr Morrieson's repeated use of a very appropriate symbol. A travelling salesman has been around the district selling prints of a picture of a white horse and a black horse in a terrible storm; and these, hanging on at least half a dozen walls, to confront the characters in states ranging from euphoria to depressive mania, are from time to time fatalistically read as terrifying visible signs of the crises which afflict them.

III

Instead of attempting to write detailed expositions of these two novels, I have intended more a few suggestive notes which I hope may indicate that Mr Morrieson's work deserves much more attention than I suspect it has so far received. One can only guess at reasons for an apparent neglect. That the raw material of the two books closely resembles what is perennially to be found in the popular press is not to be denied. But then Mr Morrieson from the point of view of literature is a writer of such distinction, one can perhaps imagine that the explosive character of his work is, for the non-literary reader, somewhat obscured by its assured and very skilful handling. Perhaps it all adds up to another comment on the present-day neglect, comparatively speaking, of the writer who endeavours by his craft to extract some sort of meaning from the chaos of popular 'documentary'. We hear sometimes of somebody who intends a march on Parliament in order to emphasize some fact of human nature or human society. It would be a comic sign of health in the community (not to mention an immense compliment to Mr Morrieson, and his skill in revealing to us much about the inner nature of human life in our country), if Parliament were to march upon him and his home town.

In matters of this kind all depends upon *quality*—upon writing skill, and the gifts of mind and heart upon which it depends. In Mr Morrieson's case there is no doubt that quality is abundantly there.

Landfall, June 1971 (v.25, no.2), pp.133-7. This essay was accompanied by one by C. K. Stead and discusses the two novels of Morrieson's then published: *The Scarecrow* (1963) and *Came a Hot Friday* (1964).

27

R. A. K. MASON

I knew nothing about and never met Ron Mason until the early thirties. But not long before he died, it interested the pair of us to discover we must have come uncommonly close to meeting in childhood: there were probably occasions when we could have seen each other by looking over a Mt Eden garden wall of volcanic rock. He and his people, driving I think in a gig, would have been visiting from Penrose; and in the next street, up from the Waikato, I would be staying with my grandparents.

When I knew him a little during slump days he wanted (or appeared to want), to be known as a figure in Left politics. I remember his telling me he would find it impossible to stand up in public and defend the poetry he had written.

And that poetry?

I don't remember ever seeing *The Beggar* until the year 1938, when he gave me a copy. But this was a year or two after I had read *No New Thing*: a copy was the inestimable gift of Bob Lowry: and the poems affected me somewhat in the manner of an electric shock: if ever I experienced a poetical 'confrontation' this was surely it. I had not long previously discovered Auden, and although I had early become addicted to reading 'the poets', Chaucer, Spenser, and so on, thought I was clear in my mind that if you *wrote* poetry, Auden was the poet you would naturally look to for a line on the kind you would write.

What on earth then was I to think of Mason? He was contemporary, but clearly he also belonged among 'the poets'; I could recognize that he had achieved results which were 'traditional' yet hadn't turned out quite like those of T. S. Eliot. But I wanted some independent confirmation. So having lately begun a correspondence with Mr William Plomer, I sent him my copy of *No New Thing*, and was much pleased by his reaction. It also pleased me that Mr Plomer was further primed for the article, 'Some Books from New Zealand', which he wrote in *Folios of New Writing*, and which was afterwards reprinted in *Penguin New Writing* (No. 17).

But after *No New Thing* there were so few new poems. And I saw almost nothing of the poet, who was busy with trade union affairs, and editing Left newspapers. During the war, like so many of us who were of the Left, and despite a Labour Government, he was sometimes on the receiving end of police inquiries.

It was not until he returned to Auckland after his tenure of the Burns fellowship that I saw much of him, and along with Colin McCahon and Christopher Cathcart became involved in endeavours to produce his play about the Otago settlers. At first it looked as though the university might help, and there was even talk of an *ad hoc* organization for the purpose. But all most disappointingly came to nothing. Later Mr Austin of N.Z.B.C. became interested, and a radio version was made: but here again there was disappointment because the production, despite its merits, was programmed for Christmas or New Year (I forget which), I would think not a propitious time for listeners who could have been interested. The poet, on holiday somewhere on the Coromandel Peninsula, semi-heard his play on a transistor. I have never heard of another broadcast.

I remember two anecdotes, one that emphasizes the dimension of his Latin scholarship; and the other touching on that same scholarship, but also pointing to the dignity and poise of his last years when he had become very stout.

Late one evening I was in a state of indignation with myself for never in a lifetime having managed to elucidate the *Davus sum* of Stanza 13 Canto XIII, Byron's *Don Juan*. Who was Davus? I did not know. I hurried round to Ron's to ask his assistance. He got up and took from his shelves a decrepit much annotated copy of Terence's *Andria*, and showed me (Act 1 Scene 2) *Davus Sum, non Oedipus*—the point being that it was no good asking a slave to solve the riddle of the Sphinx.

And on the other occasion Ron was out walking with an Evangelical friend, who took it upon herself to reproach him for neglecting his health, and so allowing himself to put on too much weight. 'You should remember,' she said, 'that our bodies are the temples of the Holy Ghost, and we have a duty to keep them in good repair.' For some time and distance the poet was silent. Then while he paused for breath he said, 'I think the bats have got into my temple.'

And about that Mt Eden garden wall. What the eye doesn't see, the heart won't—but I missed seeing the little boy, two years younger than I was, who in another twelve years or so would be writing verse which does not suffer if placed alongside some of the finest in our language.

Landfall, September 1971 (v.25, no.3), pp.239-41. Sargeson's note was one of nine tributes in *Landfall* after Mason's death in 1971.

28

FRANK S. ANTHONY

In the late thirties it would delight me to read in *The Controller* (the quarterly paper of the Auckland Transport Club), contributions by a Tramways Motorman who signed himself B. Mugg. I quote from 'Horse-laugh', an account of a day at the races.

> I followed along with the crowd, which seemed to scatter in every direction, so seeing a gate I spoke to the man in charge.
> 'Is this where I go in?'
> 'This is the way to the bird-cage,' said the man.
> 'Bird-cage? I want to go to the race-course.'
> 'Are you a trainer?' he asked.
> 'Well, I suppose you could call me that,' I said modestly. 'Last year I trained the Senior Girls' Bible Class for the scripture examination, and although I say it myself, they jumped like birds.'

And again:

> 'How much are the tickets on Bells of Bow?' I asked the man in the tote.
> 'They *should* give them away for nothing,' he said, 'but at the moment they are ten shillings.'
> 'What, ten? Haven't you any cheaper ones?'
> 'Not till after the race, then they'll be absolutely *thrown* away.'

Well, I wrote a complimentary note to this rare Motorman, but with the years he seemed to disappear from literary view.

Somewhere about the same time I was very pleased to be given a book of literary sketches called *Me and Gus*. One of the printers of the Farmers' Union paper which Rex Fairburn edited, had secured himself a job on the *Hawera Star,* and had there worked on the collection of Frank Anthony's sketches put together and brought out by the author's mother in 1938. The printer had thought Fairburn could be interested. And all this was eleven years after Anthony had died 'amongst strangers' in a village boarding-house on the English Channel coast. That year had been 1927, the month January, and this factual matter is to me interesting and touching, for the reason that on the one occasion in a lifetime of my being out of New Zealand I landed in England in April of the same year. The name of Frank Sheldon Anthony was at the time and for nearly a decade afterwards completely unknown to me, a misfortune which I regret: a few of Anthony's stories were first published in 1923 and 1924, and how I missed appearances in the *Auckland Weekly News* I can't imagine, for in my time of youth I had been devoted to that paper. I have to assume that either my devotion had by that time worn thin and I had ceased to read the paper; or else I was not quite ready to be aware of and appreciate the good writing and reading that might be discovered in the use of the New Zealand vernacular. Also I should say that a year or two before *Me and Gus* (in 1938), I *had* become familiar with the author's name: from the year 1936 there was on the shelves of the Auckland Public Library a copy of *Follow the Call*—a love story, and many many times I leaned against the shelves and turned over the pages, but I never took the book home: and I can remember comparing with Mr Mugg: 'love' was no part of his business, his line was 'bawdy' ('the lady in the green hat with the feather in the other end will pay my fare, conductor'), and gossip had it that hundreds of women readers of *The Controller* lickerishly awaited the appearance of each quarterly number: by contrast Anthony appeared incredibly innocent.

But it is high time to forget about myself: the purpose of this notice is to recommend the name and work of Frank S. Anthony.

For me there has never been a moment's doubt about *Me and Gus,* and it used to delight me that Fairburn agreed. This man had known what he was doing with New Zealand language, his ear couldn't be faulted, neither could his eye. A comic ruralist who had been dead for a generation, he had done excellently everything he set out to do: all was authentic and genuine and no question: and one's final satisfaction was the truth of the underlying bitter struggle of so many soldiers returned from World War I, who were to experience the disillusion of being 'helped' by the Massey Government on to back-breaking marginal land.

And so much for *Me and Gus*—except to say that *Gus Tomlins,* the novel that the sketches were finally expanded into, unlikely as it may sound, does not suffer from being a more premeditated, more literary, work. And who can begin to explain the man's energy and industry? It seems that although he wrote much in childhood, his mature work was not seriously worked at until he had only four to five more years left him.

As for *Follow the Call,* for the first time reading in this fine edition the author's original text, I have changed my mind. The simple and touching genuineness of the story carries it through, and no trouble at all. But surely it is as well for the reader to be wary of supposing that he is reading much of the author's personal story. Nothing, I imagine, could be further from the 'truth'. And for confirmation the reader has only to refer to the astonishing list of long and short items in the Bibliography to be found in the last few pages of both books. Remember that Anthony was born at the end of 1891, near Gisborne: the family shortly afterwards removed to Taranaki, and he remained almost totally a country boy until 1909, when he became first a merchant service sailor, and afterwards served with the Navy in World War I until 1917. By that time he was familiar with many seas and many lands. It would appear that he did not begin to write seriously for publication until 1922, when he had also committed himself to his endeavour to break in the Taranaki stump farm: also he was probably beginning to suffer from tuberculosis. And yet by 1927 when he died he had to his credit that formidable list of literary items mostly never published in his lifetime: apart from work now published there remains a host of items including several novels; much of this material is in the form of sea stories—and perhaps it is mainly on their account that I find myself wanting to mark up a slight query against the marvellous scholarly and editorial work of Terry Sturm, very ably assisted by Bill Pearson. Let me put it this way: it seems to me that readers may be too ready to suppose from these two books that Anthony was transcribing immediate experience. I suggest that instead he was concentrating into his pages country experience reaching far back into the time of his childhood. What then might we perhaps learn of his personal story if we could read his unpublished sea stories and novels? Some of the titles are teasers, *Spending the Pay-Day, Lofty's Winger, The Captain's Daughter.*

After all, Terry Sturm informs us that Anthony's sea stories 'are competently written, losing nothing by comparison, say, with W. W. Jacobs, they lack the memorable qualities of the characters he created in his comedies of New Zealand rural life'. But W. W. Jacobs? I much enjoyed reading him as a boy, but have not read him since. I notice however that he makes the *Oxford Companion to Eng. Lit.* By inference then, Anthony's sea stories should be published—as literature for our pleasure and instruction?

Review in *Islands*, Winter 1977 (v.6, no.2), pp.201-3, under the title 'More Please'. The two volumes of Anthony's under discussion, both edited by Terry Sturm, were *Follow the Call* and *Dave Baird*; and *Gus Tomlins* and *Me and Gus*.

29

RODERICK FINLAYSON: Tidal Creek

How very grateful I am to have this book again! When it was first published in Australia in 1948 Oliver Duff asked me for a review in the
Listener—and it was my immediate pleasure to meet Uncle Ted, who on
his few untidy acres of coastal land conformed only to his own personal
notions about a good sort of life to live. He came right along my own
street—and I mean that literally! Because 1948?—well, a time when the
awful consequences of the late world war were not all that much understood, nor even manifest: and despite my living only half an hour's bus-
and-ferry travel from Auckland city centre, I was still amazingly located
only a few yards from a tidal creek of my own. My street turned off the
main North Shore Road certainly, but down at the far end there was no
exit: instead a great much-decayed farm gate. Certainly there was no
farm, not any more, and not for many years: instead a wilderness of
giant solanum (which children called 'the tobacco tree'), fern and
teatree, grass in patches, and some very ancient pohutukawa where the
land dropped down twenty feet or more to a foreshore of mangroves and
mud.

It goes without saying that over many years I had become very
familiar with this abandoned farmland. I had soon discovered the
remains of a brick chimney, and an asphalt walk which had served as
flooring for the homestead verandah: and after co-opting a friend with a
talent for library-research I more or less had the story. All the land in

my area had been acquired from the Maori chief Patuone by Governor Grey, who appears to have made much of it over to a lady-friend, a Mrs Napper. Napper eventually became Napier, and so the property had over many decades become the great Napier farm. And all was well confirmed when I worked my own and neighbouring soils, and dug up countless metal bits and pieces which derived from every kind of farm implement.

But about my honorary neighbourhood uncle. He lived in the next street and we backed on to one another, or very nearly; and an admirable arrangement for short-cuts and mutual borrowings of garden tools. Much the older, and a short slight man, he was uncommonly tough and wiry. All his life he had dairy-farmed in the Waikato—and one could well imagine that by all the unwritten rules the remainder of his life would now be devoted to 'pottering'. But nothing of the kind: his energy was hardly to be believed, and in all our joint activities, and despite my endeavours to keep up, I was forever tagging along behind. According to the season we could be felling a large pine tree to cut up for winter firewood, or maybe collecting great quantities of cocksfoot grass to dry out thoroughly before spreading a large tent-fly on which we flailed out the seed. And whatever the activity he would be clad consistently in tweedy trousers and a heavy woollen singlet (a waistcoat added in winter), while up on top summer or winter and no matter what the job, he wore for hat a black hard knocker. I can think of no more extraordinary human spectacle than the sight of him on a day of summer's heat most expertly wielding his double-pieced flail, while he furiously puffed and blew without ever removing his hat to wipe the sweat—no, nor desisting until he was through with the job.

Not however that his devotion to work was an excluding absolute. Plainly he retained a keen sense of hearing, and one especially apt for outdoor noises. There was a marvellous spring morning when we were away beyond the old far gate cutting an ample supply of teatree stakes for our tomatoes, and from time to time I was puzzled to hear repeated bird calls which I couldn't identify. At last I asked, did he hear that bird? He said immediately that it was a shining cuckoo—which I questioned, although admitting a resemblance. He dropped his slasher, saying we would go and see—and so we did very cautiously. And it proved to be the one time in my life I saw a monstrous great cuckoo chick flapping its wings while it demanded to be fed by a pair of hard-working gray-warblers: their nest was not so much occupied as overflowed by the interloping tenant. Our work was forgotten, we sat and watched and listened.

I remember that what I thought so extraordinary was that we had to walk on only a few yards—and there, across mudflats and mangroves, across the deep water of the inner Harbour, a view of central Auckland city was marvellously clear and near.

I must now however concede that this honorary uncle of mine did not adequately compare with the homespun ecological philosopher that Roderick Finlayson so very engagingly depicts. His thoughts about this and that when he communicated them were always Bible-derived; and clearly he was an Old Testament man who could readily relate to patriarchal characters who had known how to be of some practical use in the world. Usually too each name was prefixed by 'old'. Who was there who did not know about old Adam, and old Noah?—and the latter was especially to be valued as the right man for a crisis: well, without his boat-building abilities (and just think what the necessary carpenter's tools must have been like in those old days!) well, where would there have been any of us to know the story in these latter and probably last days?

For me it was all so very touching and entertaining. There was never a moment's boredom, nor did it irk me when I was sometimes a target for the mild mischief which was part of the old man's nature. There was another spring occasion when we had concluded from the sounds of things that two kingfishers were feeding their young ones: at last we were able to pinpoint the nest which was a high-up hole in the bank above the mud, although totally obscured from view by a convoluted mass of pohutukawa, foliage timber and roots. I said I had never had a sight of a kingfisher's nest, nor any young—and my companion encouraged me. Why not climb up the bank and have a close look? He was daring me, and I did have a look—but only just, and for less than a second, and I wished I had avoided even that. The parent birds attacked, and the haste of my retreat ended in my falling into the mud, besides some nasty scratches inflicted by the incredible tangle of timber and roots.

Looking back now it seems that for years I was this man's workmate, accompanying him sometimes for miles in his old battered car to some roadside where there was an excellent stand of precious cocksfoot. There was also a great Chinese market garden where he would sometimes stop to bargain for an out-of-season cabbage; and on one of these occasions it astonished me to recognize one of the Chinese as the much younger man I would often watch at his work years ago in the Waikato: he would be on the other side of a fence when I was on my way to school. I was now touched to see him that much older, yet the same man working skilfully still at his job of life-work.

It was perhaps as well for my own job of life-work, my writing, when my neighbour for no reason that I ever knew, decided to sell his property and shift himself to a house on the far side of the city. I have forgotten to mention that he had a wife, but I think I saw her only once. A huge woman, I think she must have suffered some kind of illness: it seemed that she spent most of her time in bed. Besides all else her husband cooked shook the mats and swept: there were also from time to time great washes which I would help him hang on the line when we were in a hurry to get cracking.

After what seems to me now a long time he wrote me a friendly note which informed me that he had 'lost' the wife (and a Bible quotation disposed of any doubts I might have had in the matter). And it was so far as I can remember almost no time when I was over in the city and in great haste to keep an appointment with an eye doctor, that I met him in Queen Street. I thought he looked more or less the same as usual—he wore the hard knocker of course, although accompanied by a white shirt a tie and a jacket. And he was using a stick. He informed me that he had lately married again; and after complimenting him I was about to explain about my hurry when he asked me if I would accompany him to a public convenience: it seemed he had an appointment more pressing than my own—but there was these days the problem of some awkward buttons which he couldn't quite manage. Fortunately there was a neighbouring place where I knew the attendant, a humane and obliging man. We hurried, and immediately the urgencies were understood I excused myself.

I never again saw my friend, my own honorary uncle: but now at long last I have said my few words about him. It should however go without saying that they don't for a moment compare with what Roderick Finlayson has written magnificently about his own superb and ever-enduring Uncle Ted.

I do however prefer to say nothing at all about the motor-way, the local horror that now bridges my own tidal creek.

And by the way, the book is beautifully brought out by Auckland University/Oxford publishing, and is most excellently introduced by Dennis McEldowney.

Book review of a reprint of *Tidal Creek* in *Islands*, November 1979 (v.7, no.5), pp.550-3, under the title 'To Every Man His Own Uncle Ted'.

30

OWEN MARSHALL: Supper Waltz Wilson

Mr Marshall's name first became known to me when the title-story of his book appeared in the *Listener*; but strangely, I was not much prepared for the powerful impact the book has had on me.

I see now that the author is remarkable for achieving his success not by any striking economy of language (which is often thought to be the *sine qua non* of short story writing)—on the contrary by creating a verbal density which according to all the rules could well play havoc with any clear narrative line.

But it appears that no hard and fast line of approach to Mr Marshall will do. In story after story he achieves his results when the reader is confronted by an accumulation of abrupt items of information without (for me, that is to say), much close and enriching relevance to what would appear to be the matter in hand. Not however that Mr Marshall's detail is ever *totally* irrelevant: far from it: because it is only when we have finished reading any given story that we understand that besides a story in the more usual sense, we have experienced an environment which has mysteriously become a kind of character in its own right.

And perhaps I can make my meaning clearer if I exaggerate and say that while reading I was now and then prompted to begin counting the number of occasions when it appeared to be the author's purpose to introduce another motor-vehicle—about the working parts of which I was provided with a good many apposite items of information. And perhaps it is to the point if I say that living as I do on a modern suburban road which is not, and never has been, a motorway (although virtually all motorists have long since converted themselves to the belief that in fact it is), I have never reconciled myself to the daily undignified scramble which has so far enabled me to stay alive.

Well anyhow, there it is. As fine a book of stories as this country is likely to see this year the next or the one after—and so on. And because of the density, one that will stand close re-reading for many years to come. One of my favourites is 'Promise Bluff', about a man who vowed to create some kind of substantial and permanent memorial to a war-cobber casualty—and at last succeeded despite a mysterious nagging soreness which never ceased to plague him in his chest and left arm.

Also, it may sound unkind, but I should, I think, inform the reader that in my view easily the finest story Mr Marshall has so far published does not figure in this handsome Pegasus edition. No, it appeared in *Islands* 28 (March 1980), and is entitled 'Thinking of Bagheera'. It is about the destruction of a cat. And here, for a change, environmental detail is severely cut. All is centred upon a lovely living creature brought into fatal relation with a boy and the family he belongs to. I find it hard to imagine anyone's arriving at the conclusion of this story without becoming aware of a tear of sensibility upon his cheek.

Review in *Islands*, October 1980 (v.8, no.3), p.284, under the title 'Fine Stories'. The additional story mentioned, 'Thinking of Bagheera', was included in Owen Marshall's second collection, *The Master of Big Jingles* (1982).

BIBLIOGRAPHY

This bibliography aims to list Sargeson's autobiographical writings and contributions to journals, and some interviews with him. Appendices note his contributions to radio and to newspapers. It includes letters to editors which bear on Sargeson's main concerns. Items identified by asterisks are included in this book.

Sargeson contributed to *Tomorrow*, the *New Zealand Listener*, and *Parsons Packet* under pseudonyms and abbreviations, as well as under his full name. Pieces published under such bylines are so identified in this bibliography.

A fuller version of this bibliography (fuller in annotation and cross-reference) is deposited with the National Library of New Zealand under the title *Frank Sargeson's Critical and Autobiographical Writings: an Annotated Bibliography* (Wellington, Library School, 1977).

THE THREE VOLUMES OF MEMOIRS

1 *Once is Enough: a Memoir*. Wellington, Reed, 1973. [London, Martin Brian and O'Keeffe, 1973.]

2 *More than Enough: a Memoir*. Wellington, Reed, 1975. [London, Martin Brian and O'Keefe, 1975.]

3 *Never Enough! Places and People Mostly*. Wellington, Reed, 1977. [London, Martin Brian and O'Keeffe, 1977.]

[*Note*: The three volumes of memoirs have been collected into one volume under the title *Sargeson* (Auckland, Penguin, 1981).]

CONTRIBUTIONS TO JOURNALS AND BOOKS

4 [Letter to editor.] *Tomorrow*, 9 October 1935 (v.1, no.50), p.24. Sargeson justifies the style and manner of his early sketches, which had been criticized by a correspondent (*Tomorrow*, 18 September 1935, v.1, no.47, p.24).

*5 'Sherwood Anderson'. *Tomorrow*, 6 November 1935 (v.2, no.2), pp.14-15.

6 [Sarge.] 'Anomaly'. *Tomorrow*, 13 November 1935 (v.2, no.3), p.5. A brief satirical poem on political exploitation.

7 [F.F.S.] [Review] *Corydon*, by André Gide. *Tomorrow*, 20 November 1935 (v.2, no.4), pp.20-21. A note on Gide's then untranslated book on homosexuality.

8 [Sarge.] 'Love Among the Artists'. *Tomorrow*, 29 January 1936 (v.2, no.12), p.12. A satirical paragraph on Osbert Sitwell.

9 [S.] 'Blood-brotherhood'. *Tomorrow*, 5 February 1936 (v.2, no.13), pp.23-24. A paragraph on the anthropological origins of Hitler's doctrine of blood-brotherhood.

10 [Sarge.] 'Bedtime Story'. *Tomorrow*, 2 September 1936 (v.2, no.30), pp.30-31. An ironic glance at the current craze for Shirley Temple.

11 [S.] [Review.] *Waiting for Lefty*, by Clifford Odets, produced by Arnold Goodwin for the Auckland W.E.A. *Tomorrow*, 11 November 1936 (v.3, no.1), p.21.

12 [Sarge.] 'O Noble New Zealand Herald'. *Tomorrow*, 28 April 1937 (v.3, no.13), p.390. Two quotations from the *New Zealand Herald* ridiculed.

13 'Counsel'. *Tomorrow*, 12 May 1937 (v.3, no.14), p.419. A satirical poem on the banning of poultry from the inner part of Rotorua to stop the crowing of roosters disturbing the sleep of hotel guests. The poem is quoted and discussed in *More than Enough* (pp.88-89) where Sargeson recounts a discussion of it with D'Arcy Cresswell.

*14 'Mr Rhodes' Heroic Novelists'. *Tomorrow*, 4 August 1937 (v.3, no.20), pp. 632-3.

15 'Just a Few Hot-points'. *Tomorrow*, 18 August 1937 (v.3, no.21), pp.656-8. A series of passing notes on the current Springbok tour, taxis, and religion.

16 'A New Zealand Anthology. I: Horse Lords'. *Tomorrow*, 27 October 1937 (v.3, no.26), pp.822-3. The first in a series of five parodies of the style of popular fiction. The series aims to gather 'examples of prose that will give readers some idea of the merits of some of our most distinguished fiction writers'. This first example parodies *Sheep Kings*, by Joyce West.

17 'A New Zealand Anthology. II: Spur of the Moment'. *Tomorrow*, 24 November 1937 (v.4, no.2), pp.55-56. Parody of Alan Mulgan's *Spur of Morning*.

18 'A New Zealand Anthology. III: The Teeny Land'. *Tomorrow*, 8 December 1937 (v.4, no.3), pp.83-84. Parody of *The Little Country*, by John Guthrie.

19 'A New Zealand Anthology. IV: Ticket to Heaven: or, cling to your cheque'. *Tomorrow*, 5 January 1938 (v.4, no.5), pp.144-5. Parody of *Passport to Hell*, by Robin Hyde.

20 'A New Zealand Anthology. V: Hollyhocks and Hailstones: and Egbert the Blade'. *Tomorrow*, 19 January 1938 (v.4, no.6), pp.185-6. Parodies of *Thistledown and Thunder* and *Albert the Good*, both by Hector Bolitho.

*21 'Mr Fairburn and the Modern World'. *Tomorrow*, 22 June 1938 (v.4, no.17), pp.536-7.

22 [Review.] *Judgement Day*, by Elmer Rice, produced by the People's Theatre, Auckland. *Tomorrow*, 6 July 1938 (v.4, no.18), pp.566-7.

23 'Notes by the Way'. *Tomorrow*, 3 August 1938 (v.4, no.20), pp.625-7. A series of more or less connected ruminations on success, time, the protestant ethic, and the welfare state.

24 [S.] 'Two Sketches for a People's Theatre. I: Crisis in Czecho-Slovakia'. *Tomorrow*, 14 September 1938 (v.4, no.23), pp.728-30. The first of two dramatic sketches satirizing contemporary political events and attitudes: a political farce parodying Hitler and Chamberlain.

25 [S.] 'Two Sketches for a People's Theatre. II: Women in Politics'. *Tomorrow*, 28 September 1938 (v.4, no.24), pp.757-8. A street conversation between two vacant women.

26 [S.] 'Notes by the Way' [includes a review of *The Insect Play*, by Karel Capek, produced by Arnold Goodwin for the Auckland W.E.A.]. *Tomorrow*, 7 December 1938 (v.5, no.3), pp.72-74. Sargeson's strictures were attacked in a letter by the play's producer, Arnold Goodwin (21 December 1938, v.5, no.4, p.127), to which Sargeson replied (5 January 1939, v.5, no.5, p.160).

27 [A Radical Man About Town.] 'This Charming Country: a Monthly Causerie'. *Tomorrow*, 15 March 1939 (v.5, no.10), pp.302-3. This is the first of thirteen columns appearing under this pseudonym and title and running until March 1940. The columns consist of a series of ironic paragraphs commenting on current social and political affairs.

28 [A Radical Man About Town.] 'This Charming Country: a Monthly Causerie'. *Tomorrow*, 12 April 1939 (v.5, no.12), pp.364-5.

29 [Review.] *Falls the Shadow*, by Ian Hamilton, produced by the People's Theatre, Auckland. *Tomorrow*, 12 April 1939 (v.5, no.12), p.378.

30 [F.F.S.] [Review.] *Remembering Things*, by J. H. E. Schroder. *Tomorrow*, 12 April 1939 (v.5, no.12), p.379. A short note on a collection of Schroder's essays.

31 [A Radical Man About Town.] 'This Charming Country: a Monthly Causerie'. *Tomorrow*, 10 May 1939 (v.5, no.14), pp.437-8.

32 [A Radical Man About Town.] 'This Charming Country: a Monthly Causerie'. *Tomorrow*, 7 June 1939 (v.5, no.16), pp.500-1.

33 [A Radical Man About Town.] 'This Charming Country: a Monthly Causerie'. *Tomorrow*, 5 July 1939 (v.5, no.18), pp.564-6.

34 [A Radical Man About Town.] 'This Charming Country: a Monthly Causerie'. *Tomorrow*, 2 August 1939 (v.5, no.20), pp.630-1.

35 [A Radical Man About Town.] 'This Charming Country: a Monthly Causerie'. *Tomorrow*, 30 August 1939 (v.5, no.22), pp.685-7.

36 [A Radical Man About Town.] 'This Charming Country: a Monthly Causerie'. *Tomorrow*, 27 September 1939 (v.5, no.24), pp.761-2.

37 [A Radical Man About Town.] 'This Charming Country: a Monthly Causerie'. *Tomorrow*, 25 October 1939 (v.5, no.26), pp.811-13.

38 [Review.] *Murder in the Cathedral*, by T. S. Eliot, produced by the Department of English of Auckland University College and the Little Theatre Society. *Tomorrow*, 25 October 1939 (v.5, no.26), pp.816-17.

39 [A Radical Man About Town.] 'This Charming Country: a Monthly Causerie'. *Tomorrow*, 22 November 1939 (v.6, no.2), pp.48-49.

40 [A Radical Man About Town.] 'This Charming Country: a Monthly Causerie'. *Tomorrow*, 10 January 1940 (v.6, no.5), pp.142-3.

41 [A Radical Man About Town.] 'This Charming Country: a Monthly Causerie'. *Tomorrow*, 7 February 1940 (v.6, no.7), pp.210-11.

42 [A Radical Man About Town.] 'This Charming Country: a Monthly Causerie'. *Tomorrow*, 6 March 1940 (v.6, no.9), pp.272-3.

43 'Foreword'. *Speaking for Ourselves: Fifteen Stories*, edited by Frank Sargeson. Christchurch, Caxton Press, 1945, p.[7].

44 [Review.] *Drift*, by Peter Cowan. *New Zealand Listener*, 14 September 1945 (v.13, no.325), p.12. A review of a collection of stories by an Australian writer.

45 [Review.] *Unwilling Guests*, by J. D. Gerard; *Corinth and All That*, by Fred Woollams; and *They Will Arise*, by Martyn Uren. *New Zealand Listener*, 21 December 1945 (v.14, no.339), p.24. The first two books are war memoirs by New Zealanders, the third a novel about 'a New Zealand soldier who gets left behind in Greece and the Greek girl he gets in tow with'.

46 [Interview.] 'Pig Islanders into French'. *New Zealand Listener*, 20 September 1946 (v.15, no.378), pp.16-17. A brief and somewhat mannered interview with Sargeson by 'J.' (Jean Stevenson, now Jean Bertram) on the publication of the French translation of *That Summer*. Sargeson comments on some of the details of the translation, and on how the book came to be published. 'The interesting thing is . . . that it is a translation of such a *colloquial* book—well, a book written in real Pig Island language. And that they've made such a good job of it.'

*47 [Review.] *The Big Game and Other Stories*, by A. P. Gaskell. *Landfall*, March 1947 (v.1, no.1), pp.68-70.

48 'The Feminine Tradition: a Talk about Katherine Mansfield' ['first broadcast in the 1YA session "Mainly about Books" on July 28']. *New Zealand Listener*, 6 August 1948 (v.19, no.476), pp.10-12.

49 [Review.] *The Novel in Our Time*, by Alex Comfort. *New Zealand Listener*, 22 October 1948 (v.19, no.487), p.20.

50 [Review.] *The Tale of a Tub* and *The Battle of the Books*, by Jonathan Swift. *New Zealand Listener*, 10 December 1948 (v.20, no.494), p.15.

51 [Review.] *The Romantic Comedy*, by D. G. James. *New Zealand Listener*, 31 December 1948 (v.20, no.497), p.14.

52 [F.S.] [Review.] *An Atomic Phantasy*, by Karel Capek. *New Zealand Listener*, 4 March 1949 (v.20, no.506), p.15.

53 [Review.] *Writers on Writing*, selected and introduced by Walter Allen. *New Zealand Listener*, 11 March 1949 (v.20, no.507), p.15.

*54 [Review.] *The Fifth Child*, by James Courage. *Landfall*, March 1949 (v.3, no.1), pp.72-73.

55 [Review.] *Christ Stopped at Eboli*, by Carlo Levi. *New Zealand Listener*, 1 April 1949 (v.20, no.510), pp.10-11.

56 [Review.] *Why Do I Write?*, an exchange of views between Elizabeth Bowen, Grahame Greene, V. S. Pritchett. *Parsons Packet*, April-May 1949 [no.3], p.9.

*57 [Review.] *Roads from Home*, by Dan Davin. *New Zealand Listener*, 10 June 1949 (v.21, no.520), pp.17-18.

*58 [Review.] *Tidal Creek*, by Roderick Finlayson. *New Zealand Listener*, 22 July 1949 (v.21, no.526), p.18.

59 [Review.] *The Ideas and Beliefs of the Victorians: a Series of Talks on the B.B.C. Third Programme. New Zealand Listener*, 12 August 1949 (v.21, no.529), p.14.

60 [Review.] *The Huntsman in His Career*, by Erik de Mauny. *New Zealand Listener*, 16 September 1949 (v.21, no.534), pp.12-13.

61 [F.S.] [Review.] *First View: Stories of Children*, selected and with a foreword by G. F. Green. *New Zealand Listener*, 28 July 1950 (v.23, no.579), p.12.

62 [F.S.] 'Radio Review'. *New Zealand Listener*, 4 August 1950 (v.23, no.580), p.10. The first of Sargeson's three contributions to this regular *New Zealand Listener* column.

63 [F.S.] [Review.] *The Man from the Tunnel*, by Theodora Benson. *New Zealand Listener*, 4 August 1950 (v.23, no.580), p.17.

64 [F.S.] 'Radio Review'. *New Zealand Listener*, 25 August 1950 (v.23, no.583), p.11.

65 [F.S.] [Review.] *The Spring of Love*, by Charles Mergendahl. *New Zealand Listener*, 25 August 1950 (v.23, no.583), p.16. A note of an apparently very bad novel dealing with the wartime romance of an American soldier in New Zealand.

*66 [Review.] *Robbery under Arms*, by Rolf Boldrewood. *Landfall*, September 1950 (v.4, no.3), pp.262-5.

67 [F.S.] 'Radio Review'. *New Zealand Listener*, 6 October 1950 (v.23, no.589), p.10.

68 [F.S.] [Review.] *The Lottery*, by Shirley Jackson. *New Zealand Listener*, 3 November 1950 (v.23, no.593), p.15.

69 'Up Onto the Roof and Down Again (1)'. *Landfall*, December 1950 (v.4, no.4), pp.282-8. This is the first of the four parts of 'Up Onto the Roof and

Down Again; printed in *Landfall* in 1950 and 1951. The whole forms the first section of *Once is Enough* (item 1).

*70 [Review.] *Portrait of a Genius, But . . .*, by Richard Aldington. *Landfall*, December 1950 (v.4, no.4), pp.357-61.

71 'Up Onto the Roof and Down Again (2)'. *Landfall*, March 1951 (v.5, no.1), pp.8-23. This item corresponds to pp.15-29 of *Once is Enough*. The recipe for Spanish rice contained in it drew a request for further details from a *Landfall* reader, whom Sargeson obliged (June 1951, v.5, no.2, p.157).

72 'Up Onto the Roof and Down Again (3)'. *Landfall*, June 1951 (v.5, no.2), pp.104-14. This item corresponds to pp.30-42 of *Once is Enough*.

*73 [Review.] *New Zealand Farm and Station Verse 1850-1890*, collated by A. E. Woodhouse. *Landfall*, September 1951 (v.5, no.3), pp.233-5.

74 'Up Onto the Roof and Down Again (4)'. *Landfall*, December 1951 (v.5, no.4), pp.245-50. This item corresponds to pp.42-48 of *Once is Enough*.

*75 [Review.] *The Lagoon and Other Stories*, by Janet Frame. *New Zealand Listener*, 18 April 1952 (v.26, no.667), pp.12-13.

76 [F.S.] [Review.] *Short Stories from the New Yorker*; *Adventurers Please Abstain*, by Monica Stirling; *The Brazen Bull*, by Gerald Kersh; *The Kind and the Foolish*, by Laurence Housman. *New Zealand Listener*, 31 October 1952 (v.27, no.695), p.13.

77 'The Beginning of This Century: the Arrival of the Films'. *School Journal*, February 1953 (v.47, no.1, part 4), pp.2-7. The first of four articles for the *School Journal*.

78 'The Beginning of the Century: the Arrival of the Motor-Car'. *School Journal*, March 1953 (v.47, no.2, part 4), pp.42-48.

79 'The Beginning of the Century: Sights and Sounds'. *School Journal*, April 1953 (v.47, no.3, part 4), pp.66-72.

80 'The Beginning of the Century: Games'. *School Journal*, June 1953 (v.47, no.5, part 4), pp.114-20.

81 [Letter to editor.] *Landfall*, September 1953 (v.7, no.3), pp.227-8. Sargeson's letter is one of a number which contributed to a discussion of Robert Chapman's essay 'Fiction and the Social Pattern' (*Landfall*, March 1953, v.7, no.1, pp.26-58). Sargeson is specifically commenting on a letter from H. O. Pappe (*Landfall*, June 1953, v.7, no.2, pp.149-51).

*82 [Review.] *The Schooner Came to Atia*, by Roderick Finlayson. *Here and Now*, November-December 1953 (v.4, no.2), p.31.

83 [F.S.] [Review.] *Jane Austen's Novels: a Study in Structure*, by Andrew H. Wright. *New Zealand Listener*, 15 January 1954 (v.30, no.756), pp.10-11.

84 [F.S.] [Review.] *The Stories of Frank O'Connor*. *New Zealand Listener*, 26 March 1954 (v.30, no.766), p.14.

*85 'A Book of Stories' ('From an address to mark the occasion of the recent publication of the World's Classics book of New Zealand stories'). [*New Zealand Short Stories*, edited by D. M. Davin.] *Landfall*, March 1954 (v.8, no.1), pp.22-26.

*86 'What is the Question?' ['Originally delivered as an address to the Otago University Literary Society']. *Here and Now,* March 1954 (v.4, no.4), pp.22-26.

87 [F.S.] [Review.] *Epitaph of a Small Winner,* by Machado de Assis. *Parsons Packet,* July-August 1954 (no.29), p.5.

88 [F.S.] [Review.] *The Adventures of Augie March,* by Saul Bellow. *Parsons Packet,* September-October 1954 (no.30), p.6.

89 [F.S.] [Review.] *The End of an Old Song,* by J. D. Scott. *Parsons Packet,* November-December 1954 (no.31), p.5.

*90 [F.S.] [Review.] *The Young Have Secrets,* by James Courage. *Parsons Packet,* January-February 1955 (no.32), p.11.

91 [F.S.] [Review.] *The Goodly Seed,* by John Wyllie. *Parsons Packet,* May-June 1955 (no.34), p.7.

92 'What is the Literary Situation?' ['Originally broadcast from the National Stations in the programme *Bookshop*']. *Numbers,* June 1955 (v.1, [no.3]), pp.3-4. This brief note suggests that New Zealand should pay more attention (and money) to its writers. Sargeson emphasizes the need for our best writers to remain in the country.

93 [F.S.] [Review.] *Self-Condemned,* by Wyndham Lewis. *Parsons Packet,* July-September 1955 (no.35), p.5.

94 [F.S.] [Review.] *Bonjour Tristesse,* by Françoise Sagan; *Messiah,* by Gore Vidal. *Parsons Packet,* October-December 1955 (no.36), p.4.

*95 'Can a New Zealand Writer Live by His Writing?' *Kiwi,* 1955, pp.13-17.

96 [Review.] *Theatre in Danger: a Correspondence Between Bruce Mason and John Pocock. Landfall,* December 1957 (v.11, no.4), pp.331-4.

97 'D'Arcy Cresswell'. *Landfall,* December 1960 (v.14, no.4), pp.348-51.

98 'Obituary Notice: N.Z.B.S.' *Landfall,* September 1962 (v.16, no.3), pp.283-5.

99 [Review.] *Shepherd's Calendar,* by Oliver Duff; *Hot-Water Sailor,* by Denis Glover. *Landfall,* March 1963 (v.17, no.1), pp.81-84.

*100 'Shakespeare and the Kiwi'. *Landfall,* March 1964 (v.18, no.1), pp.49-54.

101 'Greville Texidor 1902-1964'. *Landfall,* June 1965 (v.19, no.2), pp.135-8. Sargeson provides a much fuller account of the person and the writer in *Never Enough!* (item 3).

102 'Beginnings'. *Landfall,* June 1965 (v.19, no.2), pp.122-9. The substance of this essay has been largely taken over into his first two volumes of memoirs: *Once is Enough* (item 1: pp.114-15, 118-22), and *More than Enough* (item 2: pp.35, 93-95).

*103 'Henry Lawson: Some Notes After Re-Reading'. This essay is based on *The Stories of Henry Lawson,* edited by Cecil Mann. *Landfall,* June 1966 (v.20, no.2), pp. 156-62.

*104 'An Imaginary Conversation: William Yate and Samuel Butler'. *Landfall,* December 1966 (v.20, no.4), pp.349-57.

*105 [Review.] *Overland Muster: Selections from* Overland *1954-1964,* edited by Stephen Murray-Smith. *Landfall,* June 1967 (v.21, no.2), pp.206-7.

*106 'Conversation in a Train: or What Happened to Michael's Boots?' *Landfall,* December 1967 (v.21, no.4), pp.352-61.

107 'The New Zealand Literary Fund'. *Landfall,* September 1969 (v.23, no.3), pp.275-7. Sargeson's is one of seven contributions to a symposium on a report of the working of the New Zealand Literary Fund.

*108 'Conversation with Frank Sargeson' [by Michael Beveridge]. *Landfall,* March 1970 (v.24, no.1), pp.4-27.

*109 'Conversation with Frank Sargeson (2)' [by Michael Beveridge]. *Landfall,* June 1970 (v.24, no.2), pp.142-60.

110 'Henry Lawson: Some Notes After Re-Reading'. *Transition: an Australian Society of Authors Anthology,* selected by Nancy Keesing. Sydney, Angus and Robertson, 1970, pp.105-11. A reprinting of item 103.

*111 'Two Novels by Ronald Hugh Morrieson: an Appreciation'. *Landfall,* June 1971 (v.25, no.2), pp.133-7.

*112 'R. A. K. Mason'. *Landfall,* September 1971 (v.25, no.3), pp.239-41.

113 [Review.] *An Account of New Zealand: and of the Formation and Progress of the Church Missionary Society's Mission in the Northern Island,* by William Yate. [The review is of the 1970 reprint of the 1835 edition, with an introduction by Judith Binney.] *Landfall,* September 1971 (v.25, no.3), pp.299-304.

114 'The Drive'. *Landfall,* December 1971 (v.25, no.4), pp.321-38. This item was subsequently incorporated into the 'Third Class Country' section of *Once is Enough* (item 1), pp.51-69.

115 ['Frank Sargeson']. *Contemporary Authors: a Bio-Bibliographical Guide to Current Authors and Their Works,* edited by Carolyn Riley. Volume 25-28, Michigan, Gale Research Company, 1971, pp.645-6. Sargeson's 'bio-bibliographical' entry in this reference book is accompanied by a brief statement: 'Personal data of no interest to anyone except self and half a dozen friends. But my publishers think my longest book, *Memoirs of a Peon,* is one of the funniest books written anywhere this century. They may be right.'

116 'Henry Lawson: Some Notes After Re-Reading'. *Henry Lawson Criticism 1894-1971,* edited with introduction and bibliography by Colin Roderick. [Sydney], Angus and Robertson, [1972], pp.420-6. A reprinting of item 103.

117 ['Frank Sargeson']. *Contemporary Novelists,* edited by James Vinson. London, St James Press, 1972, p.1096. A brief statement of purpose.

118 'Frank Sargeson on *The Swiss Family Robinson*'. *Education,* 1975 (no.3), p.24.

119 'The Word is Liberating' [interview with Sargeson by Tony Reid]. *New Zealand Listener,* 29 March 1975 (v.78, no.1843), pp.28-29.

120 'Sabbath Breakers'. *New Zealand Listener,* 11 October 1975 (v.80, no.1871), p.6. In this guest editorial Sargeson reflects on the Auckland District Law Society's call for the repeal of sections of the Police Offences Act prohibiting working for gainful employment on Sundays. He emphasizes that this is a matter of what you define as work. 'Has anyone ever heard of a bank knocking off interest for 52 days of the year because of 52 Sundays?'.

121 ['Frank Sargeson']. *Speaking of Writing: Seventeen Leading Writers of*

Australian and New Zealand Fiction Answer Questions on Their Craft, edited by R. D. Walshe. Sydney, Reed Education, 1975, pp.78-81.

122 'Sargeson on Success: Peter Isaac Meets New Zealand's Man of Letters, Frank Sargeson'. *New Zealand Bookworld*, September 1976 (no.28), p.8-9.

*123 Review. 'More Please!' [review of *Follow the Call* and *Gus Tomlins*, by Frank S. Anthony]. *Islands*, December 1977 (v.6, no.2), December 1977, pp.201-3.

124 'My Choice'. *Islands*, March 1978 (v.6, no.3), p.297.

125 'An Interview with Frank Sargeson' [by J. P. Durix]. *Commonwealth, Essays and Studies, Melanges*, v.3, 1977-1978, pp.49-54.

*126 'To Every Man His Own Uncle Ted' [on Roderick Finlayson's *Tidal Creek*]. *Islands*, November 1979 (v.7, no.5), pp.550-3.

*127 'Fine Stories' [review of Owen Marshall's *Supper Waltz Wilson*]. *Islands*, October 1980 (v.8, no.3), p.284.

SARGESON'S RADIO BROADCASTS

Sargeson contributed regularly to radio in the nineteen-forties and nineteen-fifties. Items 48 and 92 in the bibliography were originally broadcasts. From programme details in the *New Zealand Listener*, Sargeson was a regular contributor to the ZB *Book Session* from c.1949 into the mid-nineteen-fifties.

Sargeson made several broadcasts in 1948. In *More than Enough* (item 2, p.124) he mentions broadcasting with Dan Davin. A fuller account exists: 'Mr Davin and Mr Sargeson argued about "The New Zealand writer and his craft" . . . these two also took part in radio discussions with Mr O. N. Gillespie, Mr George Joseph, two members of P.E.N.; and Mr Pat Lawlor, our President'. (*P.E.N. Gazette*, Wellington, P.E.N. (New Zealand Centre), October 1948 (no.22), p.1.)

The following items are taken from N.Z.B.C. archives: general catalogue no.1, 1967. Timaru, N.Z.B.C. Archives Section, 1967, p.9. (I have provided the numbering and the annotations.)

*A1 Talk about Katherine Mansfield. 1948. [See item 48, which is part of this broadcast.]

*A2 Two talks. 'On Writing a Novel'. 1950 (?). [The catalogue describes this as 'fairly autobiographical'. Quotations from it are given by Winston Rhodes in *Frank Sargeson* (New York, Twayne, 1969, pp.7,37,93,136,151). A typescript is among Sargeson's papers in the Alexander Turnbull Library, Wellington.]

*A3 Three talks on Olive Schreiner and the *African Farm*. 1956.

A4 Two talks: 'The Play and the Playwright'. 1957.

CONTRIBUTIONS TO NEWSPAPERS

In Bill Pearson's bibliography appended to Frank Sargeson's *Collected Stories*,

1953-1963 (Auckland, Blackwood & Janet Paul, 1964), Sargeson's contributions to newspapers are described (without any dating) as having been in the *Auckland Star* (reprinted in the *Christchurch Star-Sun*); the Christchurch *Press* (reprinted in the *Southland Times*); the *People's Voice*; and, as some of the radio commentary which 'appeared over the name of Ben Bolt' in the *Observer* (Auckland).

Some of these pieces are preserved in the Sargeson papers in the Alexander Turnbull Library, and the following description is based on an inspection of the clippings. In many cases there was no indication of date, in no case was there a page reference. All were fully signed, unless otherwise described.

Sargeson has said: 'The first thing I ever had published was an article in the *N.Z. Herald* called "A New Tramp Abroad" or some such title' (above, p.181). This appears to be 'In France: Along the Road', by 'F.S.', in the *New Zealand Herald,* 30 May 1930, a brief descriptive piece about wandering in France.

Contributions to the *Auckland Star* included two items on horse racing ('In the Tote' and 'Race Meetings . . .'). Writings on literary subjects included 'Naming Your Novel: Some Titles and Plots'; 'Life and Fiction'; 'Gibbon, His Famous History'; and 'Using Words: How They Are Squandered'. All are at a fairly popular pitch. 'School Reading: the Journal: Introduction to Moderns' praises the *School Journal*'s inclusion of modern writers, and suggests the addition of American writers (5 January 1935).

Other contributions to the *Auckland Star* include 'The Simple Life: Does it Really Exist?' (1936?), 'Second-hand: Our Auction Rooms', and an article on 'Men and Machines'.

A review of John A. Lee's novel *Civilian into Soldier* was apparently from the *Press*. The novel was published in 1937.

There were no clippings from the *People's Voice*, cited by Pearson. Possibly this paper has been confused with the *Workers' Weekly*: an article on horse-racing by Sargeson under the pseudonym 'Bucephalus', 'The Racing Racket', was published there in (?) 1939. (Sargeson identified the article as his in a letter to the writer, 20 September 1977.)

'For the Little Ones', a parody of 'Twinkle, Twinkle, Little Star', appeared in *Soviet News* (February 1935), signed 'F.S., Takapuna'.

A 'Ben Bolt's Almanac' clipping from the *Observer* was dated 1 January 1941.

(The source of this information, in the Frank Sargeson Papers, Alexander Turnbull Library, is: Ms. papers 432/147/'notebook'/(item 29 (B)); Ms. papers 432/158-163 Early press clippings; Ms. papers 432/164-167 Later press clippings.)

INDEX

Page numbers of main references to topics are in italic